T0342301

Luminos is the Open Access monograph publishing program
from UC Press. Luminos provides a framework for preserving and
reinvigorating monograph publishing for the future and increases
the reach and visibility of important scholarly work. Titles published
in the UC Press Luminos model are published with the same high
standards for selection, peer review, production, and marketing as
those in our traditional program. www.luminosoa.org

The Fluvial Imagination

CRITICAL ENVIRONMESERNTS: NATURE, SCIENCE, AND POLITICS

Edited by Julie Guthman and Rebecca Lave

The Critical Environments series publishes books that explore the political forms of life and the ecologies that emerge from histories of capitalism, militarism, racism, colonialism, and more.

1. *Flame and Fortune in the American West: Urban Development, Environmental Change, and the Great Oakland Hills Fire*, by Gregory L. Simon

2. *Germ Wars: The Politics of Microbes and America's Landscape of Fear*, by Melanie Armstrong

3. *Coral Whisperers: Scientists on the Brink*, by Irus Braverman

4. *Life without Lead: Contamination, Crisis, and Hope in Uruguay*, by Daniel Renfrew

5. *Unsettled Waters: Rights, Law, and Identity in the American West*, by Eric P. Perramond

6. *Wilted: Pathogens, Chemicals, and the Fragile Future of the Strawberry Industry*, by Julie Guthman

7. *Destination Anthropocene: Science and Tourism in The Bahamas*, by Amelia Moore

8. *Economic Poisoning: Industrial Waste and the Chemicalization of American Agriculture*, by Adam M. Romero

9. *Weighing the Future: Race, Science, and Pregnancy Trials in the Postgenomic Era*, by Natali Valdez

10. *Continent in Dust: Experiments in a Chinese Weather System*, by Jerry C. Zee

11. *Worlds of Green and Gray: Mineral Extraction as Ecological Practice*, by Sebastián Ureta and Patricio Flores

12. *The Fluvial Imagination: On Lesotho's Water-Export Economy*, by Colin Hoag

The Fluvial Imagination

On Lesotho's Water-Export Economy

———

Colin Hoag

UNIVERSITY OF CALIFORNIA PRESS

University of California Press
Oakland, California

© 2022 by Colin Hoag

Suggested citation: Hoag, C. *The Fluvial Imagination: On Lesotho's Water-Export Economy*. Oakland: University of California Press, 2022. DOI: https://doi.org/10.1525/luminos.134

Library of Congress Cataloging-in-Publication Data

Names: Hoag, Colin, 1980–
Title: The fluvial imagination : on Lesotho's water-export economy /
    Colin Hoag. Other titles: Critical environments (Oakland, Calif.) ; 12.
Description: Oakland, California : University of California Press, [2022] |
    Series: Critical environments: nature, science, and politics ; 12 |
    Includes bibliographical references and index.
Identifiers: LCCN 2022010685 (print) | LCCN 2022010686 (ebook) |
    ISBN 9780520386341 (paperback) | ISBN 9780520386358 (ebook)
Subjects: LCSH: Lesotho Highlands Water Project. | Water transfer—Lesotho. |
    Water resources development—Environmental aspects—Lesotho. |
    Water-supply—Lesotho.
Classification: LCC HD1699.L5 H63 2022 (print) | LCC HD1699.L5 (ebook) |
    DDC 333.910096885—dc23/eng/20220716
LC record available at https://lccn.loc.gov/2022010685
LC ebook record available at https://lccn.loc.gov/2022010686

28 27 26 25 24 23 22
10 9 8 7 6 5 4 3 2 1

For Corinne, for Eamon, for Eske

CONTENTS

Introduction   *1*

1. Water Production   *27*

2. The Soil Problem   *44*

3. The Soil Solution   *63*

4. Bureaucratic Ecology   *80*

5. Livestock Production   *100*

6. Negative Ecology   *120*

Conclusion   *141*

Notes   *147*
Acknowledgments   *177*
Works Cited   *183*
Index   *211*

MAP 1. Map of Southern Africa, showing contemporary provincial boundaries of South Africa and district boundaries of Lesotho (inset). Cartography by Tracy Tien, Spatial Analysis Lab at Smith College. Populated places and ocean bathymetry made with Natural Earth. South Africa and Lesotho subnational administrative boundaries from UN OCHA ROSEA (Southern and Eastern Africa).

Introduction

What follows is a story about the world's first "water-exporting country," a geopolitical category forged in the blast furnace of our planet's accelerating environmental crisis. It's an account of a system of water production, the contradictions that threaten to destroy it, and the many kinds of work required to hold it all together. Water is not simply captured behind dam walls and sold. It is *produced* like any other commodity. This production, I'll show, requires a theory of how water flows over land and into reservoirs in distant watersheds—and how people living in those landscapes therefore should comport themselves to encourage satisfactory flow. And, it requires a negotiation with local contexts—in this case the racial capitalism of South African apartheid. That's where I'll start.

THE TERRESTRIAL POLITICS OF WATER PRODUCTION

In 1986, the enclave state of Lesotho signed a treaty with South Africa for the Lesotho Highlands Water Project (LHWP), a multibillion-dollar scheme to construct a series of massive dams and tunnels that could carry water to Johannesburg. In remote and difficult terrain, some of the most sophisticated hydro-engineering in the world was deployed to make this export economy a reality. The small mountain kingdom is rarely thought of as a player on the "world stage," yet there it stands at the vanguard of natural resource politics. Not by the bottle, but by the cubic meter per second, Lesotho services the subcontinent's parched industrial and commercial epicenter.

Exactly a century before that treaty was signed, the largest gold deposits in the world were found at the Witwatersrand, a craggy ridge that runs east-west through contemporary Johannesburg. Sparsely populated at that time, the rolling, semiarid grasslands that surround it featured no significant source of fresh water—much less enough for a water-intensive industry like gold mining—but the human population mushroomed with the rush to capitalize upon the promise of gold.

In the decades between these two historical moments—the gold rush and the water rush—the white supremacist political philosophy known as apartheid was instituted in South Africa for the conjoined project of segregation and exploitation: separating people by a hierarchy of racial types for the purpose of separating gold from the earth in which it was caught. Surrounded by South Africa, Lesotho was drawn into that apartheid project. Its national borders were leveraged by the mining industry to manage the flow of labor to South African mines, and the country was positioned as a labor reserve, a kind of holding tank for an army of surplus African workers.

This system fell apart with South Africa's hard-fought turn to democracy in the early 1990s, but just then another was being assembled to extract *water* instead. That system was designed according to a seemingly more defensible rationale—Lesotho's national sovereignty and development—though it inherited many of the same fixtures that spun the flywheel of this earlier machine: it relied on the construction and regulation of storage reservoirs, as well as the modulation and reassertion of ethno-national identities. It also inherited many of its problems and contradictions, including intense economic pressures and inequality.

. . .

The supply of water, of course, is among the most concerning of "natural resource" issues in our present moment. Our world has been built according to a Holocene climate that was relatively stable. As we enter the Anthropocene, the proposed geologic epoch to follow the Holocene characterized by planet-wide environmental damage,[1] we find a world in which droughts and floods seem always equally plausible. It is a world with more people living in cities, more water-intensive mining and energy production, more water-intensive manufacturing, more water-intensive agriculture, and on and on. Lesotho's relationship to South Africa stands as a case study of the looming threats and possibilities of such a world. It illustrates how these shifting and patchy water geographies could potentially realign global relationships and commonsense understandings of water's value.[2] On the other hand, it could also further entrench and intensify the inequities of the status quo.

South Africa's contemporary water problems were thrust upon the global imagination during Cape Town's 2017–18 brush with "day zero," a crisis that nearly brought that metropolis to a stop, and which stemmed from a combination of mismanagement and protracted drought.[3]

On the other side of the country, Johannesburg's crisis is equally severe. Were it not for transfers of water from Lesotho, Johannesburg and the entire Gauteng Province would have long ago been brought low. Its own day zero will surely come, however. Johannesburg is home to some 10 million people and aspires to become a "world city," yet it has a very spotty record of water management, with nearly

40 percent of its water being forfeited to leaks and other losses.[4] Forecasts predict a regional future that is hotter and even more drought-prone.[5]

Thankfully, proponents of Lesotho's water-export economy on both sides of the border explain, Lesotho has abundant water, and it only "uses" around one percent of its total 140m3/s capacity.[6] With crisp economic logic, they describe the LHWP as a mutually beneficial agreement between South Africa and Lesotho: Lesotho has abundant water supply, and South Africa faces acute water demand. They argue that this international commodity exchange between the two countries not only can bring in revenues but can also bolster Lesotho's status as a sovereign territory.

In April 2014, I was in the highland town of Mokhotlong when then prime minister of Lesotho, Tom Thabane, held a *pitso*—an open-air speech and community-outreach meeting—as he had been doing for each of the country's ten administrative districts. With his typical good humor, he explained (in Sesotho) to the crowd how, when he met recently with South African prime minister Jacob Zuma, Thabane reminded him that "South Africa *needs* Lesotho—people in Joburg can't even take a piss without our water!" It got a good laugh from the crowd. Thabane was referencing the LHWP, as the two countries had signed an agreement just a month earlier to move forward with construction of the project's next phase: the colossal Polihali Dam, to be built just a few kilometers away from where he spoke. Ahead of the initial treaty in 1986 and ever since, there has existed an optimism among national elites that water export would elevate Lesotho's position in the region. This optimism was on display in Thabane's speech.

That the issue of Lesotho's sovereignty merited mention at all is testament to its weakness. Lesotho is simply not on equal footing in water-export negotiations with the country that envelops it; nor is it on many other matters, be it fiscal policy or border policy. If apartheid-era Lesotho was part of an infrastructure of economic production that sought to regulate the flow of labor, justified through a dubious logic of racial difference,[7] Lesotho today is part of an infrastructure of economic production that seeks to regulate the flow of *water*, justified through a dubious logic of national sovereignty.[8]

Much as the early colonists of Africa and the Americas "found" a purportedly empty and therefore "underutilized" territory—*terra nullius*—so too has Lesotho's abundant water been delivered into productive use.[9] In these settler framings, resource exploitation is presented as a bridge between states of nature and civilization, past and future—a kind of natural resource modernity. Large dams, described as "temples of modernity" by postcolonial figures such as India's independence leader Jawaharlal Nehru, are quintessential tools for this work,[10] even though ironically dams have at times helped preserve colonial power well into the postcolonial period.[11] The Lesotho Highlands Water Project, too, promises to transcend old barriers to Lesotho's self-determination. The notion of *water abundance* is its stepping stone.

Alas, as I will show in the chapters that follow, the export of this abundant water reinscribes the racial nationalism that has long governed the subcontinent.[12]

Authors who have scrutinized accounts of water "scarcity" and "abundance" have shown that these designations are technological and political artifacts rather than self-evident calculations.[13] Examining the everyday work of managing and allocating water, those anthropologists and geographers working in water studies have helped us to understand that, while water volumes in a reservoir may be absolute numbers, downstream these figures take concrete shape in relation to political terrain. Into the downstream urban or agricultural matrix, a network of pipes and valves—an infrastructure of distribution—determines who has access to this water.[14]

Building on that work, this book instead turns upstream to examine infrastructures of *production*, where a landscape of soils and of vegetation, of livestock and of people, of identities and of citizenships, of croplands and of wetlands determines how much water enters the reservoir and at what cost. Raising livestock like cattle, sheep, and goats has long been an important accessory to rural livelihoods, alongside labor migration to the mines. Whereas it was once a retirement activity, however, producing wool, mohair, and meat has turned into a primary occupation since the decline of mining work. This has raised fears that land degradation could result in accelerated soil erosion and the sedimentation of Lesotho's dam reservoirs. That is, that land degradation could tank the water-export economy.

In essence, the terrestrial demands of water production are coming into conflict with those of livestock production. Degraded rangelands not only threaten to diminish the quality of the water that enters Lesotho's highland streams, which would otherwise be purified by filtering through soils rather than carried over land as runoff. They also lead to an increase in the energy of water flowing downslope, carving out gullies and carrying sediment and organic matter as it passes into reservoirs. This sediment diminishes reservoir capacity when it piles up and threatens machinery like the water intakes that connect reservoirs to South Africa.

A 2011 report by the World Bank found that LHWP reservoirs are silting up "at an alarming rate," and that as a result "the LHWP might bury itself in a few decades."[15] LHWP engineers told the *Lesotho Times* newspaper in 2017 (and me in 2014 and again in 2019) that documented sedimentation at the 'Muela Reservoir alone could prevent Lesotho in the near future from supplying water to South Africa. If or when that happens, Lesotho would stop receiving payments for water export. At the same time, the country would face financial penalties payable to South Africa, being contractually bound to supply water through 2044. All the while, it would need to continue servicing its debt to the World Bank for construction of the LHWP.[16] The pain would extend across the border, too, given that millions of people living in South Africa's economic core in and around Johannesburg depend on Lesotho's water.[17]

I was told by an LHWP water engineer in 2019 that the small Matsoku Reservoir, formed by a weir and connected by tunnel to the Katse Reservoir, is even more impacted than 'Muela.[18] "It's probably gone," he said. Bringing dredging machinery to Matsoku might be too costly to be worthwhile.

What causes erosion, and how severe is it? How does one see erosion, and what can be done to stop it? How *does* water flow over land exactly? These questions echo through Lesotho's mountain valleys in the water-export era, drawing attention further and further upstream.

Turning upstream has led me to believe we need a better sense of water as a terrestrial phenomenon, and not only a hydrologic one. Just as a commodity like petroleum, say, is pumped, inspected, and subjected to various forms of refining and redefinition before it can be sold, water is produced—not a thing but a project.[19] Ways of understanding it are cultivated; social forms that can accommodate it are identified and leveraged. These activities point toward what I think of as a terrestrial politics of water: terrestrial, in reference to Lesotho's *territory* but also to *terra*, the earth: the soil through which it flows and which it carries downslope into the watercourse.

Water commodities must be coaxed out of the mud.

That coaxing requires a "fluvial imagination," a sense for how water flows over land and why. I'll turn to an ethnographic example of this shortly, but first I need to thicken the historical narrative that I've so far developed. I want to show something about both the dynamism and the conservatism of this fluvial imagination—how it gets shifted strategically over time, but how certain elements endure. The text below embodies the tempo and recursivity of this history, with its sudden turns and returns. Crucially, I hope to show just how deeply enmeshed the fluvial imagination is with racial apartheid.[20]

ENGINEERING STORAGE

It was the 1950s, and the British colonial administration struggled to make its Basutoland territory profitable. The colony now known as Lesotho had little economic potential, with its extremely mountainous terrain, limited arable land, and few natural resources. Peter Ballenden, the administration's director of public works, hired an engineer named Ninham Shand to investigate the possibility that water could be stored in the country's highlands and sold to neighboring South Africa for irrigation on farms in the Orange Free State and for industry in the Transvaal.[21]

Across the border in South Africa, the National Party was in its early years of majority rule since ascending to power in 1948. They had created a substantial political base of white "Afrikaners," the Dutch- and Huguenot-descendant settler colonist group. They did so on a platform of racial segregation, the promotion of Afrikaner economic interests, and greater independence from the British

Commonwealth. As the government implemented its policies of apartheid under native affairs minister Hendrik Verwoerd—later prime minister Verwoerd—fears were surfacing about future water scarcity in South Africa's expanding economic heartland surrounding Johannesburg and Pretoria.[22] With its meager sources of freshwater, the Johannesburg-Pretoria conurbation faced severe limits to its growth.[23] Nevertheless, gold and diamond mining there generated astronomical profits, drawing in secondary industries and an ever-larger human population.

During Shand's visit to the Oxbow area in northern Basutoland, now Butha-Buthe District, he was struck by the hydrologic potential of the area. Surveying the elevation maps, he reportedly exclaimed, "If these levels are correct we can supply water not just to the Free State but to the entire Witwatersrand, by gravity!"[24] That is, water could be stored in the mountains and transferred to Johannesburg without the need for costly pumping, as would be the case for alternative supplies. Lesotho's water eventually passes into South Africa, but it is too low in elevation to reach Johannesburg by gravity alone.[25]

The "Oxbow Scheme," as it was dubbed, was formally presented to the newly independent Lesotho government in 1967, but geopolitics intervened to delay it. The World Bank refused to finance the project due to international opposition to apartheid, which only intensified during the 1970s and early 1980s. Lesotho eventually became a "frontline state" in the fight against apartheid, and prime minister Chief Leabua Jonathan—though friendly to the apartheid government in the early years of his premiership—drew international aid into the country by exploiting this "frontline" position;[26] at least, that is, until 1986, when Jonathan was toppled in a military coup supported by South Africa.[27] Just ten months after the coup, at the request of Lesotho's military government, the World Bank approved financing. A treaty was signed. Lesotho was to become South Africa's water silo.

According to its initial design in 1986, the Lesotho Highlands Water Project entailed the construction of five storage dams positioned at various points along the Orange/Senqu River and its major tributaries. So far, two of these storage dams have been built in the mountains at Katse and Mohale, as well as a weir at Matsoku and a tailpond dam for hydroelectricity generation at 'Muela in the foothills. Tunnels connect the reservoirs, and a river carries the water to Johannesburg. These are all engineering marvels. Seeing the dam walls in person is stirring. At 185m and 145m, respectively, Katse Dam and Mohale Dam are among the tallest dam walls on the continent, with reservoirs that together hold over 2.9 billion m3 of water. A third dam, under construction at Polihali as I write, will add another 2.2 billion m3 of water storage, on demand for a thirsty South Africa.

As noted above, this was not the first time that Lesotho had been enrolled as storage infrastructure for South African industry. For more than a century, Basotho men and women had migrated to South Africa for work in the mines, as domestic workers, and as manual laborers.[28] Whereas the country was once an important exporter of grain to South Africa in the late nineteenth century—the so-called "granary of the Free State"—South African tariffs and British colonial

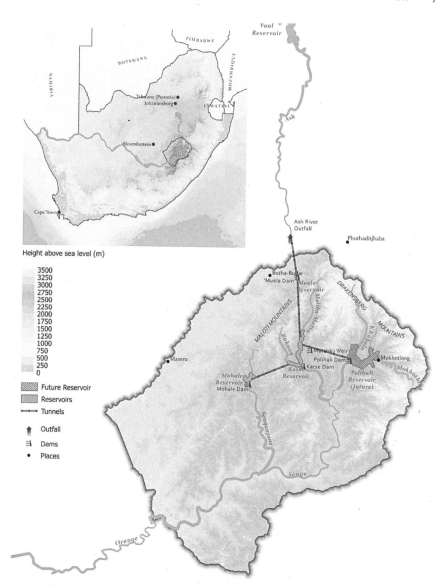

MAP 2. The Lesotho Highlands Water Project. Cartography by Tracy Tien, Spatial Analysis Lab at Smith College. Ocean bathymetry and major rivers made with Natural Earth. Outfall, dams, reservoirs, secondary river, and tunnels adapted by author from Google Earth. Elevation contours derived from NASA SRTM Digital Elevation 30m.

"hut taxes" undermined that agricultural production and pushed Basotho people into migrant labor.[29]

Lesotho was positioned as a periphery to the South African core like the former South African homelands, sometimes referred to as "Bantustans."[30] These Bantustan territories were an important part of South Africa's racist political

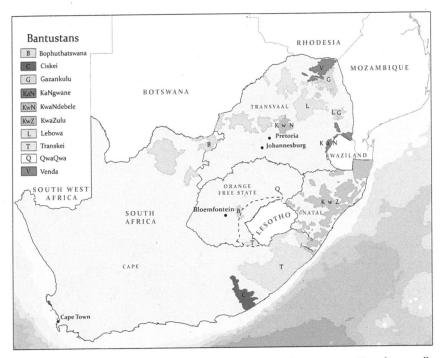

Bantustans

B	Bophuthatswana
C	Ciskei
G	Gazankulu
KaN	KaNgwane
KwN	KwaNdebele
KwZ	KwaZulu
L	Lebowa
T	Transkei
Q	QwaQwa
V	Venda

MAP 3. Map of the Union of South Africa circa 1975, showing the Bantustans. Note that not all Bantustans had been granted "independence" at that time. Dotted line shows the "conquered territories" of Lesotho. Cartography by Jon Caris and Tracy Tien, Spatial Analysis Lab at Smith College. Bantustan boundaries adapted by author from https://commons.wikimedia.org/w /index.php?curid=25392438 by Htonl. Conquered territories boundary digitized by author based on map in Lelimo (1998). Ocean bathymetry made with Natural Earth. All other administrative boundaries and city locations from ESRI Living Atlas.

economy, whereby Africans, having had their best land expropriated, were compelled to work in industrial centers—but with their movements regulated through passbooks and work permits in accordance with labor demand.[31] Under apartheid, South Africa sought to establish the Bantustans as quasi-independent countries so that they could legitimately remove Africans from white spaces through "deportation." Each Bantustan would house a distinct ethnic group: one for the Batswana, one for the amaZulu, and so on. These groups would then be able to preserve their language and culture, so the story went. The international community refused to recognize the Bantustans, however, bowing to pressure from activists who saw them clearly as tools for racial discrimination and exploitation.

Like a Bantustan, Lesotho is ethnolinguistically homogenous and has very little arable land or industry. Yet, whereas the Bantustans were dissolved with South Africa's transition to democracy in 1994, Lesotho is a "real country,"[32] so it remained whole. There was talk of dissolving Lesotho into South Africa as a tenth province at that time—after all, South Africa completely surrounds it—but the calculus was unsolvable: an entire monarchy, its associated chieftaincy, and a parliamentary political class would be reduced to minor, provincial players. Ordinary people in Lesotho would have to subject themselves to an alternative political system, and one that was emerging from the rubble of outright revolution. Besides, Lesotho had little to offer South Africa's economy (as South African leadership saw it) apart from labor and water, which South Africa already had access to as needed.

Making matters worse for Lesotho, the new South Africa favored domestic workers over foreign ones, and Basotho experienced a severe contraction of employment opportunities in South African mines. As if the crisis could not deepen further, the price of gold dropped, and mines underwent a period of mechanization. Less labor was needed, foreign or domestic. Whereas in 1979, there were some 129,000 Basotho workers on the mines according to official statistics,[33] this figure declined to 34,000 in 2011, and 19,000 in 2018.[34] Mining jobs that were once a rite of passage for Basotho men are today the luxury of a privileged few. Worse than a labor reserve, Lesotho had become a *discarded* labor reserve.

With Lesotho's water-export economy just getting off the ground, a decisive shift was afoot. Having been transformed in the early twentieth century "from granary to labour reserve," as Colin Murray famously described the decline of Lesotho's position as a prominent exporter of grain,[35] the country was transformed in the late twentieth century from labor reserve to *water reservoir*—a structural condition whose social, political, and ecological consequences are the subject of this book.

. . .

But back to Ballenden and Shand for a brief moment: their idea in the 1950s to build dams in the mountain valleys of Basutoland did not come out of thin air. It was a legacy from another colonial moment of fluvial imagining. They proposed to provision water to the Transvaal, but several decades earlier the scheme was put forward instead as a means of preventing floods from damaging farms in the Orange Free State.

In the early twentieth century, the white Afrikaners who owned those farms complained that unregulated grazing in the Basutoland highlands was causing soil erosion and undermining the mountains' ability to store and slowly release water over the course of the year. They believed that rangeland degradation was causing water to flow too quickly through the watercourse, leading to floods and an excessive amount of silt. Basotho people were called upon to cease farming and even to leave the mountain areas altogether, despite the lack of reliable data at the time showing that their grazing methods did indeed contribute to erosion.[36] The British proposed the construction of a dam in the mountains to mollify those farmers and their political leaders in the Union of South Africa—not yet so closely united as today's Republic of South Africa—who had begun using this issue to pressure the British to cede Basutoland to the Union. The dam would "capture any siltation and result in a clearer flow of water into the Union," as the historian Thackwray Driver aptly put it.[37]

Those pressures subsided as the years passed. By the time Ballenden and Shand arrived on the scene, complaints by South Africans about highlands erosion and flooding had abated somewhat.[38] South African engineers were turning their attention instead to urban water supply in Johannesburg and Pretoria, with projections of future water demand making action on the issue appear increasingly urgent.[39] Ballenden and Shand effectively reimagined those proposed flood-control dams as a water-transfer scheme in service of South African industry.

In sum, a flood-control project designed to *trap sediment* was converted into a water-export project *in spite of that sediment*. That conversion reverberates in attempts to understand and manage problems posed by soil in the present—in attempts to engineer the storage of water commodities. It is a reminder that storage infrastructures like these are not mere "technical" matters. They are sites of social activity: of imagination, of production, of reproduction.[40]

Above all, engineering storage requires regular reckoning with contradiction, namely the contradiction between storage and extraction. During apartheid, South Africa sought to store up workers it could tap at any moment. Industry then wanted laborers but not rights-bearing citizens. It needed them close, but wanted them far away. Industry today wants Lesotho's water, but without having to worry about the landscapes from which it issues. It demands minimal impact by livestock, but as I'll show it provides almost no long-term employment, leaving livestock production as one of the few options for rural people living in upstream catchments.

South Africa's labor reserves required "upstream" mechanisms to manage their contradictions.[41] Some of these mechanisms were material in nature, while others were symbolic or social. Borders and passbooks, for example, helped regulate the flow of people, while ethnic or national identities helped to justify that regulation. The disciplining of kinship relations, too, for example by prohibiting spouses and children to accompany mineworkers, reinforced miners' status as "temporary sojourners" in white areas.[42]

South Africa's water reserve requires similar upstream mechanisms. As during its labor-reserve era, the demands of storage and extraction in this reimagined apartheid infrastructure come into conflict. The contradictions generated by Lesotho's structural position as water reservoir must be managed. Over my sixteen months of ethnographic and ecological field research between 2011 and 2019,[43] I found that such management is in large part an exercise in theorizing environmental process. More specifically, those making a living in the shadow of Lesotho's water-export economy must creatively read and navigate the fluvial landscape. Not left to the expert class alone, this is a task for livestock owners, water engineers, conservation bureaucrats, herders, and even livestock and vegetation. Each must conceive of how water flows through soils, plants, and other landscape features—and therefore how one should properly interact with this landscape.

In short, I show, the search for "water security" in South Africa's urban core interpellates landscape theorists in the rural periphery.[44]

Walk with me.

SQUARING AN ECOLOGY WITH A SOCIOLOGY

We stood in the full sun, leaning against the stone wall of a livestock corral in the high mountains. Tankisi flashed a smile, straightened up, and answered my question with one of his own.

"If someone sets out in front of you maizemeal, sautéed greens, and meat, then asks you to choose one, which would you choose?"

Correctly, I answered, "Meat."

We all burst into laughter. Tankisi's joke, which played on Basotho love for meat, was made in passing but packed with meaning. It was a map through dynamic rangeland spacetime, a theory of ecological process—one fit to explain Lesotho's degraded rangelands, as he saw it. Standing beside his son, Kao, who often lives and works as a herder at this remote livestock post, Tankisi explained what he meant: livestock select the sweetest perennial grasses from a pasture, like *seboku* (*Themeda triandra*, the meat in his analogy), leaving behind shrubs and less palatable, less nutritious annual grasses. In doing so, they diminish the desirable species, while aiding the undesirable ones.

More than outlining an ecological theory, Tankisi was in fact voicing implicit support for a rangeland reform proposed by a foreign conservation organization called the Sponges Project that I'll describe at a few different moments in this book. The reform suggested that livestock should be prevented from grazing whichever plants they prefer; instead their movements should be confined in such a way that they consume everything in the sward. Its goal was to protect Lesotho's "water resources" by improving the condition of its highland pastures. In the catchments upstream from Lesotho's reservoirs, rural people are very successful at raising livestock, but they are described by conservation bureaucrats at home and abroad as woefully ignorant of good environmental practice.[45] This ignorance, they contend, manifests in runaway soil erosion and reservoir sedimentation. Better rangeland management would promote the good flow of water into reservoirs and, by turns, Lesotho's ability to produce water commodities.

But the reform was as much about understanding the past as it was about building some brighter future. It represented an attempt to interpret and author a history of the landscape. It was a form of landscape historiography. This landscape historiography aspired to bring a theory of ecological process into alignment with a theory of social process for the sake of water export. It would account for how a specific set of plants assembles into a community under grazing pressure; how water flows differently through that community; how livestock preferences call for certain herding techniques; and, as I'll show later on, how ideal conditions for water's careful flow into dam reservoirs might be encouraged through livestock commodification and changes to political institutions.

In a joke, then, a landscape.

We occupied the exposed midslope of a spur that bisected Mokhoabo-Motšo ("The Black Mire"), a small valley named after the dark, organic soils of Lesotho's alpine wetlands. These wetlands, or "mires," are known to hold massive amounts of water that they slowly release downstream, turning ephemeral streams perennial. Discharged from Mokhoabo-Motšo, this water flows to the Seate, Mapholaneng, Khubelu, and Senqu Rivers, each tributary tumbling down toward the trunk. The Senqu River then heads south and west out of Lesotho (where it is called the Orange River), twenty-three hundred kilometers to the Atlantic Ocean along the border between South Africa and Namibia.

From our perch in these Senqu headwaters, we looked out across the steep valley slopes surrounding us—slopes mottled with blotchy eruptions of distinct shrub communities that I had come to know well from the help of hard copy field guides and the assistance of people like Tankisi. On the south-facing slopes, a sea of pea-green malitšoekere (Helichrysum trilineatum) in full yellow bloom was interspersed with shocks of bluish-gray thotho-li-roalana (Inulanthera thodei), and on the north-facing slopes a mix of the dark-green sehala-hala (Chrysocoma ciliata) and selingoana (Pentzia cooperi) dominated. Like a drop of water on dry paper, they crawled up from the valley bottom before thinning out and giving way to grasses and, eventually, the rocky, mineral soils on the ridgeline that crumble into the valley.

Interrupting this floristic pattern were occasional "cattle posts" (see fig. 1), where herders stay with their herd of typically sheep, goats, and a few cattle:[46] a low, round, stone structure with a haphazard thatched roof and a stone kraal, the commonly used Afrikaans word for a livestock corral. Cattle posts can be seen from a distance as a brown expanse of bare earth, surrounded by bright-green, creeping grasses that thrive in the nutrient-loaded soils created by animal urine and feces. A diffuse network of trails was cut between the cattle posts, pastures, and water points, passing onward to locations beyond the valley. Histories were encoded in rangeland palette and form—patterns of deep significance to the water-export economy, interpreted by Tankisi. And by conservation bureaucrats. And by me.

Mokhoabo-Motšo was supposed to be empty of livestock at this time of the year, when these winter grazing areas become deserted by chiefly decree for the even-higher summer rangelands. The call to move had been issued two weeks earlier. But further down the narrow valley below us some sheep grazed and rested

FIGURE 1. A highlands cattle post. Photo by author.

between the shrubs. Somewhere in our sight, a herder sat watch. A mass of afternoon clouds peeked out from behind a distant ridge, too far away to signal rain.

It was both surprising and sensible that Tankisi would envision rangeland ecological process in the way he described. Surprising, because I knew he believed that changes in the rains were having more profound effects on the range than management decisions about when and where to graze livestock. And he knew better than I did that the conservation bureaucrats' plans were impossible. To limit which grasses are eaten by livestock, generations of grazing practice and the political order that structures it would need to be overturned. Areas would need to be fenced to delimit the space in which livestock could graze—an expensive proposition, and in any case one deeply offensive to the rangeland commons. Absent fences, herders would need to practice what the bureaucrats described as "active herding," continually encircling the animals to keep them from straying.

Herders, who are paid next to nothing to live for months exposed on the high plateau of the Drakensberg Mountains, would simply not agree to this labor-intensive method. At *motebong*, the Sesotho name for these remote areas where most of Lesotho's livestock are kept, herders do not obey the rules of others. Neither do their livestock. A Sesotho aphorism states, "At *motebong*, there is no herding" (*Motebong ha ho lisoe*). Owing to some grammatical ambiguity, it could also be translated, "At *motebong*, one is not herded."

Yet, his position was not only surprising but *sensible*, because Tankisi is well-known as a "liaison," I might say, a person who lives in a rural village and is often called upon when development and conservation initiatives pass through the area—which they do with some regularity. At his house one day he proudly showed me a brochure from an earlier wetlands-protection project, which featured him by photo and by name as a farmer who was committed to teaching his village about the importance of wetlands after having attended one of their workshops. Tankisi speaks no English, and is enthusiastic and unambiguously "rural" in the ways these projects appreciate that subject position (though he worked in South African mines for a decade, spoke Fanakalo and Sepedi, and had church and family connections that brought him periodically to the South African city of Polokwane).

Most importantly, he has a clear understanding of how such initiatives work. This, even if he may disagree with project efforts in practice. Indeed, he often does. For example, Tankisi is a leading member of the local grazing association, a "community-based" group formed by that earlier wetlands conservation project but resuscitated by this more recent scheme—and yet, as I describe later on, he was known by my observation and those of others to transgress grazing association rules. He epitomized the complex exegetical work in which people in Lesotho read the landscape with an awareness of the social and material costs of one landscape interpretation or another.

In a joke, then, a landscape. Specifically, an *upstream* landscape: one characterized by the upsetting speed of its fluvial water, and its position as part of Lesotho's enclave geography—but which could be improved. The landscape Tankisi (and this wetlands protection scheme) presented was one that answered a pressing question: How to reconcile the terrestrial demands of Lesotho's water-export economy and those of its rural population? If only it were that easy.

That question instigates a debate about how livestock impact water's flow. The chapters below follow that debate—the delicate effort to square an ecology with a sociology—throughout Lesotho and its upland catchments. Attempts to resolve the debate have different implications for people, depending on their social position, illustrating the high stakes of interpreting landscape patterns in Lesotho's water-export era. I show how the water economy's orientation toward water's flow, capture, and extraction is suffused with literal and metaphorical sediment. It is mired in the alluvium of scheduled water transfers and reservoir management strategies, in the fears and fantasies about people and their environment, and in the "imperial debris" of a century of bureaucratic reforms scattered across the landscape.[47] This sediment is carried from slope to stream, tumbling through the watercourse as suspended load and bedload, before settling on the reservoir floor, both problem and logical outcome—the by-product of a system of storage. Lesotho has been rendered what I call a "fluvial economy."

THE FLUVIAL ECONOMY

The specter of fluvial water upstream looms over the volumetric water sold to South Africa. The geomorphological term *fluvial* refers to water flowing over land and its effects, or the disturbance of a site through hydraulic action. Fluvial processes leave traces.[48] I call attention to them because the very nature of water as it passes through the landscape is at stake in the manufacture of national water commodities, in this attempt to reorganize Lesotho's political economy in the aftermath of labor export.

What water *means*—what water *is*—how water *moves*—is being newly negotiated in these ecological and political contact zones between water production and livestock production. Variously positioned within those contact zones, the ethnographic characters I present include civil servants from Lesotho's conservation bureaucracies, livestock owners, herders, water engineers at the LHWP, and others.[49] Water's relationship to the nation, to livestock grazing, to rangeland management, and to interactions within the multispecies community was sometimes debated, sometimes agreed upon among these groups during my research as they interpreted the fluvial landscape.[50] Their interpretations converged upon a variety of scenes I present below: in village workshops to promote grazing associations; in herders' use of medicines to encourage their animals to consume unpalatable forage; in encounters between herders and conservation bureaucrats on the roadside; in meetings between bureaucrats and chiefs; and in observations of eroded hillslopes.

I use the term *fluvial* literally and figuratively when I join it with *economy* to describe how the contradicting imperatives of storage and extraction instigate problems—in this case problems of sedimentation and problems of interpretation.[51] Though it is the first "water-exporting country" in the world,[52] a political category that draws attention to the flow of water commodities, in fact the LHWP is fundamentally about storage, or the arresting of flow: holding water behind national borders, behind dam walls, and even in the wetlands of the upstream catchment. In the same way that a labor reserve might be described as "supplying labor" when in fact the arrangement does more to prevent immigration, the LHWP is predicated on its ability to hold back water as a precondition for regulated flow. The necessity of storage in the course of extracting water commodities means the project is always threatened by sedimentation, an accumulation of stresses and pressures.

The concept of fluvial economy, then, speaks to a broader process at work in the world today: the accumulating stresses that follow economic inequality and rapidly changing Anthropocene environments. It is a concept for seeing the byproducts of systems of extraction or production. After all, "by-products" are actually "products" by another name, as Raymond Williams described.[53] A factory that generates toxic waste in the process of making toys for children, say, is equally a manufacturer of toxic waste as it is a manufacturer of toys. Similarly, the by-product of water production is reservoir sedimentation.

Recall how theorists of globalization were rightly taken to task for obsessing over the "flows" (e.g., of capital, images, people) that were said to characterize a newly interconnected world without examining what Anna Tsing described as the "channel-making activity of circulation . . . the missed encounters, clashes, misfires, and confusions that are as much part of global linkages as simple 'flow.'"[54] Building from this work, the notion of a fluvial economy draws attention to a relationship between the flow of resources from one place or people to another, the material effects of those flows, and the interpretive work of discerning how these flows occur and what they mean.

The clash between water production and livestock production—and the concerns about soil erosion that it animates—ultimately represents a form of "green imperialism," Richard Grove's term,[55] describing the habit of imperial powers to intervene in imperial peripheries with remedies for environmental problems they themselves have caused.[56] The water economy is the cause of sedimentation concerns, and yet its scientists and engineers ask rural people to shoulder the burden. Allow me to explain. First, the LHWP raises the stakes on soil erosion: once a minor problem for rural livelihoods alone,[57] now soil erosion threatens South Africa's water supply and therefore Southern Africa's entire regional economy. Second, the LHWP didn't do enough to account for soil erosion in its design and planning, despite many warnings (see chapter 2). Third, the inundation of river valleys increases land pressure in the catchments above the reservoirs by removing land from use, forcing farmers to plough and graze animals on marginal land. Finally, the water-export economy has left livestock as one of the few ways of making a living in rural Lesotho: the livelihood practices needed to survive the water-export era are precisely those that undermine water export.

Any system of storage and extraction will inevitably be caught by problems of sedimentation. Like water basins, however, which see different rates of sediment movement based on their inherent soil and topographic properties, climate regime, disturbance regime, and land cover, some fluvial economies are more impacted than others. This is why the history and materiality of Lesotho's water is so important. It's why in the pages below I will regularly historicize the social and ecological forms at play. And it's why I'll insist on a close scrutiny of biophysical data as much as "social texts." It matters that this water commodification effort is happening amid a global climate crisis, and it matters that it's happening specifically in Lesotho. Whether it's water or livestock, labor or land, commodification works through the reduction of diverse things to abstract exchange values, but that transformation is always a local negotiation.[58] These negotiations churn in the disorientations of landscape historiography of upstream Lesotho, to which I now turn.

PATTERNS IN THE LANDSCAPE

Like water flowing over land, discourse on landscape change passes through exist-ing channels, widening them and only occasionally cutting new pathways. If land-scapes are libraries, as Kate Showers has put it,[59] Lesotho's shelves are full, and this book reflects critically on this tradition of landscape historiography even as it registers a new entry. Erosion mitigation in Lesotho is long and fraught,[60] calling into question whether current and future efforts can succeed—except perhaps as mechanisms for rural governance.[61] Soil erosion is difficult to see, measure, and monitor, yet despite the country's reputation as profoundly erosive,[62] sedimenta-tion monitoring has been a minor priority since the LHWP began.[63] This has left only guesswork, punctuated by alarm, to fill the epistemic gaps.

Consider one small example—one attempt to make sense of an observation of the landscape.

I drove through the mountains of Mokhotlong one day with conservation bureaucrats, on our way back from a visit to some degraded wetlands. We'd been discussing the ongoing drought when we passed over the Tsilantšo bridge, where a dramatic flood had laid waste to the riverbed just a few months earlier. Sediment sat in sandy piles, small boulders were strewn across it, and the typical riparian vegetation had been scoured out. The small river was perfectly dry, in spite of the fact that it was well into the rainy summer season. As many people told me, Lesotho recently had seen changes in the rains toward irregularity: long, dry spells broken by torrents. One of the bureaucrats, Tuke, looked out the window at it and sucked his teeth: "Hey, the river is so dry," he said, in what we in the car under-stood to be a reference to the drought.

His colleague Sepheo replied, gesturing up the mountainside, "Or, perhaps the soil above can't hold the water and it just courses downstream and away." Sepheo was critical of chiefs' inability to exclude livestock from pastures for periods of rest and forage regrowth, envisioning the effects of this failure in the loss of soil func-tion. The dry, eroded streambed was an expression of the problem.

"Yep," Tuke replied in agreement. We looked out the window briefly in silence. Sepheo had effectively reframed this fluvial landscape from one shaped by the condition of rains to one shaped by the condition of land management.

Anxiety about fluvial process draws my interlocutors' attention upstream like this to the pastures, agricultural plots, and especially the alpine wetlands of Lesotho's rural highlands.[64] Holding extraordinary amounts of water on the high plateau, these wetlands help regulate streamflow, preventing floods and extending the seasonal life of ephemeral streams through the dry winter months.[65] The wet-lands are deposits of deep, black organic soils that contrast with the thin, mineral soils of the steep slopes around them. From afar, their outlines are particularly clear: their edges transition abruptly from the small forbs and creeping grasses that cover them to the vegetation types more typical of the hillslopes elsewhere: tussock

FIGURE 2. Herder in alpine wetland. Photo by author.

grasses and dwarf shrubs. Herders use them as water points for their animals, particularly in the drier months (see fig. 2). Wetlands are now understood by water engineers as crucial components in the LHWP storage infrastructure, used to promote an even, predictable flow of water into reservoirs across the year.

Their perceived importance is attested by the proliferation of metaphors to explain them. Conservation bureaucrats and LHWP boosters sometimes refer to them as "silos of white gold" (*lisiu tsa khauta e tšoeu*) or "sponges."[66] An entire conservation project was established to mobilize this particular metaphor in the Mokhotlong District, the Khubelu Sponges Project.[67] In early 2014, I sat down with Sepheo, who was a well-respected official employed by that conservation scheme. I hoped to learn about his work. He started by explaining wetlands' function—casting about his office for a sponge. Unable to find it, he pantomimed for me a lesson on wetlands' water-storage capacity.

"If you take two cups with some water in them," he said, holding two invisible cups on the desk in front of him, "and place a sponge in one—and then turn them both upside-down—what will happen?" I started to answer, but he finished for me: "The water spills out of the one without the sponge, but it slowly pours out of the other."

The sponge metaphor nicely articulates processes of landscape change in response to livestock movements. A ministry official explained to me on a separate occasion that the wetlands are being degraded when livestock trample them. "They are like sponges," he said, also pantomiming. "When you pour water on a sponge, it absorbs it. But when you squeeze it," he clenched his fist, "like when livestock trample wetlands, the water runs out of it."

Because they serve as water points for livestock in these high-altitude regions, wetland degradation linked to livestock trampling has become an object of concern for the LHWP, the Lesotho government, and a host of nongovernmental organizations interested in conservation.[68] If erosion gullies form, rainfall is immediately lost as surface runoff; no longer trapping as much organic matter either, they are less able to maintain water purity. One study concluded that Lesotho's wetlands stored 36 percent less water than is their potential due to historic degradation.[69] Though geomorphologists have found that factors other than livestock contribute to wetland degradation, such as burrowing rodents,[70] livestock impacts are clear to anyone who visits them.

The wetlands protection project was initially run by a global consulting firm based in Germany, justified by the importance of Lesotho's "water resources,"[71] before being taken up by the government of Lesotho. The firm won a contract to carry out this project, valued at more than 1 million euros and funded by the German international development fund, the Deutsche Gesellschaft für Internationale Zusammenarbeit (GIZ). The early work of the Sponges Project, Sepheo said, was to establish connections with people in government and elsewhere, while also hiring experts on wetlands and rangeland management for a temporary consultancy in order to advise them in their work. When I spoke with him in 2014, they were trying to map out how different "stakeholders" relate to each other in rangeland use, such as how herders relate to farmers, and how farmers relate to chiefs or to institutions called "grazing associations." In effect, they sought to square what they knew about institutional forms and processes with what they knew about ecological ones.

An underlying assumption of theirs was that pedagogy surrounding water and wetlands was of the utmost importance, hence the metaphors of silos and sponges.[72] Five years later, at a meeting of the wetlands project in 2019, there was still widespread concern among them about the issue of public education. The agenda featured topics submitted by the various agencies and ministries present. One topic stated that "people still don't understand the value of wetlands."

In the discussion of this topic, the conservation bureaucrat named Tuke said that he believed this issue was slightly more complicated than what had been written. "People have an interest in their animals," he explained, "whereas we have an interest in wetlands. These are two different positions," he said, effectively arguing as I am that the terrestrial demands of everyday people conflict with the terrestrial demands of national water production. The local government councilor, Lebohang, agreed, but countered by reminding everyone of the high stakes of water production in and beyond the nation: Namibia, Botswana, and South Africa also depend on this water. Controlling the movements of livestock and controlling the flow of Lesotho's water, we learned, were conjoined geopolitical propositions.[73]

What constitutes proper land use in Lesotho hinges on ideas about how grazing affects water's interaction with soils, grasses, and other landscape features—not to mention ideas about the chieftaincy, the duties of a citizen, and even Lesotho's geopolitics. Though there may be agreement between livestock owners and conservation workers that rangeland condition used to be better, in my research I found disagreement as to how to define "land degradation," how to attribute a cause for it, and how to remedy it.[74] This disparity creates problems for range management: a contested economy of signs for reading the landscape. When built into conservation plans, the gaps and assumptions within such interpretations become physical manifestations, demonstrating how bureaucracy ramifies in ecological processes.

At a broader level, this situation shows how the everyday life of herders and the forage preferences of sheep in out-of-the-way places become urgent matters of interest for water engineers in office buildings in the capital. The more closely one scrutinizes water, the more uncertain it becomes. Like a siren's call, water production leads us to shipwreck, luring us upstream into soils, plants, social forms, and landscapes, a seduction this book reenacts.

ETHNOGRAPHY OF THE LANDSCAPE

At the center of water politics in Lesotho are landscapes—their description, structure, historiography, and morphogenesis. Since the colonial period, the highlands landscapes have incited anxiety in outside observers fearful of their unruliness and inscrutability.[75] How does one reckon empirically with anxious and inscrutable landscapes? I argue that it is with an ethnography of the landscape, a methodology that draws together the immersive, interpretive data of anthropology and various kinds of biophysical data familiar to ecology.[76]

In the following chapters, I try to hold two things in tension: the disorientation of competing landscape historiography on one hand, and the material presence of landscape patterns on the other. My aim is to represent the disorientation richly and accurately, while also providing a positive (or, realist) account about landscape change based on "what we know"—two different approaches to working through the disorientation. I'm invested in this approach, not only because I think it's useful to this specific case, but also because it speaks to a simmering problem for studies of the environment in the Anthropocene. This is a moment in which our planet's ecosystems are buckling. It's also moment in which natural scientists are coming to greater awareness that culture and power might be relevant to understanding environmental change, and in which humanists increasingly engage with natural science subjects and concepts.[77] There is excitement but also unease.

The historical cleavage between interpretive approaches in the humanities and positivist approaches in the natural sciences has left humanists mostly unauthorized to describe landscapes except as sites of meaning-making. Recoiling from the stultifying and sometimes racist forays of sociobiology and cultural ecology, "the environment" became merely a staging ground for human political contests among humanists.[78] Some of the most provocative exceptions to this rule come from scholars working in African contexts who have drawn together ecological science and critique to tell rich landscape stories.[79] *The Fluvial Imagination* builds on this tradition, while taking inspiration from emergent conversations about natural history in environmental anthropology,[80] to advance this work as a robustly ethnographic project.

Ecological formations, like social formations, are historically specific—in material terms and symbolic terms. Anthropologists and other humanists need a means of accounting for ecological formations, but without sacrificing interpretive sensibilities along the way.[81] If ecologists seek to establish the laws that determine ecological processes, anthropologists might work to discern the signs, practices, and histories that make those laws matter at a given location and a given moment in time.[82] This means drawing in practices of noticing from ecology, while affirming the value of qualitative observations of the landscape made by researchers and their subjects.[83] Perhaps counterintuitively, it means not overstating the case in assessing the human influence upon Anthropocene landscapes, even as humans have been so catastrophically destructive to our planet.[84] Lots of action in an ecosystem—say, in the assembly of a plant community in the highlands of Lesotho—has little to do with humans.[85]

It means understanding the limits of critique, with a sense of the political costs of dismembering and cannibalizing science, a suite of knowledge practices that we desperately need (certain parts of it, anyway).[86] Equally, it means practicing a science that is self-aware about the cultural production of scientific nature—with all its anxieties, aspirations, prognostications, translations, and political commitments.[87]

It means leveraging the insight from science and technology studies that all science is "ethnoscience" into an empirical project that is at once reflexive and authoritative, critical and positive. The missing *ethno-* on unmarked science is a testament to the importance of the humanities in conversations about the environment. That all science is ethnoscience doesn't mean that science is irredeemably compromised. On the contrary, it means that it's more dynamic and interesting than is commonly thought. In looking upon a landscape, we need both the *science* and the missing *ethno-* to understand what we're looking at.[88]

As part of my field research, I walked the landscape with herders and livestock owners through villages and cattle post areas, learning how they appreciate the effects of rains, livestock, and the political order on their rangelands. I sat in offices and meetings of government ministries, the LHWP, and other important conservation organizations, trying to understand the pressures that direct their energies, their primary concerns, and their goals. I drove with conservation bureaucrats on their field visits and walked the landscape with them, hoping to see how they envisioned rangeland problems and possibilities. And, critically, I worked at the interface between rural people and conservation bureaucrats, tracking how both groups represented themselves to and conversed with other audiences—seeing how different visions of ecological process play out in real time. In addition to these human-focused ethnographic methods, I drew upon multispecies ethnographic approaches, including natural history observations and ecology. I used archival and remote sensing research to track changes in rangeland condition, as well as methods from ecological science to consider the relative importance of different variables for determining floristic composition and structure, including some invisible to the human eye such as soil moisture and nutrient loads.

This book is "interdisciplinary," then—a term, however, that collapses many different kinds of practice into one, and these differences matter. Humanists' use of ecological science, for example, can entail things like reading ecological science literature seriously and deeply to present the latest consensus on a debate; using ecology concepts to do social theory; using quantitative ecological science methods and analysis; or even simply working on the basic assumption that the biophysical world is relevant to stories about humans. This book enlists all of these interdisciplinary techniques. Readers will feel the shifts across them, as I have tried to hold on to their distinct tenors and vocabularies rather than smoothing out differences for a fantasy transdisciplinary harmony.

The research for this book began as a strictly anthropological project, but as it developed, I needed to understand the nature and timing of environmental change in Lesotho's rangelands, hoping to parse debates I encountered in the field. These questions hadn't yet been resolved in the scientific literature, so I decided to sort through them myself. I enrolled in rangeland ecology and soil science courses, but became so possessed by the questions that I pursued a PhD in biological science.[89] I came to realize after many years of laboring to understand this landscape history of water—to understand the morphogenesis of the landscape and its relationship to water and water production—that my interlocutors and I were preoccupied with similar questions, though posed from different positions. Our collective efforts represented a phenomenon demanding scrutiny in its own right: that anxiety about fluvial processes was emblematic of Lesotho's water-export era, even if its affects, textures, and discourses were inherited from earlier periods.[90]

Like me, my interlocutors sought to understand how livestock grazing, political institutions, and climate configured the passage of water through the landscape.

Like them, I had been interpellated by the water-export economy as a theorist of water's flow.

Ultimately, as I will show, Lesotho's landscapes are inherently prone to erosion. The architects of the water-export economy strategically overlooked this point, and the decision to site these dams in Lesotho in the first instance is the source of the water economy's soil problems. Yet, soil erosion is also exacerbated by several other factors: the intensive production of livestock in rangelands historically unaccustomed to it, including fires set for their benefit; a recent climatic shift toward more intense rainfall events; erosion control programs that have encouraged rather than prevented erosion; and colonial efforts to promote wool production. If there were a way to improve rangelands through novel management techniques—a possibility I find doubtful—it is thwarted by a long history of interventions into rangeland institutions that has rendered grazing almost ungovernable. Because of the weight of these structural factors, the space for action is limited. This book affirms Piers Blaikie's insight that oftentimes the true cause of environmental degradation is not found locally but rather off-site.[91] It's true: intensive livestock production can encourage erosion. But such a statement is of little value without describing the context. Left with only livestock production in the aftermath of labor migration, rural people might push at the limits of Lesotho's landscapes—but it is because those who profit from water export have pushed so hard at the limits of Lesotho's ecosystems and social systems. At once drawn into South Africa's political economic orbit and excluded from it, people in rural Lesotho shoulder South Africa's environmental load.

. . .

For those who might like to read select chapters, here is the book's argument and architecture in one place. Each chapter builds upon the one that came before it, but I've tried to write them so that they might stand alone (which has required some repetition).

Efforts to produce water commodities incite landscape theorizing that can align environmental process with social process. Through an accounting of water's flow across the landscape, differently situated people seek to resolve or bypass the contradictions of Lesotho's water-export era: for example, that water production requires minimal landscape disturbance, even as it leaves rural people with only livestock production for their livelihoods; or, that the flow of water commodities requires storage, generating the problem of sedimentation.

The book's structure mimics the problem of water production as experienced by the LHWP. As one looks more closely at water, its nature becomes less certain, drawing additional factors and actors into view—from soils to livestock to social structures for grazing management to vegetation. The chapters are subtextually autoethnographic, reenacting my own attempts to find my bearings amid this spasm of landscape theory in the water-export era. Each moves step-by-step up the catchment, from water production in the lowlands, to soil conservation efforts in the subalpine rangelands, and to herder lifeworlds in the alpine wetlands. They are also inflected with an historical sensibility that is common to scholarship in African studies, but always in service of elucidating my ethnographic data. The look and feel of that historical approach shifts across chapters—some sequential, some patchy, some cyclical—as the ethnographic material calls for it.[92]

The first two chapters describe the construction of a fluvial imaginary in Lesotho and the circumstances through which water commodification became thinkable and sedimentation inevitable. They show how the upstream production of water commodities rests upon a fluvial pedagogy that promotes coherent understandings of water's symbolic and material realities. First, national elites cultivate the notion that Lesotho's water is abundant, even across the nation, and a deep essence of the territory, as outlined in chapter 1. This runs counter to prevailing notions of actually existing water in Lesotho, a water which is seen as scarce, unpredictable, and destructive. While literature on water commodification describes water as a holistic, local, and cultural substance before being alienated as a commodity, in Lesotho I saw instead how that holisticness, localness, and culturalness was being fashioned as a precondition for alienation.

Water engineers are aware of the destructive quality of Lesotho's water, and it figures for them as a "problem of operations" in reservoir management, as I show in chapter 2. That chapter documents how the elevation of water production as a national priority instigates discussion about who is responsible for land degradation and how to address it, depicting Lesotho's landscapes as spaces through which water flows too quickly. In the belated response to reservoir sedimentation, conservation bureaucrats must acknowledge the destructiveness of Lesotho's water when they attempt to engender popular concern for reservoirs as objects of national interest. I start by outlining Lesotho's history of soil erosion and assessing the current threat it poses to the LHWP. Then I turn to consider how conservation bureaucrats teach publics to read vegetation patterns as a way of understanding erosion, especially patterns of dwarf shrubs.

Solutions to the inevitable sedimentation of water storage infrastructures focus squarely on livestock in the upstream catchment. These include the countrywide institution of conservation measures aimed at slowing down the flow of water across the landscape, including the one endorsed by Tankisi. I turn to these measures in the next two chapters. Armed with ecological theory from colonial times that draws land-use management to the center of attention, rather than changes in the rains as emphasized by everyday people, contemporary conservation bureaucrats employ techniques that fit with their own imaginaries of proper social order. Soil conservation efforts consist of two different approaches, described respectively in chapters 3 and 4: physical structures, such as gabions and silt traps, and social structures, such as grazing associations.

Chapter 3 shows how the practice of soil conservation defers the political economic contradictions of life in the water-reservoir era. The physical works promoted by conservation bureaucrats are unsuited to prevent soil erosion, and yet strangely they are critical to the LHWP. This is because they shore up a precarious social contract in the aftermath of labor migration through a politics of distribution—giving people money so they don't starve. This conservation work is termed *fato-fato*, and it reflects a long history of government distribution, as well as political debate about its merits.

The grazing associations that I describe in chapter 4 represent a more explicit kind of social engineering. Grazing associations, whereby ordinary villagers are tasked with managing rangelands on behalf of chiefs, are seen by conservation workers to get at the root of the problem: rangeland management failures. But these associations are haunted by many decades of previous land use reforms that hobble these new efforts. What emerges is an entangled bank of grazing rules and authorities, impossibly complex. Such efforts have little impact on rangeland condition, as there is probably no management fix in an economic periphery like Lesotho, where both grazing pressure and interannual variation in rainfall are high. However, they do secure donor aid for elites who implement them, shape the political terrain within which herders work, and stymie future reforms.

The final two chapters show how herders and livestock owners have attempted to circumvent the structural pressures around them, whether imposed by colonists, national elites, or the climate. This is visible in the ways they commodify livestock. As I explain in chapter 5, everyday Basotho people have produced sheep and goats for wool and mohair since the earliest days of the Basotho nation when they freed themselves from chiefs' control of lowland pastures. In assessing the social and environmental roles played by livestock, much of the focus from conservationists and anthropologists has been on cattle and their resistance to commodification. However, small stock have been readily commodified by Basotho, thanks partly to the forms of freedom that they inspire in young Basotho men. Since the decline of the labor migration economy, livestock owners are turning wool and mohair production, which had long been a retirement activity, into a full-blown occupation. Pushing one step further, too, they are integrating mutton breeds into their flocks to tap a new market at butcheries over the border.

Chapter 6 describes the landscape effects of these livestock practices, illustrating how Lesotho's rangelands are products of South African industry and its apartheid legacy. Herders and livestock owners engineer rangeland spacetime in response to encroaching shrubs, drought, and insufficient forage. Not waiting for conservation bureaucrats to improve their fortunes, herders burn the range, encouraging erosion but drawing young grasses out of the soil; they introduce molasses and salt to encourage their stock to eat unpalatable forage; they improve their sheep and goat breeds; and they find ways to import or produce fodder in agricultural plots. Like *fato-fato* and sheep commodification, these medicines and pasture management strategies subtend water production, which would otherwise buckle under the weight of the country's social contract.

Drawing together archival materials, natural history evidence, ethnographic data, and ecological surveys, I present an alternative landscape history to the one provided by conservation workers. I describe how settler colonialism by white Afrikaners, class struggle within Basotho society, and the colonial promotion of wool and mohair production put intense pressure on the mountain rangelands where LHWP dams are now sited. Overstocking was encouraged during the emergence of the wool market despite colonial and conservation statements to the contrary, and it has only been exacerbated by Lesotho's ongoing marginalization. With continuing pressures to expand commercial circuits, it is difficult to see how a transition to improved range condition could be attempted without changes to the regional political economy. Lesotho's rangelands express the country's experience as a storage reservoir.

1

Water Production

Investment into water resources development has made water a costly resource that can no more be treated as a free gift of God, and the cultural
attitudes toward this resource need to be changed.

—*LESOTHO: SECOND STATE OF THE ENVIRONMENT REPORT, 2002*[1]

In April 2014, I went on the official tour of the 'Muela Dam at the offices of the Lesotho Highlands Development Authority (LHDA), the administrative body charged
with building and maintaining the Lesotho Highlands Water Project (LHWP).[2]
The tour includes a visit to a large room with posters, diagrams, and models that
describe the structure and construction process of the LHWP; a visit to an over-
look above the reservoir; a guided tour of the dam facilities; and a fifteen-minute
informational video. Being situated in the relatively accessible lowlands and containing power-generating machinery of interest to infrastructure tourists, it is one
of the more frequently visited LHWP sites. White South Africans in Land Rovers
packed with camping gear pass through on their way to the highlands, and Basotho schoolchildren are ferried there by the busload to learn about their country's
signature engineering project.

I had made a special appointment for the tour, so I sat alone in the exhibition
room as the tour guide started the DVD player and then left the room. The video
opened with reconstructed images of dinosaurs passing through a watery, Jurassic
environment, shifting to others of King Moshoeshoe I of Lesotho, the founder of
the Basotho nation. The water we drink today, the video explained, is the same that
was drunk by the dinosaurs and by King Moshoeshoe I himself. It then narrated a
series of videos and images of people doing quintessentially "Bosotho" activities:
women collecting shrubs for cooking fuel and threshing wheat, men with blankets
riding horses, herders tending a flock. The narrator intoned, "As if time had stood
still, oxen plough the fields." It showed the impressive Maletsunyane Falls, another
common tourist destination, and segued to an overflowing Katse Dam, as though
equivalent expressions of something distinctly emblematic of Lesotho. Overflowing with images of crystal-clear water babbling over stones in mountain tributaries

or bursting over the Katse Dam wall when at overfull capacity, the video threaded water through a well-known national mythology. Water, it implied, brings Basotho people into communion with their ancestors. Basotho subjectivity, Lesotho's national identity, and Lesotho's territory are anchored in a watery past, carried forward by this water project. Lesotho's water, the video instructs, is primordial, cultural, sovereign, and abundant.

I had encountered this conception of water before. Lesotho government publications, tourist brochures, and corporate advertisements—including the popular pictorial calendars that are handed out throughout the country by aid organizations, grain wholesalers, and life insurance companies—invoke it widely. So commonplace, it feels like it has always been around, but in fact it's a recent innovation.

Since the LHWP began, a new discourse about water in Lesotho has emerged. It is "abundant" (*metsi a mangata*); it brings development; it is a symbol of national identity; and it is a driver of "regional economic integration."[3] LHWP promotional materials and speeches by its proponents are filled with the cliché metaphors and symbols of water: *metsi ke bophelo* (water is life), or *khauta e tšoeu* (white gold).[4] Suggesting that the nation's water can fuse progress with culture, images of reservoirs and rivers act as a backdrop for tar roads, high-tension power lines, San "bushmen" rock paintings, herds of cattle, and traditional thatched-roof housing. At the heights of phase 1 construction of the Katse and Mohale Dams, such as during my time as a U.S. Peace Corps volunteer from 2003–5, LHWP Toyota Hilux trucks were regular sights on the streets of the capital, Maseru, a commonly understood sign of the project's wealth and significance. Early phase 1 promotional materials figured the reservoirs as tourist destinations, featuring pictures of white people on Jet Skis and motorboats. The tourism industry has been particularly fond of this image of a watery Lesotho. This passage from the government of Lesotho's website is typical: "Mountains, valleys, and rivers provide memorable scenery for tourists. This is where Lesotho gets its crystal clear water as well as green pastures for livestock. . . . [Tourists] enjoy playing around in the clean water of Lesotho's mountains. This is one of the biggest source [sic] of income to the country."[5]

The video ended, and I was taken upstairs to the main lobby of the office and into the main control center of the hydroelectric station, a glass-walled room inside another room. It was filled with computer monitors and a large panel, the focal point, which was complete with diagrams of the reservoir flow process, and red, digital displays indicating the amount of electricity being generated and the height of various reservoirs. I was given a lesson in the role 'Muela plays in the LHWP. The guide explained that water is carried by tunnel from the Katse Reservoir, passing through hydroelectric turbines as it flows into the 'Muela Reservoir. 'Muela is a small "tailpond" reservoir that holds water temporarily before it falls vertically into a bell-shaped intake and passes through a tunnel under the border with South Africa. In this tunnel two instruments—one ultrasonic, one magnetic—are used to determine how much water passes out of Lesotho. From there, the water resurfaces at an outfall on the Ash River near Clarens (see map 2) and passes into the Vaal Reservoir south of Johannesburg.

I had heard that farmers in South Africa's Free State Province, through which the Ash River passes, illegally extract water from the river before it reaches the Vaal Reservoir, so I asked the tour operator about whether she thought that was true. She replied by saying that they do not know—but anyway, "It's not Lesotho's problem what happens to the water after it crosses the border."

While the video downstairs pronounced the primordial and essential nature of water in Lesotho, the people upstairs clearly treated water export as a kind of commodity exchange. I suppose this was to be expected from these technocratic agents of the LHWP, but after having watched that video, I found her response striking. It was as if two different kinds of water—one self-consciously cultural, one unabashedly commodified—were being presented in two parts of this same building. What, I wondered, could be the relationship between them?

These two contradictory depictions are of a piece. "National water"—my shorthand for the primordial, abundant, sovereign, cultural water depicted in the video—and abstract water commodities rely upon each other for conceptual stability. The connection between these two different versions of water become clear when we look closer at how Lesotho was made into storage infrastructure for South African industry in the first place, whom this system serves, and how "national water" aligns with actually existing water in Lesotho. That's where we're headed in this chapter.

Efforts to commodify or privatize water—to nullify its status as a public good—have intensified globally in the past several decades.[6] Activists have lobbied hard in response to assert that water is a "human right."[7] Meanwhile, scholars have argued that water is intricately stitched into a social and cultural fabric, and it must be ripped from this fabric if it is to be sold. Anthropologists have led this charge, drawing on Marcel Mauss's conception of the gift as a "total social fact" to envision water as a phenomenon in which "all kinds of institutions are given expression at one and the same time": religious, moral, economic, and more.[8] This "holistic" view of water stands as a case study for the violence of private property: all of these connections are severed in commodification. And, anthropologists say, the obstacles encountered by those who try to commodify water speak to the local specificity of water, meaning that one can learn about *culture* by looking at those obstacles.[9]

The commodification of Lesotho's water does not simply rip water from an intricate sociocultural fabric, however, but in fact creates a fabric from which to rip it. Standing in the glass-walled control room at the 'Muela Dam, this looks like proper commodified water—what Jaime Linton calls "modern water,"[10] a water abstracted from a local context through hydrologic science and capitalist logics. No doubt, too, it is part of a shift toward water privatization in postapartheid South Africa.[11] Yet, commodification has been contingent upon the LHWP's ability first *to link* water to those local contexts, visible in the video screening room downstairs. The LHWP depicts water in Lesotho as a form of national patrimony and an abundant resource, but no such thing as "Lesotho's water" existed beforehand. Few people in Lesotho would describe the country as water-abundant, given that household water access is poor, drought is common, and water is mostly confined to rivers in the northeastern highlands where LHWP dams are sited. Nor is it seen as a national patrimony. Instead, it is depicted as violent and destructive, as rainfall often comes by torrential downpour, particularly in recent years when climate change has been shifting Lesotho's weather patterns for the worse.[12]

Having internalized the cultural lexicon of holistic water put forward by anthropologists and activists, the LHWP *fabricated* linkages between water and Lesotho's landscapes. That is, rather than merely alienate an otherwise cultural water through commodification, the LHWP generated a cultural water that could be alienated and exported. It is not just commodified water that would be foreign to Basotho, then, but also this harmonious, connective, cultural water that anthropologists and activists work to safeguard.

The new type of water created by the LHWP—one that is cultural, abstractable, and unfamiliar to everyday people—helps us see something else, as well. It exposes the fantasy that water export represents a neutral economic exchange between two sovereign parties when in fact Lesotho's position is tenuous. Whereas South Africa's Bantustan labor reserves were dissolved with the end of apartheid, Lesotho remained intact, and it continues to struggle with the "paradoxes of its sovereignty":[13] that its sovereignty is contingent upon its subordinate relationship to South Africa. The production of national water—that is, the nationalization, culture-ification, commodification, and export of water—remedies this by teaching citizens to recognize themselves as party to a kind of national project in spite of that subordinate relationship. It is pedagogic, as in the South African case described by Antina von Schnitzler.[14] The LHWP has been used as an occasion to produce other, more concrete kinds of national heritage, too, as Rachel King shows,[15] from the construction of national parks to the establishment of historical heritage sites.

To explain how the production of national water works, I need to start by describing the setting—a mountainous and mono-ethnic constitutional monarchy, surrounded by a multiethnic republic with steep racial hierarchies—and by outlining a two-step historical process that scaffolds the chapter's plot: the transformation of Lesotho over the past 150 years first from a self-sufficient agricultural producer to a labor reserve and, later, to a water reservoir.

FROM GRANARY TO LABOR RESERVE . . .

Seen from the vantage of the water-export era, it almost seems as though the Senqu catchment were an organic unit of political space in the partitioning of Lesotho's territory, with national boundaries mapping precisely onto the Senqu headwaters—as though it were naturally a water-exporting country.[16] More so, it is a product of Basotho defense of their mountain stronghold.

FIGURE 3. The Lesotho highlands. Photo by author.

Lesotho is generally described in terms of two geographical regions: the low-lands and the highlands.[17] These regions look and feel dramatically different as cultural and physical landscapes. Both are mostly treeless. The lowlands resemble the southwestern United States, with reddish-brown soils, rolling hills, and periodic mesas that formed from a sandstone, sedimentary geology.[18] They make up less than a third of Lesotho's surface area, just a crescent of land in the country's west, but they contain most of its arable land and 80 percent of its 2.2 million citizens.

By contrast, the highlands are deeply incised, high-altitude grasslands, made of a volcanic, basalt geology (see fig. 3). They resemble the windswept Scottish Highlands or the Andean Páramo, reaching altitudes of over thirty-one hundred meters above sea level. They consist of two chains running more or less north and south, which converge in the north of the country: the Maloti Chain to the west, and the Drakensberg Chain on Lesotho's eastern border with South Africa.[19] When cold air drifts in from the eastern coast of South Africa and meets the steep escarpment of the Drakensberg, it produces orographic precipitation in the highlands, which Lesotho now sells to South Africa.

In the highlands, Basotho refer to the lowlands as "Lesotho," as though it were another country altogether. It points to the remoteness of these areas and hints at a time when the highlands were mostly uninhabited. Today, there are several sizable towns in the highlands, including the district capitals of Mokhotlong, Thaba-Tseka, and Qacha's Nek. At the turn of the twentieth century, these were nonexistent.

The mountains and western foothills were spaces of refuge during the colonial period, and spaces that Basotho could defend against settlers. The area was very sparsely populated until refugees fleeing the early nineteenth-century Zulu wars on the southeastern coast retreated inland, to the opposite side of the Drakensberg mountains.[20] Just to the west of them, white Afrikaner settlers were arriving in the area after fleeing British rule in the Cape.[21] These refugees fended off Afrikaner (and British) efforts to seize their land, partly through alliance with French and Swiss missionaries.[22] Though they were an amalgam of different "clans" (liboko), they eventually coalesced under a chief named Moshoeshoe into a single group called "the Basotho," the inhabitants of "Basutoland." The Afrikaners called their own territory the Orange Free State, signaling their Dutch ancestry and their independence from the Cape.

Basutoland became a major agricultural producer, exporting grain to the Orange Free State—today thought of as the breadbasket of South Africa—where the Afrikaners had been struggling to farm successfully. One missionary observer writing during a serious drought in 1863 referred to Basutoland as the "granary of the Free State and of part of the [Cape] Colony."[23] Upset with this dependence on Basotho and eager to take hold of more land, Afrikaners fought to increase their territory.[24] After several decades of conflict, Moshoeshoe was compelled to request "protectorate" status under Great Britain in 1868, effectively becoming a British colony. He also signed away a large tract of fertile land to the Afrikaners as part of this negotiated compromise—today, these "conquered territories" (see map 3) are a source of ongoing consternation for Basotho.[25] The annexure of Basutoland not only gave the British a territory but insured themselves against the increasing power of the Orange Free State. South Africa, after all, had not yet been unified and was instead a set of contested territories.

At that very moment, the world's largest diamond and gold deposits were discovered at Kimberly (1866) and the Witwatersrand (1886), respectively. Basotho went to work in the mines so they could purchase consumer goods that were newly available, such as plows and guns.[26] The plows helped Basotho increase their agricultural production even in spite of having lost territory to the Afrikaners, exporting even more grain to the booming mining towns around Kimberly and the Witwatersrand. The guns helped them fend off additional threats from Afrikaners and the British. When the colonial administration of the Cape attempted to disarm the Basotho, they ignited the Gun War of 1880–81. Safe in their mountain redoubt, they rebuffed the soldiers from Cape, which spent a staggering 4.75 million pounds with nothing to show for it. The Basotho retained all of their weapons and even refused to pay the license fee that was imposed afterward.[27] It was an extraordinary act of anticolonial resistance.[28]

In addition to being *pulled* to work in the mines by plows and guns, however, they were also *pushed*. This happened in at least two ways: a "hut tax" imposed by the British, and tariffs on Basutoland grain imposed by South Africans.[29] The colonial administration forced Basotho to pay a tax for every dwelling, and mining labor was one of the few ways to earn cash.[30] Tariffs from the 1880s onward then undercut Basutoland's agricultural exports, while cheap U.S. and Australian grains flooded South African markets. Making matters worse, a rinderpest epizootic decimated Basotho cattle used for ploughing, and crippling droughts followed.

Across Southern Africa, these taxes and tariffs combined with land seizures to force many Africans into exploitative wage labor. With the 1913 Natives Land Act, for example, 93 percent of South African territory was reserved for whites, including the most productive agricultural lands. Africans were forcibly relocated to impoverished ethnic reserves known as "Bantustans" or "homelands," and later legislation such as the 1923 Urban Areas Act made it impossible for them to reside in the city centers without a pass, defining Africans as "temporary sojourners" in white lands.[31]

The scholar-activist Harold Wolpe articulated the overarching structure and implications of this arrangement:[32] Africans were both drawn into an exploitative industrial center and expelled to a barren geographical periphery, trapping them in an endless, oscillating migration. The Bantustans of Venda, Bophuthatswana, and Transkei were later "granted independence" in the late 1970s, but these "countries" were not recognized by the United Nations, which understood them as mechanisms for segregation and exploitation. Mining recruitment centers were established in Basutoland's district capitals, where work permits could be issued before arriving in South Africa. Pass laws for South Africans and work permits for Basotho made it possible to control the flow of workers, creating what Karl Marx called "an army reserve of laborers."[33]

Lesotho had been transformed within a century, as Colin Murray famously put it, "from granary to labor reserve."[34]

. . . AND FROM LABOR RESERVE
TO WATER RESERVOIR

As exploitative as the migrant labor system was, it is seen nostalgically by some people in Lesotho.[35] From the late 1980s onward, Basotho employment in South African industry plummeted. Mines mechanized. The price of gold dropped. Even in the early 2000s, when the gold price rebounded, domestic pressure on the South African government meant that domestic workers were favored over foreign nationals. Citizens of Lesotho hoping to work in South Africa were left with domestic work (for women), illegal mining in abandoned shafts (for men), and other work in the "informal economy." The one hundred twenty nine thousand Basotho mineworkers in South Africa in 1979 dwindled to just nineteen thousand by 2018.[36] The proportion of households that have at least one member working in South African mines declined from 50 percent in 1952 to just 12 percent in 2002.[37] No new work contracts have been given to foreign mineworkers in South Africa since 2003.[38] Mining employment went from a standard expectation to an elusive goal.[39]

There has been little else to make up for these declines in Lesotho's economy. A textiles industry has been largely propped up by trade agreements that must be periodically renewed. Garment factories can disappear literally overnight when companies no longer find the profits they had hoped for. Some revenues come in through the South African Development Community (SADC) revenue sharing agreement. A few diamond mines in the highlands make sporadic if sometimes lucrative finds. Foreign aid continues to be one of the main sources of economic activity.

The decline of the mining labor economy has run parallel to the emergence of the water-export economy with the signing of the Lesotho Highlands Water Project Treaty in 1986. Providing the largest source of foreign exchange and one of the largest sources of foreign revenues altogether after remittances and foreign aid,[40] the LHWP is a rare bright spot for the country. Phase 1 of the project was completed in 2004. It included the construction of two large dams at Katse and Mohale, as well as a smaller tailpond dam at 'Muela and a weir at Matsoku. Some 120km of tunnels connect these reservoirs, and 72MW of electricity are generated at 'Muela before the water passes into South Africa, nearly satisfying Lesotho's domestic needs. By the end of 2020, a total of 16.401 billion m3 of water had been transferred to South Africa, generating 11.265 billion Maloti (USD 771 million) in royalties.[41]

But serious questions about who benefits from the project have been correctly raised.[42] Most employment associated with the LHWP was temporary. Only a handful of people are required to manage and operate the field operations branches at 'Muela, Katse, and Mohale, and a small executive staff remains permanently in Maseru.[43] Rural electrification has moved extremely slowly, meaning that, while electricity prices have stayed low thanks to the 'Muela hydroelectric station, many areas of the country cannot take advantage.[44]

Impoundment of Katse Dam displaced more than two thousand people who were resettled in neighboring villages or in the capital. Another twenty thousand to twenty-five thousand people lost croplands, rangelands, fuelwood, and medicines.[45] Because of the steep slopes and thin soils found in the country, Lesotho does not have much arable land,[46] so the valleys inundated by LHWP reservoirs were a significant loss, especially the fertile croplands along the valley floor. The LHWP provided compensation for those who were affected, but many have reported that compensation was inadequate. For example, compensation funds for commonly held resources like grazing land were pooled, and communities were advised to spend them on failed development initiatives such as flour mills that quickly went into disrepair. Some people were paid in grain—which was eaten and then gone.[47]

It's important to note that the benefits and burdens of the LHWP are shared unevenly in South Africa, too, where water prices have been raised significantly to buy Lesotho's water.[48] South Africa, unlike Lesotho, does not have access to cheap loans from the World Bank, so it has funded construction and purchases of water supply partly through raising end-user water prices.[49] This, even as South Africa fails to fix its water infrastructure and limit its need for transfers from afar. One estimate suggests that as much as 37 percent of South Africa's water is lost because of leaky pipes.[50]

The LHWP is a storage and extraction project. Phase 2 is expected to deliver water beginning in 2027 and gradually increase from the current 780 million m3 per annum to 1255 million m3.[51] Its centerpiece is the Polihali Dam, which nearly doubles Lesotho's water storage by adding another 2.2 billion m3 of capacity. When phase 2 was initially proposed, it was slated to include a 1,000MW pump-storage hydroelectricity system at Kobong, a major selling point for Lesotho, which could produce enough electricity to export.[52] But this pump-storage scheme has been deferred. That Kobong—the phase 2 component most beneficial to Lesotho— is no longer planned underscores a sad truth: the LHWP's primary function is not hydroelectric generation for Lesotho, but rather as a water storage tank for South Africa.

The country has been transformed from labor reserve to water reservoir.

SOVEREIGNTY AND THE ICONOGRAPHY
OF WATER ABUNDANCE

Lesotho's status as storage infrastructure has prompted some in the country to advocate for a South African annexure of Lesotho as a tenth province.[53] Each year around Lesotho's commemoration of independence on October 4, stories in the print and radio media can be found reporting on Lesotho citizens' discontent with Lesotho's independence. During the 2010 Independence Day festivities, the principal chief of Thaba Bosiu stated that "celebrations today have lost their old spark; they are so low-key. Basotho are not even proud of this day anymore."[54] I met many people during my field research who advocated "incorporation," and some of Lesotho's politicians such as former prime minister Thomas Thabane have campaigned on such a position.[55] A petition with thirty thousand signatures was submitted to the South African High Commission in 2010 by the Lesotho People's Charter Movement for incorporation, but the issue has stalled for the likely reasons that the move would all but erase the authority of Lesotho's government ministers, chiefs, and civil servants.

From the South African side, there is little incentive to incorporate Lesotho as a tenth province. It is true that Lesotho has some natural resources and skilled, educated citizens. But South Africa currently admits as many Basotho workers as it likes, has favorable access to Lesotho's water, and has broad powers to shape Lesotho's economic policy through the Southern African Customs Union.[56] Lesotho's currency (the Loti; pl. Maloti) is pegged one-to-one to the South African Rand, too. This provides Lesotho with monetary stability, but prevents it from using monetary policy to manipulate its position with regard to trade deficits and inflation. The same is true for interest rates and minimum agricultural prices.[57]

Water commodification responds to this malaise,[58] and the notion of "water abundance" is a critical conceptual vehicle for doing so.

As I mentioned in the introduction, the LHWP Treaty was signed by a military government that ten months earlier had overthrown prime minister Chief Leabua Jonathan in a coup. The coup was likely supported by South Africa: Jonathan had resisted the water project for some time and had been harboring anti-apartheid activists. Despite these inauspicious beginnings, national elites advanced the misleading notion that the LHWP could improve Lesotho's political and economic position as it harnessed the power of its water. The chief spokesperson for the LHDA explained in a 1988 interview printed in the *Toronto Star*:

> "It's going to change the face of Lesotho," he says. "Once we are supplying South Africa with water, it won't be so easy for them to do things like blockade our borders." Then, in an aside that seems to underline Lesotho's vulnerability, Sephoko looked out his office window, across the dusty, potholed streets of Maseru, towards the nearby South African border. "Years ago, when I was a herd-boy tending cattle and sheep in the mountains, I never imagined anything like this," he said. "I thought we in Lesotho would have to depend on South Africa for generations."[59]

An LHDA brochure from 1986 stated categorically that "Lesotho must control, store and redirect its water. Only in this way can Lesotho ensure that proper use is made of its water within the country and that a proper payment is received for the large quantities of water leaving Lesotho [which will] give Lesotho effective control over its water resources."[60] The legal scholar Patrick McAuslan pointed out that, in fact, the treaty explains clearly that Lesotho *loses* control over its water by putting it under the administration of an international body, namely the Lesotho Highlands Water Commission.

After the signing of the 1986 treaty, the World Bank was being pressured to rescind its support because of international economic sanctions on South Africa. King Moshoeshoe II published a 1988 op-ed in the *New York Times*, imploring the international community to allow financing of the LHWP to go forward. He urged the world to "punish Pretoria, not Lesotho." Lesotho is not blessed with natural resources like its neighbor, he said—but it does have "abundant water."[61]

Not only is Lesotho's water abundant, supporters of the LHWP explain, but the country is unable to actually "use" it. The government of Lesotho's website suggests that "unfortunatly [*sic*] river discharge statistics show that most of this water is lost to Lesotho in the form of run-off."[62] Consider how water is framed in the LHWP Feasibility Study:

> Water is one of the few resources which Lesotho has in relative abundance. Even allowing for possible irrigation projects and for general expansion and improvement in living standards, Lesotho's total water resources far exceed its likely future requirements. The average total water available in Lesotho is of the order of 140 m3/s compared with Lesotho's present consumption of approximately 1.5 m3/s. The LHWP would confer substantial value on the water which is surplus to Lesotho's

requirements by turning it into an exportable commodity, albeit to a single buyer. It is to be noted that South Africa receives the water in any event, since all water originating in Lesotho but not used in Lesotho, flows into South Africa.[63]

In other words, the country has so much water it might as well sell it—and anyway Lesotho should be happy to do so because the water ends up in South Africa either way. They fail to mention that this water enters South Africa at too low an elevation for use in Gauteng, where it is needed: expensive pumping would be required to move the water from the Free State to Johannesburg.

"Water abundance" is not simply a hydrological fact, but rather a political tool,[64] as well as an object of rumor and fantasy.[65] It's true that Lesotho's territory is relatively well watered compared with its neighbors. It is commonly cited in project-related documents that four countries (Namibia, Botswana, South Africa, and Lesotho) depend on Senqu/Orange River basin—but whereas 46 percent of the basin's mean annual runoff originates in Lesotho, the country contains just 3 percent of the basin's total land area.[66] A promotional booklet for the Maloti-Drakensberg Transfrontier Project, a failed effort to establish conservation zones in Lesotho's alpine wetlands, conjures Lesotho as a "water factory" of the subcontinent as a means of justifying the construction project, citing mean annual rainfall figures of 1,800–2,000mm.[67]

As extraordinary as the hydrological figures may be, they obscure the fact that water abundance is highly localized in Lesotho. Lesotho has an extremely diverse topography, leading to diverse rainfall patterns and a patchy geography of water. The northeast highlands feature high rainfall rates when compared to the lowlands, which receive less than the foothills. Parts of the mountains, too, are affected by a "rain shadow" in the lower Senqu River of Qacha's Nek District. The rain shadow is caused by its position far enough inland to be shielded from low-pressure systems reaching the Drakensberg Range to the east, meaning that the southern highlands are almost as dry as the lowlands. In addition to being localized spatially, water in Lesotho is localized temporally, with high seasonality of rainfall and regular droughts stemming from the El Niño Southern Oscillation (ENSO).[68]

The massive dam reservoirs of Katse and Mohale seem to proclaim water abundance by their very existence. Yet, ironically, dam reservoirs themselves have become indices of drought for everyday people and in national discourse (e.g., news media), as drops in their levels expose barren soil that help one visualize the extent of a drought. The Katse Reservoir has not been at full operating capacity since 2013. During my field research in the summer of 2019, reservoir levels were dangerously low: Mohale was at 17 percent, Katse was at 40 percent. This meant that the total storage currently was only somewhere around 30 percent according to an LHDA water engineer I spoke with.[69]

Neither does alleged water abundance translate into general availability of water for households. Even villages sited immediately beside LHWP dam reservoirs may lack well-maintained water taps or any form of irrigation and are prohibited from extracting water from the reservoir for consumption or irrigation.[70] In some cases, people near dams have seen their taps dry up as a (presumed) result of underground shifts in hydrology triggered by the reservoirs' incredible weight against mountainsides.[71] Small earthquakes known as "reservoir-induced seismicity" were recognized just one month after impoundment at Katse Dam.[72] Countrywide, most people (51.9 percent) in rural areas get their water from a shared public tap, with nearly a quarter (23.8 percent) getting it from springs.[73] The situation is not much better in urban areas where most services are located,[74] though it has improved somewhat with the 2015 Metolong Water Scheme, a lowlands dam that provides water to lowland urban centers. Back in the highlands of Mokhotlong, employees from the Rural Water Supply (RWS), the government agency responsible for building and maintaining water taps in rural areas, told me that they had a multiyear backlog of village complaints regarding taps that were needed, dried up, or broken. Additionally, many people do not have the money to purchase rainwater storage tanks, nor the metal-roofed houses needed to use them.

In short, "water abundance" contradicts everyday lived realities in a country where droughts are common, rain is localized, and water access is spotty. Yet, the iconography of national water has been deployed across Lesotho as though abundance is spatially even, a quintessential property of Lesotho. Water abundance links together culture, territory, and a rationale for the LHWP in the face of its various costs, including resettlement, loans from the World Bank, and more.

"WATER IS A GIFT THAT DESTROYS"

If that notion of abundance is a recent coinage for the water-export economy, how does it articulate with existing ideas about water? When I began my research on water in Lesotho, I wanted to address just that question. I wanted to track how water was talked about in light of the LHWP. What, I wondered, might a vernacular notion of water in Lesotho look like, and how might Lesotho's water economy be changing it? But my probing questions about water came to little. If I asked someone whether Lesotho had a lot of water, they would typically respond in the affirmative, understanding that I was probably referencing the LHWP. The conversations went nowhere. My early fieldnotes express deep frustration on this point. If I asked specifically about the LHWP and whether it benefited people or not, I could start a conversation but it would not be particularly interesting. Some in the mountain areas would cite the benefits of roads built as part of the LHWP or the royalties paid by South Africa to Lesotho for water; others would explain how those royalties were "eaten" by politicians. But few of these conversations elicited strong emotion or felt particularly revealing of how people might spontaneously talk about water outside the usual tropes. Instead, I felt as though I had already learned these perspectives from reading newspaper stories about the project, or even in reading about healthy river activism elsewhere in the world.

This changed, to my surprise, when I attended a workshop in Mokhotlong, the main town in the mountainous area where my research was mostly sited. My friend in a government conservation agency invited me to the workshop, which was put on by the Disaster Management Authority (DMA), a government agency created with royalties from the LHWP to coordinate other government agencies on "disaster preparedness." The DMA was presenting its Disaster Risk Reduction Policy to local government councilors and civil servants. After a prayer and introductions, the DMA staff outlined the basic tenets of the policy for around thirty minutes, after which time audience members had the chance to ask questions and comment on the policy.

Mostly, they ignored the policy document and complained about what the government should do to fix roads, bridges, and other infrastructure under threat from natural disasters. There were complaints about the government's failures to clear roads and culverts of sediment after storms—and how flooding within the town of Mokhotlong was damaging the foundations of homes. There were concerns about the dangers posed to schoolchildren when crossing flooded rivers, and demands that the government build and repair more bridges to protect them. There were lamentations for the topsoil in people's agricultural fields carried away by storms. There was an extended discussion of the village of Khahleti, where a flooding river in 2013 led to the collapse of a large riverbank on which a graveyard was sited (see fig. 4). The storm was undeterred by the array of gabions that had been put in place to reinforce the bank, and the graves of twenty-one people were carried downstream, reburied in sediment or strewn across riverbanks and unidentifiable. More "diversion furrow" ditches, they said, were needed upstream to redirect runoff water and protect the cemetery.

I came to realize that nearly every discussion about natural disasters was actually about surface water and the dangers it posed when left to its own devices. It occurred to me that these cases articulated a notion of water quite distinct from the water depicted in LHWP propaganda documents or water activism. Whereas those documents depict pure, life-giving water, flowing transcendently from above, the water discussed at the DMA meeting was something different: it was violent, unpredictable, and deeply mixed with the soils through which it passed. Instead of flowing, connective, and productive, this water was disruptive, disjunctive, and dangerous.

The destructive quality of water should not have surprised me. It is referenced regularly in everyday life. Just two weeks prior to the DMA meeting, a woman taught me a Sesotho proverb (*maele*) as we stood in a shop taking shelter from a violent thunderstorm that quickly brought water flashing through the town drainage ditches before our eyes: *metsi ke mahlopha-a-senya* ("water is a gift that destroys").[75] When I visited the destroyed riverbank cemetery at Khahleti with the government conservation agency, one of the conservation bureaucrats used this same expression as we looked upon the wreckage. After having learned it, in fact, I would hear the phrase with some regularity during my research.

FIGURE 4. Collapsed streambank after a storm in the village of Khahleti. Photo by author.

I saw this kind of water everywhere after that meeting. Lesotho's roads are tormented by it: during storms, piles and piles of sediment wash over roads that must be cleared by front-loader tractors. Gullies carve away at roadsides, undermining bridges and culverts. It is like a signature scrawled across Lesotho's landscapes. Even on my way to the ministry office on the very morning of the DMA meeting, I stopped to look at some gullies and diversion structures and was struck by the dramatic ways in which this landscape had been shaped both by soil erosion and soil conservation. Around every corner, a gully, a rut, a culvert, a gabion, a silt trap, signs of road repair, and other testaments to the unruliness of Lesotho's water. *Metsi ke mahlopha-a-senya.*

And it is not simply rural people from the highlands who identify this quality of water. Most of the DMA workshop attendees were from the urban lowlands, after all. At a separate government workshop on watershed conservation in the lowlands town of Hlotse, a consultant to the ministry said of Lesotho's water in a PowerPoint presentation, "Our water is disruptive" (*Metsi a rona aa lukeha*), as though it were its natural condition. The statement spoke to his overarching point: that water in Lesotho must be brought under control through watershed management in order to prevent it from damaging crops, homes, and livelihoods. Water is a gift that destroys.

This is a long-standing notion—long enough to be immortalized in a proverb—but also one that is sharpening amid climate changes. The rains used to be much better in Lesotho, as just about anyone in the country will tell you. They used to start in September or October, falling most commonly as *pula ea molupe*—slow, drizzling rains that percolate into the soil and nourish the forage and agricultural crops upon which most people in rural Lesotho depend. If the sun shines after a *molupe* rain, the rangelands seem to transform before your eyes, with new grass shoots coming up green. Livestock will become so giddy, one herder told me, that they'll scamper around, making it hard to catch calves or foals.

These days (*linakong tsena*), people said to me repeatedly, the rains don't arrive until December or January and only then as *pula ea sekhahla*—torrential downpours that fall on lands denuded of vegetation by drought and starving livestock, carrying away the soil.[76] The "water simply slides over the surface" (*metsi aa thella feela*), as some described it. The seasons are being pushed out of order. These days, snow might fall in the middle of the summer, as it did in 2017 in the highlands of Mokhotlong. You can't tell if it's winter or summer anymore, one elderly man told me.

Rainfall data from the Lesotho Meteorological Society support these perspectives.[77] Though total annual precipitation has not changed much over the years, with annual rainfall totals more or less consistent at decadal time scales (albeit highly variable from year to year), the country has witnessed a delayed onset of summer rainfall and longer periods without rain during the rainy season (see fig. 5). That is, the dry season is getting longer but it is broken by heavy rains that ultimately stabilize annual rainfall totals. To make matters worse, it is also more common to see sustained periods of high temperatures. The lowlands occasionally experience fourteen straight days at over thirty degrees Celsius, a heatwave that is unheard of in recent memory. As temperatures rise, evapotranspiration increases, meaning that soils and vegetation do not hold moisture as long.[78]

These days, if Lesotho's water doesn't come crashing downslope, it gets evaporated before it can be utilized.

CONCLUSION

Far from a neutral economic exchange, the sale of water to South Africa stands as an example of South African domination of its smaller neighbor. Lesotho has been fashioned as South Africa's storage vessel—once for laboring bodies and now for water bodies.

As with the commodification and export of Basotho labor, the commodification and export of water from Lesotho is part of a regional infrastructure of economic production. This infrastructure requires maintenance—forms of material, social, and symbolic engineering upstream. For one, commodification relies on aesthetic, symbolic work to make water export between these two countries thinkable. Water must be made conceptually *as a resource* before it can be exploited.[79] Supporters of the water project have drawn water into Lesotho's national iconography, describing it as fundamental to the territory, spatially even

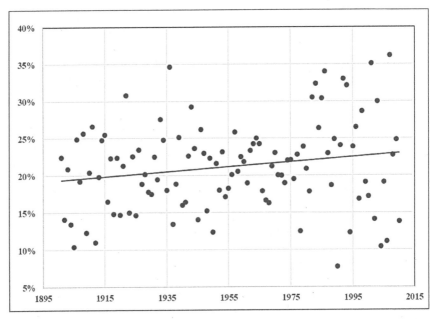

FIGURE 5. October–November rainfall as percent of annual total, 1900–2010. Source: World Bank (2016).

across the nation, and abundant. They created a new category of water: national water. In rendering Lesotho "water abundant," its water became underutilized and exporting it to South Africa became a logical consequence, even necessary: by selling water that it "does not use," as they described it, Lesotho's geopolitical position would be bolstered.

Under the highly unequal terms of exchange between Lesotho and South Africa, sovereignty was declared as both a precondition for and product of the LHWP. But rather than testifying to Lesotho's sovereignty, the export commodification of Lesotho's water illuminates its weakness as the country shifts from labor reserve to water reservoir. Ironically, national water is foreign to ordinary people. For anyone not actively promoting the LHWP, water is scarce, localized, and threatening. National water clearly contradicts Lesotho's actually existing fluvial regime, in which staccato rainstorms yield low soil infiltration and high rates of overland flow. National water, then, is foreign water that has been contrived as local. Rather than rendering water as an abstract category to extract it from its local, material contexts, as described by critics of water privatization, the LHWP first produces a locally emplaced water for the purpose of extraction.

The LHWP's conceptual development of "national water" also exposes a weakness in anthropology's conceptual development of water as a total social fact,[80] the antithesis of which is commodified water. Literature on the topic figures water as transcendent, as being in harmonious connection with society prior to its violent extraction and alienation under capitalism from that cultural substratum—a kind of Edenic fall from grace. While I am careful not to discount the deep imbrication of water in human life, nor the violence that can accompany commodification, I worry about the ease with which we tell stories of water's Edenic fall, particularly when efforts to commodify water in Lesotho draw upon Edenic imagery and when ethnographic subjects emphasize a nonharmonious, disjunctive water—a gift that destroys. The holistic interconnectivity envisioned by anthropological accounts of water needs to be provincialized, then.

Not only should anthropologists do more to document the creativity with which capitalists manage to commodify water, and question the conventional tropes used to contest it; they should also do more to account for water's different modalities, including surface water, rainfall, tap water, glaciers, condensation, reservoir water, and so on.[81] For example, national water is principally volumetric, and during production comes into conflict with surface water—fluvial water. Had the LHWP boosters learned more about the local qualities of Lesotho's fluvial water, they might have avoided problems currently being experienced by the LHWP, in fact. It turns out that the water flowing over land as runoff and cutting erosion gullies into the soil could render the LHWP nonoperational in a matter of decades. The dam reservoir at 'Muela is facing serious sedimentation problems as a result of soil erosion in the upstream catchment,[82] and a multimillion-dollar effort is now underway to dredge the reservoir.

2

The Soil Problem

[A river] can be considered a body of flowing sediments as much as one of flowing water.

—PATRICK MCCULLY[1]

If a river is a body of flowing sediments, as Patrick McCully puts it in the epigraph for this chapter, then producing water requires its separation from sand, silt, and clay, particle by particle. And, yet, soil erosion and reservoir sedimentation appear in almost none of the engineering and planning literature for the Lesotho Highlands Water Project. How could it be that a multibillion-dollar water storage and export scheme came to be sited in a notoriously erosive country—literally a global testing ground for soil erosion mitigation techniques?[2] And, why would it ignore the problem?

The previous chapter showed how water is being conceptually transformed in Lesotho to facilitate export production. That meant the development of a concept of "national water"—a water that is abundant and locally emplaced; one that is spatially even across the territory and across time; one full of elisions and omissions. Now, I turn to those elisions and omissions, and to the pedagogical work that seeks to address them. National water is essentially volumetric,[3] and therefore it clashes with fluvial water, which is defined by its patchiness, its punctuated temporality, and its destructive movement over land. Fluvial water shifts across rainy years and dry years, with droughts broken by storms, coursing sometimes riotously from hillslope to river to reservoir. Its material properties are surprising and suspect. In this collision of volumetric and fluvial water, we can see just how scrambled and contradictory conceptions of Lesotho's water have become. At the very moment that water is established as an export commodity, its nature is called into question, asserted, contested, and reasserted.

Whereas in chapters 3 and 4 I'll describe *solutions* developed by conservation bureaucrats to tackle soil erosion, this chapter critically examines the *problem*. I start by explaining how the problem of soil erosion and sedimentation manifests for water engineers, before outlining what is known about the threat it poses to water export. I show how conservation bureaucrats have sought to develop a flu-vial pedagogy—teaching rural people how to identify soil erosion and to diagnose its causes—implicitly and explicitly blaming livestock owners for sedimentation. They do so in the absence of adequate measuring and monitoring of soil erosion, however, leading them to rely on a "sentinel device": dwarf shrubs.[4] Shrubs are put forward as a way to see soil erosion and its relationship to livestock grazing, but as we will see these relationships are subject to a wide diversity of interpretations.

The soil problem is serious, and it demonstrates the extent to which producing water cultivates a fluvial imagination, or a sense for how water flows over land and why. It educes theory about the landscape, generating an attention to such fine-grained processes as the movement of different sediment particles down a slope, how they weather in the face of cold or heat, how they pass through different kinds of vegetation, and the ways they aggregate together and slump within a reservoir. This chapter adopts that same attention.

A PROBLEM OF OPERATIONS

"Are your concerns primarily related to water quantity," I asked two water engi-neers I'll call Thomas and Selemo, "or water quality?" They worked for the Lesotho Highlands Development Authority (LHDA), the administrative body responsible for building and maintaining the water project.

Throughout much of my research, that was how I thought of the LHWP's sediment problems. That is, I assumed sedimentation was either a problem because it cuts into storage capacity (i.e., the quantity of water available for transfer) or because it adds organic matter to water that compromises water purity (i.e., the quality of that water). It was late in my research, and I was surprised by their answer.

"Neither," they explained. "Sedimentation is first and foremost a problem of *operations*." By this, they meant that sedimentation circumscribes their ability to manage water levels at the reservoirs. From an "operations perspective," their mandate was to plan properly to provision water at an agreed-upon rate to South Africa. I didn't quite get it.

Thomas zoomed out on the problem for me. The LHWP consists of essentially three reservoirs. In the mountains, the Mohale Reservoir flows by tunnel into Katse Reservoir. From there, water enters another tunnel and flows into the 'Muela Reservoir, passing through hydroelectric turbines just before it arrives (see map 2). Engineers' work consists of managing the levels of these reservoirs to ensure that they maintain a steady passage of water through the turbines and on to South Africa, the issuance of which must happen according to agreed-upon schedules for a given month and year. They also try to ensure a consistent production of electricity, without which Lesotho must import additional electricity for national use. They can surpass these minimum production requirements when water is abundant (provided there is space available downstream in South Africa's Vaal Reservoir to receive the water), but the important part is to make sure enough water sits in the mountain reservoirs to meet these regular requirements even during the dry season or periods of drought.

From an operations perspective, Selemo said, two related issues threaten their mandate—one inside the reservoir and one above it. The first, he said, is sedimentation from soil erosion. With increasing sediment levels at 'Muela, the water quantity in the reservoir is smaller, narrowing their flexibility in managing reservoir levels. The room for maneuver is reduced. The second, he said, is the degradation of alpine wetlands. The wetlands' function is to store water and release it slowly downstream. If the wetlands don't store water, then the water flows out of them too quickly. This increases the risk of sedimentation from flooding, but it also reduces the evenness of water's flow into the reservoir—too much in the rainy months and not enough in the dry ones—meaning again that their ability to manage reservoir levels is diminished. If the river systems upstream carry water slowly and evenly into the reservoirs, then reservoir levels will be predictable.[5] If levels were poorly managed, a period of significant rainfall could overflow the dam walls, meaning a loss of water to the project.

We were seated in an LHDA office building, and I pointed to a framed picture on the wall behind them: the iconic image of an overflowing Katse Dam that proclaims Lesotho's water abundance, printed on a thousand different postcards, calendars, billboards, and government reports (see fig. 6). "So, the overflow of Katse Dam in that picture," I asked, "represents a failure of management rather than a success?"

They agreed and we had a laugh. If that water were instead being stored in the wetlands or rangelands above, then it would be released later when the reservoir level had diminished from water transfers.

The LHDA's icon of water abundance, it turns out, is an index of land degradation and poor reservoir management for these engineers.

Thomas drew a profile of the reservoir on the whiteboard to edify me. He said the first thing to know is that the issue of sedimentation only comes into play for transfer capacity when it crests the line between "dead" and "live" (or, "active") storage. Dead storage refers to the water beneath the transfer intake tunnel, which can't be transferred and is therefore "dead." If sediment accumulates to an elevation higher than the intake, it will begin cutting into the overall transfer capacity. Shrinking the dead storage is an issue for "operations," however, because it narrows their management options. It is also a problem if it accumulates against the dam wall where the downstream outflow is. Unfortunately, he said, there is no sediment outflow valve for Katse or 'Muela, though there is talk of putting one in for the Polihali Dam. There are outflow release valves on both dam walls, he explained, but they are designed only to allow for the release of water downstream

FIGURE 6. Overflowing Katse Dam. Photo by author.

to promote river ecological function. Sediment can only pass through specially designed outflows—its abrasiveness would destroy the outflow valves at Katse or 'Muela.

I asked if they knew the actual sedimentation status of these various reservoirs. Was there a monitoring program in place? Unsure and unaware of such a program project-wide, they suggested I send a data request to the CEO's office. (I did, but received no response after numerous follow-ups.) For 'Muela, however, they did have data. In fact, on the very same whiteboard they drew my attention to some figures scrawled in an equation, at the end of which was the figure "0.725," with "12%" scrawled beside it. Thomas explained that 0.725 million m3 of sediment were currently in the reservoir. The reservoir's total volume is 6 million m3, meaning that it was 12 percent filled.

I asked if they knew of any efforts to model sediment accumulation in the reservoirs, but they knew of none. Selemo said that he wouldn't really believe the models if they did. This is because of the nature of Lesotho's soils. He said that all the soil might wash away to bedrock, but then more soil could form in the next coming years—the amygdaloidal basalts in the highlands weather easily. So, it's very difficult to predict sedimentation rates, he said.

Selemo then drew our attention from the reservoir back to the upstream catchment. One of the key issues today is that wool production has taken off in such a big way. Because of the boom in wool production, he said, overgrazing has led to a reduction of the ground's capacity to store water. The reservoirs at Katse and Mohale are much larger than 'Muela's, he said, so he felt the sedimentation problem there was not particularly pressing. However, he added, it is a problem in the long term, so they are very concerned about it. He asked us to consider Matsoku Weir, situated in a neighboring valley to the Katse Reservoir and connected to it by a diversion tunnel. The weir had become so clogged with sediment that it is almost non-operational. The cost of dredging it might be too expensive to be worthwhile.

In a separate conversation, another water engineer emphasized the significance of the lands above the reservoir. The sediment problem at Matsoku Weir, he said, originates from people ploughing on steep slopes and grazing too many livestock. The LHDA hopes to create protected areas in the upstream catchment so that they can enforce rangeland conservation, perhaps near Mont-Aux-Sources. The core issue, he said, is that the catchment health is not simply the interest of the two to three people whose animals graze in a given area, but rather "the interest of the nation." It is a "national priority," he said, reframing these landscape processes so they might become visible as national problems. It was a kind of (ethno-) fluvial geomorphology.[6] These engineers taught me how to envision the flow of water and sediment from wetland to reservoir in relation to the nation: a national fluvial imagination.

FLUVIAL THEORY IN HISTORICAL CONTEXT

Lesotho has long been known as a global soil erosion hotspot.[7] It's the kind of thing one might even read in a *Lonely Planet* travel guide or in an encyclopedia entry for the country. In the early twentieth century, agricultural journals, and South African farmers, as well as British conservationists,[8] began drawing attention to gullies and flooding in the Lesotho lowlands and the Afrikaner farming stronghold across the border, the Orange Free State.[9] All across Southern Africa, in fact, concerns about soil erosion had gathered pace in the years following the United States' Dustbowl crisis, when soil erosion expertise flourished and expanded across the globe.[10] In Southern Africa, the interest in soil erosion stemmed largely from concerns over future declines in production on white-owned farms rather than degradation in "native areas," but the specter of African agricultural collapse also loomed in the minds of settler colonists.[11]

In the Orange Free State Province, however, the concerns were particularly acute. They focused primarily on flooding and sediment loads. The Orange River, which originates in Lesotho (where it is referred to as the Senqu River), passes through the Orange Free State en route to the Atlantic Ocean. The Orange Free State—today, a South African province called the Free State—was and is the site of some of South Africa's best agricultural land. It was also where white Afrikaners settled after the "Great Treks" from British-controlled Cape Province in the nineteenth century, as I described in the previous chapter.[12]

These farmers, a powerful constituency in the Union of South Africa of the twentieth century, complained to the British colonial authorities of Basutoland (nowadays the independent nation of Lesotho) that overgrazing in the Maloti Mountains was rendering the land incapable of holding water and leading to destructive floods downstream. The floods were alleged to carry so much silt it would compromise any attempt to dam the Orange River for use in irrigation.[13] After repeated calls by South Africa for British action to stem erosion and over-grazing, including by afforestation and drastic reductions in livestock numbers, the British colonial authorities began to fear that the Union of South Africa would use this issue to pressure them to cede control of Basutoland and the two other British High Commission Territories, Bechuanaland (now Botswana) and Swazi-land (now eSwatini). The British even prepared a draft white paper in case South Africa submitted a formal application for transfer.[14] The incorporation of Lesotho on these grounds was popular among South Africa's white electorate during Jan Christian Smuts's first term as prime minister (1919–24). As South African pres-sure continued to increase, the British proposed a set of dams in the Basutoland mountains to address the problem of mountain erosion and sedimentation. It bought the British time.

In the meanwhile, as feasibility studies were carried out to scope where such dams could be built, how much they would cost, and so on, the colonial adminis-tration determined it needed to know more about the precise *extent* of land deg-radation and the value of Basutoland territory as a colonial holding. It solicited a comprehensive review of the natural resources of the territory and the political institutions that manage them by Alan Pim in 1930. Pim's task was to advise the administration on how to increase the long-term profitability of the colony. His 1935 report came to a dramatic conclusion: "The problem of erosion in its many aspects is in fact the most immediately pressing of the many great problems which now confront the Administration."[15] Pim was echoed by Smuts, who said in 1936 that "erosion is the biggest problem confronting the country, bigger than any poli-tics."[16] They envisioned a future Basutoland incapable of feeding its inhabitants and washing away down ever-expanding gullies. These assessments were energized by the racial politics of the time. The soil scientists Graham Jacks and Robert Whyte wrote in 1939 that, having conquered people and territories in Africa, the "white man's burden in the future will be to come to terms with the soil and plant world."[17]

The Pim report recommended the institution of country-wide soil conserva-tion projects that included the construction of buffer strips and contour banks around agricultural fields. The program would later be praised in 1944 by Hugh H. Bennett, head of the U.S. Soil Conservation Service, when he visited South Africa amid escalating fears about soil erosion in the region.[18] But it was subsequently criticized as a failure immediately after independence and later by the environ-mental historian Kate Showers,[19] whose close study showed that the programs used untested soil conservation strategies that not only failed to diminish rates of erosion, but actually *increased* them. Put another way, Lesotho was used by

Britain as a testing ground for experimental conservation solutions. Rather than arrest these erosion gullies, which the British described as emblematic of Basotho mismanagement, British mismanagement had expanded them.

As I noted in the introduction, concerns from Afrikaner farmers eventually diminished. By midcentury, South Africans became more interested in problems of water security for the Johannesburg-Pretoria area than about preventing sediment-heavy floods in the Orange River. But in the course of transforming the dam project into a water-export scheme, how did the architects reconcile their plans with Lesotho's reputation as a supremely erosive country, where erosion was "bigger than any politics"?

One way was by erroneously presuming that dams in the high mountains would be free of the problem. Another was by disregarding it. In the following section, I take a closer look at that presumption, the threat that sedimentation might pose to the LHWP, and the measures so far taken to assess or address it.

ASSESSING THE THREAT OF SEDIMENTATION

Soil erosion poses a threat to all dam projects. Sediment deposited behind dam walls diminishes reservoir capacity and, once it reaches intakes for turbines or irrigation, can threaten a dam project in its entirety. Such dams will eventually be decommissioned or even removed. While all dam reservoirs have a "dead storage" area below the intake, that area is crucial to reservoir management, as the engineer Thomas explained earlier in this chapter. And, sediment eventually cuts into "live storage." Because it accumulates irregularly in reservoirs, it can do so much sooner than is often acknowledged by dam proponents.[20]

A 1951 feasibility report by the civil engineering firm Hawkins, Jeffares, and Green stated that there was too much silt in the lower reaches of the Orange/Senqu River and suggested that dams be built in the basalt areas upstream instead.[21] The lowlands feature sandstone, sedimentary soils. These soils have a "duplex" formation that makes them susceptible to piping—the development of subsoil water passages—and, subsequently, gully erosion.[22] The highland soils by contrast are formed on basalt parent material. The cold temperatures in the mountains mean that these soils generally have a higher organic matter content than those in the lowlands and therefore resist deterioration.[23]

But while the lower erodibility of the soils themselves was taken by Hawkins, Jeffares, and Green, as well as others,[24] to mean that sedimentation in the highlands was insignificant to the dam project, a range of evidence suggests otherwise. First and most obvious is the fact that concerns about highlands erosion were longstanding, as described in the previous section; Pim's erosion control efforts, for example, were not confined to the lowlands but rather were rolled out across the highlands.[25] It is true that highland soils are often relatively thin and undeveloped (except for the very limited peat histosols in the alpine wetlands), oftentimes featuring few or no diagnostic subsurface horizons. Yet, because of the steepness of highland slopes, and because of their high amount of exposed, unvegetated soil, they are vulnerable to rain splash erosion, sheet erosion, and even mass movements.[26] And, while cold temperatures can promote soil aggregate stability, it is also true that the freezing and thawing leads to cryogenic weathering.[27] Two of the four varieties of basalts found in the upstream catchment of Katse are especially susceptible to disintegration, too, including the olivine basalts and those with disseminated clay spots.[28] This is because secondary materials in the basalt, such as smectitic clays like montmorillonite, swell with moisture. That is what the engineer explained earlier in this chapter—that even though the highland soils are generally thin, the bedrock degrades easily. Nearer to the valley floor, too, soils get deeper, and gullying is widespread. After heavy rainstorms, huge amounts of sediment are sometimes washed across roads, requiring clearance by excavators for cars to pass safely.

Just a few short years after the LHWP Treaty was signed, the most prominent soil scientist in the country, Qalabane Chakela, found that "[Lesotho has] the highest erosion hazard of any single country in southern and central Africa."[29] On account of "the steep slopes; high total quantities of rain; poor lithosols; and only average vegetation covers . . . [t]he conventional view that the mountain areas of Lesotho are less prone to erosion is unsupported."[30] That is, the lower inherent erodibility of highlands basalt (relative to lowlands sandstone) is offset by the highlands' precipitation, topography, land cover, and secondary materials such as the expanding clays. Besides, the 'Muela Dam, through which all of the LHWP's water flows, is sited in the sedimentary zone, where dam reservoirs "have a very short useful life."[31]

Nevertheless, the LHWP Phase 1 *Feasibility Study* stated that, "based on a limited number of existing field observations and also taking account of published sediment yields for adjacent catchments in South Africa," the transfer tunnel intake in Katse Reservoir "would remain free of sediment for at least 50 years and it would be many more years before there could be any significant loss of active storage."[32]

The LHDA has not made much data publicly available on the issue of sedimentation.[33] One study analyzing erosion hazard, by Smith et al.,[34] contradicts the findings of Chakela, Molapo, and Putsoane,[35] and finds no serious issue posed by sedimentation. That study was funded by the Lesotho Highlands Water Commission, the binational body that oversees the LHWP. I have no evidence of deliberate misinformation. But a long history of "corporate science" in the assessment of natural resource extraction impacts,[36] by which consultancies can solicit future contracts from enterprises like the LHWP, raises doubts about the impartiality of their results. A separate attempt at modeling the risks of reservoir sedimentation was made by Jehanno et al.[37] The authors modeled sediment deposition in the Katse Reservoir and found that the water intake would not be affected until at least fifty years after impoundment, affirming the *Feasibility Study*. However, their model only included sand particles and omitted silt and clay—two smaller classes of mineral soil particles—meaning that their figures underestimate sedimentation rates. Further, the French SOGREAH consultancy responsible for the Jehanno et al. study was found in a criminal court in Lesotho to have bribed the CEO of the LHWP, Masupha Sole, in order to solicit contracts. Sole served nine years in prison.

The paucity of research on the problem posed by sedimentation is shocking—a multibillion-dollar project upon which the regional economy depends, but without serious commitment to ensure its longevity. Water engineers have not been completely blind to this problem, however. In 1995, the LHDA engineer Stanley Hirst authored a position paper to rouse his organization into action.[38] Hirst pointed to internal dissent, explaining, "Soil erosion in project catchments and the associated sedimentation of operation reservoirs has been a subject of long-standing discussion and some discord" within the LHWP. "Since 1990," he went on, "a number of proposals, from in-house and from outside consultants, have been made to mount a study of erosion and sedimentation in the LHWP Phase 1A catchment. For a variety of technical, budgetary, and procedural reasons, none of these have found their way through the approval process."[39] The lack of knowledge about the issue was particularly vexing for him: "No detailed pre-project baseline studies appear to have been done for the LHWP."[40] Not only that, but "None of the engineering feasibility or design studies for Katse and 'Muela dams (LHWP Phase 1A) specifically included collection and analysis of sediment samples."[41] After the project was underway, a vegetation baseline was begun, but no data gathering was included specifically for erosion and sedimentation. There are not even "substantiated estimates," he said, for rates of soil loss or sediment yield in project catchments. The same ignorance prevailed for the Mohale Dam (Phase 1B), which was in planning stages at the time of his writing. For that catchment, an automatic sediment sampler had been installed on the Senqu River downstream from Mohale, he wrote, but "only one year's data will be available for engineering design and that for a likely drought-stricken year" (i.e., a year in which sediment movement would be limited).[42]

Actual rates of sedimentation in Lesotho's reservoirs are poorly understood for two main reasons. First, soil erosion is difficult to measure, typically requiring field study and long-term monitoring. Gullies are the most evident index of erosion, though they only occur where soils are deep and where runoff force is sufficiently strong to dislodge soils and channelize water. Moreover, gullies often form during dramatic flood events, and can remain stable for another decade or more, until a storm of that magnitude occurs again. Areas of exposed bedrock can also be an indication that erosion has taken place, though this phenomenon, too, is highly localized, confined primarily to steeper slopes where soils are thin. In areas where soil is thinly vegetated, a significant amount of sediment movement can take place without leaving much of a trace: when rainsplash dislodges particles of exposed soil, for example, they are later entrained downslope by concentrated runoff water. Measuring the increase in gully size or the rates of sheet erosion (i.e., the more or less uniform loss of soil across a surface) requires precise and regular measurements. Even when river monitoring captures changes in the bedload and the suspended load of sediments that ultimately make their way into the river, these describe only the effects of the most recent rains and must be measured over longer time periods in order to derive acceptable estimates of long-term changes and their causes. The LHWP's limited field observations therefore call into question the accuracy of models that came to optimistic conclusions about projected rates of sedimentation.

The second—and most important—reason that rates of sedimentation are unknown has been the lack of will to know them.[43] This is because the principal concern of dam builders—the government officials, politicians, contractors, and others with a stake in these high-profile projects—is simply building the dams. This helps explain why no comprehensive study has been undertaken, despite numerous pleas,[44] and why "no measured soil loss data from runoff plots exists in the Lesotho Highlands."[45] Steps to address erosion—not just to measure it—are often seen as peripheral to dam builders, perhaps partly because, while they maintain reservoir capacity (and water quality) in the long term, they can in fact diminish water yield. Afforestation, for instance, leads to the retention of infiltrated water which is lost to the reservoir by plant uptake and evapotranspiration.[46]

The LHWP would not be alone as a water project that ignores its social and environmental impacts,[47] but the specific ignorances of this project are stunning.

A pair of bathymetric sediment surveys in 2003 and 2019 at the 'Muela Reservoir, a small but critically important LHWP reservoir, is a rare exception. And the case is telling. In 2003—just six years after the completion of the 'Muela Dam wall—the first survey found that 7 percent of the reservoir volume had already been filled with sediment. By 2019, it had become 12 percent filled.[48]

After having resisted the move for many years, the LHWP took tentative steps to address the erosion issue in the early 2000s. It did so by implementing Integrated Catchment Management (ICM), a set of soil conservation programs that ostensibly takes a holistic approach to managing the catchment-scale dynamics that drive erosion and other kinds of land degradation.[49] The program was established for a five-year period between 2005 and 2010, to be rolled out in each of the (then) three catchments of the LHWP: Katse Dam, Mohale Dam, and 'Muela Dam. These programs continue at the time of this writing, albeit in diminished form, and plans are underway for another concerted effort, including in the catchment of the future Polihali Dam. I describe these programs in the next two chapters.

For now, let me turn to describe the fluvial pedagogy that is emerging to square national water with fluvial water—to square water production with livestock production in the absence of real measuring and monitoring of the problem. This pedagogy is not unlike the pedagogy of water meters described by Antina von

Schnitzler in neoliberal South Africa.[50] Instead of reading a water meter, however, rural people are taught to read the landscape. With evidence of soil loss having been so poorly recorded, this pedagogy is shrouded in confusion and uncertainty. Nevertheless, it is instructive. The effort to instill the public with this fluvial imagination shows how a dam project doesn't want or need just any kind of water, nor just any kind of soil, nor just any kind of citizen. It wants a water that moves slowly through the soil. It wants a soil that captures and slows water's flow. And, it wants a rural citizenry that cares about erosion for the sake of the nation's reservoirs, not only their livestock or agricultural fields—teaching them to become better citizens through improved natural resource stewardship.

FLUVIAL PEDAGOGY

The soil problem is an ontological one. The nature of soil and the water that flows through or over it have become scrambled. Lacking adequate documentation and understanding of sedimentation, a class of plants—the dwarf shrub—has come to be used by conservation bureaucrats to make erosion visible to the naked eye. If, in the semiotic world of conservation bureaucrats, wetlands symbolize water storage, then dwarf shrubs symbolize erosion.

One dwarf shrub species has cut a particularly dramatic figure, transposing issues of desertification and erosion onto issues of livestock grazing (see fig. 7). Known in Sesotho as *sehala-hala* and in English as bitter Karoo bush, *Chrysocoma ciliata* (Asteraceae) has been identified with livestock overgrazing since at least the 1870s, when farmers and conservationists in South Africa reported its invasion into heavily grazed sheep pastures.[51] They are essentially unpalatable, so they are unwelcome competitors to the forage grasses that livestock desire. *C. ciliata* was despised for its fecundity and for the difficulty in eradicating it—a mature plant produces more than one thousand wind-dispersed seeds each year; they can grow in extremely disturbed settings such as along the roadside; and they can regrow from basal meristems if burned in a fire.[52] Because it is known as a desert shrub (i.e., "Karoo bush"), it is seen by conservation bureaucrats as having desert provenance and therefore indicating not only overgrazing but also soil erosion and desiccation—an increasing water scarcity.[53] Livestock owners and herders I spoke with also envisaged a kind of desertification through reference to the shrub. For them, however, the shrub was not an indication that overgrazing was *bringing about* desert-like conditions, but rather an indication that an increase in droughts was favoring shrubs over grasses. Though these associations between shrubs and erosion antedate the LHWP, they are drawn into its orbit in contemporary Lesotho.[54]

Do they actually signal erosion? The positions among conservation bureaucrats and the LHWP are contradictory, variously arguing that shrubs are indicators of erosion or desiccation, that they stabilize soils, or even that they actively encourage erosion. Consider the landscape theory-work done in this Basutoland colonial

FIGURE 7. The dwarf shrub *Chrysocoma ciliata*. Photo by author.

report from 1948, which moves a reader from the selective grazing of livestock, through shrubs, to soil erosion:

> The northern, northwestern, and north-eastern slopes of the mountains were origi-
> nally covered with sweet (Themeda) grass, while the colder slopes grew "sour" grass-
> es of which *Festuca caprina* was the dominant species. Stock naturally congregated in
> the sweet grass, with the result that this has been slowly eaten or trodden out and its
> place has been taken by useless scrub, *Chrysocoma* [*ciliata*] predominating. The graz-
> ing value of these slopes has consequently steadily deteriorated. Chrysocoma also
> offers little resistance to soil erosion. In this way a very large percentage of the moun-
> tain slopes has been damaged and it is considered to be a matter of the most urgent
> and vital importance that these slopes should retain their former grass covering.[55]

Elsewhere, conservation statements suggest that they might prevent erosion, but that their proliferation is a sign of generalized desiccation. A Convention on Biological Diversity report suggests that the, "Karoo [Desert] species like *Chrysocoma*" are spreading and, though they might help prevent soil erosion by providing ground cover, they are "a sign of increasing desert-like conditions. In essence, Lesotho is progressively becoming a desert."[56]

There is no clear evidence that shrubs are linked to soil erosion, and some observers suggest that they actually prevent it, including even the LHWP. In the *Feasibility Study* for Phase 1 of the LHWP, shrubs are depicted as soil-stabilizing agents, but ones that are disappearing rather than proliferating: "The shrubs are

FIGURE 8. Shrubs stabilizing a roadside. Photo by author.

. . . deeply rooted and contribute to the control of soil erosion even on steep and heavily grazed slopes. The shrubs are, however, in strong demand for fuel and in some areas they have virtually disappeared."[57]

I am sympathetic with the view that shrubs stabilize soils, having noticed very few sites where gullying had exposed the root systems of these shrubs, for example. Instead, one can easily find eroded hillslopes that appear to be held in place by shrubs (see fig. 8). They do increase with grazing where soil conditions are favorable, though this is somewhat separate from the question of whether they are a sign of erosion.[58] It is because of the association of shrubs with grazing—and the presumed relationship between grazing and soil erosion—that shrubs have become equated with erosion.

These associations between vegetation, erosion, and landscape history can be disorienting, but let me provide a few brief stories that will give a sense as to how they operate in the everyday life of soil conservation for the water-export economy.

Story 1: "The Place of Shrubs"

In March 2014, I visited the Khubelu Valley in the Mokhotlong District with a civil servant named Sechaba from the ministry to observe a meeting of a local grazing association. The civil servant had, in fact, called the meeting to encourage them to better manage grazing in the high plateau areas that were technically under control of their association. The massive Polihali Dam is currently being built lower in the valley. Conservation bureaucrats are concerned about livestock-induced degradation of the upper catchment, as noted above, and were promoting grazing associations that might help prevent more wetland degradation. These are community-run cooperatives, comprised of members who pay dues and collectively manage rangeland access on behalf of chiefs. (I'll return to discuss chiefs and grazing associations in chapter 4.)

The slopes rose steeply upward, the more so as we neared the meeting, and they were covered mostly in dwarf shrubs. Sechaba pointed out the shrub-covered pastures to me and shook his head. "Do you see that? These people are ruining their pastures."

Shrub-dominated landscapes told a story for Sechaba of the failure of rangeland institutions and the obstinacy of rural livestock holders. We parked the car and walked up the hill to the meeting. It was held at the chief's place, as with most open-air meetings in Lesotho, called *lipitso*. And, like all *lipitso*, people came and went throughout the meeting, some of them never clearly in attendance. Mostly young and old men, they leaned up against the stone kraals of the chief's compound. They were no doubt curious about what was to come of this meeting, on the heels of several others that took place there recently, since the wetlands conservation project associated with the LHWP began its attempt to resurrect this particular grazing association.

When the chair of the association got up to speak at the outset of the meeting, he spoke at length about the importance of protecting the rangelands in their area, especially the wetlands on the plateau that, he said, produced a large amount of water which Lesotho sells to South Africa. I have seen these speeches many times before. It is a performance honed through years of experience with civil servants like Sechaba, as well as others in the conservation-development industry.[59] It is a genre of speech, not exclusive to Lesotho, that is notable for its overly optimistic and moralizing tone, and its disregard for the challenges that both speaker and audience know to stand in the way. There was no mention, for example, that the principal chief of the area is rumored not to care about wetland degradation or managing the use of rangelands in general; or that Sechaba's ministry fails to provide the association with the grazing permit forms that it's supposed to issue to all livestock owners grazing in association pastures, forms that affirm the association's legitimacy through their materiality and bureaucratic authority.

Sechaba, in his capacity as technical advisor to the local chief and the grazing association, stood up next to deliver an impassioned speech of his own, this one also honed through years of standing in front of Basotho crowds to upbraid them about their rangeland management practices. Like most civil servants—or "conservation bureaucrats," the term I'm using to refer to ministry officials, LHWP conservation workers, and those from foreign-funded conservation NGOs—Sechaba was from the lowlands of Lesotho, so he knew little of the local context. He had only been in this valley a handful of times and had never visited the rangeland areas that were at issue that day. Sechaba began, customarily, by telling the group his full name and the village where he was born, in the urban lowlands of Leribe District. He explained that people from Leribe refer to this mountain district of Mokhotlong as *lihlahleng*, the place of shrubs. The crowd erupted in shock and some laughter, with shouts of disbelief and offense: Haibo! Aikona! Hey! No way! And Sechaba continued for another ten minutes, chastising them for their lack of organization and lecturing them on the importance of protecting the range.

As we drove back to town, I asked Sechaba, "Is that true? Do people in Leribe really call this area *lihlahleng*?" I had never heard that.

"No," he said, throwing his head back and laughing. "That's just motivation."

In a joke, then, a landscape.

Playfully riffing off of half-serious rivalries between Lesotho's districts, and especially rivalries between the highlands and the lowlands, Sechaba sought to orient us to this landscape, to author a landscape history that derived process from form: a pattern of shrubby vegetation (the form) became an index of years of poor management (a process). And, therefore, the situation was a threat to the water project. He was trying to cultivate in them a fluvial imagination, and the figure of the dwarf shrub ushered us along a semiotic chain, drawing connections between livestock management, soil erosion, water, and the nation. Ultimately, it was a conduit for urban prejudice against rural people.

Story 2: A Bald Man's Head

The traffic across this semiotic chain flows in more than one direction—not just from the state to the public.[60] Just a few days before standing with Tankisi at his cattle post, which I described in the introduction to this book, I had asked him about the condition of those cattle post areas while sitting out front of his house. He said that the condition was not good. The rains were arriving too late in the summer, and there is a problem with the hydrologic cycle (*lebili la pula*). The water is pulled up from the ocean and for whatever reason is not reaching Lesotho as it once did. The cycle is broken, he said. According to Tankisi and many other rural people I spoke with, the rains used to fall more commonly as day-long drizzles that infiltrate the soil (*pula ea molupe*). These days, the rains are not only much delayed, but when they finally arrive, they fall as destructive, thirty-minute torrents (*pula ea sekhahla*). Pointing up the valley from his house, he said these days in the summer rainy season it's common to see rain far away in that direction, but it doesn't move this way as it once would have. Or, if it does manage to arrive at his village, the strong rains he saw up the mountain might have diminished to simply a sprinkle (*mofafatsana*).

Swiveling our gaze in the opposite direction, he pointed to the hillslope beneath a wool shearing shed that was in our view a kilometer or so away. Pointing out the shrubs that he said had colonized the pasture just below it, he argued that their presence was a consequence of this changing rainfall regime. This was in contrast to Sechaba, then, who invoked shrubs as a consequence of overgrazing and poor land management. Tankisi explained that these new, more destructive rains don't soak into the soil. Instead, they move across the surface "like water on a bald man's head." This favors shrubs, he said, whose thick roots and stems are better adapted to drought than grasses.

The very next day, I walked with a ministry official named Tefo through a shrub-encroached pasture that surrounded an alpine wetland. The wetland looked horrible; worse than it did the last time I saw it just a few years prior. It might be described as dead or dying. Whereas a healthy wetland features continuous grass and forb cover, with hummocks covered in rare and delicate wetland plant species,[61] water-logged and squishing as you walk across it, degraded wetlands are edged by dwarf shrubs, pockmarked with the hooves of animals and the burrows of ice rats (*Otomys sloggetti*), dry, and silent—almost hollow-sounding.

Tefo explained that there is too much grazing here, and it has led to the incursion of dwarf shrubs. He did so by mobilizing the same metaphor as Tankisi, but to do different theoretical work. More than merely an index of something else (i.e., overgrazing, climate change, etc.), shrubs for Tefo were in fact *agents* of poor water flow. Shrubs don't hold soil or water as well as grass, he explained, so that when you see a place like this with shrubs edging the wetland, the water doesn't seep into the soil but rather just courses over it. Think of it, Tefo said, like water falling on a bald man's head. If there were hair on it, water would be retained; if not, it would simply run off.

Story 3: The Shrub Silt Trap

As I've said, the LHWP's sedimentation problems are especially pressing near the 'Muela Dam in the lowlands of Lesotho. Speaking with a councilor (an elected, local government official) named Ntsikeng from a village near 'Muela one day, he told me how he and some other councilors were taken by a conservation NGO to the highlands for a training. Led by two white people whom they were told were experts in range management, he said, this was not so much a "workshop" (*thupelo*), he said, as it was a "demonstration" (*pontšo*).

I was surprised to hear that they were taken to some of the same places where I had been conducting fieldwork for the previous five months. One was a hillslope where soil had completely washed away, leaving only the bedrock exposed. Silt traps called *metsele-tsele* (known in vernacular English as "stonelines") were being built there: long rows of stones running perpendicular to the slope. They were told that the stonelines would help soil to accumulate so that plants could recolonize the area. Using a Sotho proverb, Ntsikeng explained that the experts' rationale for showing them the site was as a cautionary tale: *ho haha serobe phiri ese jele*, which translates literally as, "to build a chicken coop after the chickens have already been eaten by a hyena." That is, they wanted to caution against attempting to correct problems after it was already too late.

FIGURE 9. Rows of uprooted shrubs. Photo by author.

The councilors were also taken to a place called Motšerimeli, where the government had been paying rural people to uproot shrubs to allow for grasses to grow (see fig. 9). He spoke with admiration for the condition of the pasture and the large rows of uprooted shrubs that he described as "shrub silt traps" (*metsele-tsele oa sehala-hala*). Indeed, the rows of shrubs did look like silt traps from afar, and driving by Motšerimeli on public transit, I had heard several people refer to them in that way. This always struck me as funny because trapping sediment is not their goal or function. It was simply for the purpose of piling them up in an orderly way.

He and the other councilors learned during this demonstration that the presence of grass was preferable to shrubs, not simply because grasses are forage for livestock and shrubs are unpalatable, but also because the grass *sieves* the water (*joang bo sefa metsi*) and, when shrubs dominate, the water simply runs down slope (*metsi aa matha feela*). It was a way of understanding the flow of water through an attention to the morphology of different plants.

Standing with a ministry official one day in the pasture where shrubs were uprooted, he pointed out a pickup truck that passed by on the road below with frustration. It was carrying bales of uprooted shrubs to town where they would be sold as firewood. I was confused as to why he would be upset. The program was implemented on the notion that demonstrating a healthy pasture would compel people to improve the rangelands, but also that it would allow rural people to earn money: first, by working to uproot the shrubs, and second by selling the shrubs as cooking fuel. A sign at the bottom of the pasture explaining the program exclaimed in all caps: "cash for assets!"

The official told me, however, that recently the ministry had ordered that the shrubs be left in the "stonelines" formation so that they might slow down the flow of water.

Once misrecognized as silt traps from passing buses, conservation bureaucrats leaned into this misrecognition, transforming them into *actual* silt traps.

Dwarf shrubs acted as powerful but confused boundary objects between rural people and conservation workers, a site for interpretive work in the historiography of the fluvial landscape. Shrubs had long embodied land degradation and desertification, but after having been uprooted to exemplify a pasture through which water flowed well, rows of uprooted shrubs *became erosion control structures.* Like the physical conservation works I'll describe in the next chapter, the very presence of these shrub silt traps, so visible from the roadside, would testify to passers by that rural people were mismanaging their pastures and that government agencies were taking action. They were devices for knowing and manipulating water, as well as for disciplining the interpretation of landscape patterns.[62]

CONCLUSION

This chapter has presented a paradox: a dam project originally aimed at trapping sediment and controlling floods was transformed into a water-export project in spite of that sediment. Alarm about soil erosion in Lesotho has been a consistent refrain for a century. But in the planning and implementation of the LHWP, it was ignored, and ignorance about the specific nature of this threat bodes ill for the water-export economy's future. Sediment haunts the futures of residents of the Lesotho highlands and of urban South Africans alike.[63] It's worth noting, too, that while the accumulation of sediment behind the dam walls is a problem for water export, starving the downstream ecosystem of these mineral and organic materials is also a problem for ecosystem health.[64]

National water, presented in the previous chapter, is portrayed as being spatially and temporally even across the territory, but that territory in fact is characterized by a patchy rainfall regime, full of drought and punctuated storms. These rainfall patterns are becoming even more acute than in the past. Producers of national water, while at first disregarding this problem, have in recent years begun developing a fluvial imaginary that draws upon long-standing ideas about rural land mismanagement. Theirs is a landscape through which water flows too quickly, and rural people, said to have a poor sense of this fluvial water and its national stakes, must be educated.

Because erosion can be difficult to see, and because not enough work has been done to know the causes and extent of soil erosion, recourse has been made to an indicator species for landscape interpretation. Yet, a common interpretation of their significance is lacking, as can be seen in the three stories I presented. For Sechaba, the shrub was a consequence of overgrazing and poor land management; for Tankisi, a consequence of changes in the rains; but for Tefo the shrub was actively shaping the ways water flowed across land—an agent of fluvial problems rather than a reflection of them. Later, the rows of uprooted shrubs were left to serve as silt traps, transfigured from being indices of erosion to being erosion control structures. Landscape theory swirls in the void left by the LHWP's ignorance.

Whereas this chapter has showed how conservation bureaucrats and water engineers understand water's flow and seek to impose that understanding upon rural people, the next two chapters will show how they translate that fluvial imaginary into action. Conservation bureaucrats have taken broadly two approaches to slowing the flow of water across the landscape: the construction of physical conservation works (chapter 3) and social transformations within rural society (chapter 4). These efforts illustrate how fluvial imaginaries in Lesotho, as hinted at above, are hitched to ideas about a state's obligations to its citizens. I'll describe in chapter 3, for example, how soil conservation is used as a means of redistributing national wealth to the poor. The upstream social and ecological engineering carried out to produce water commodities, then, is not just about disciplining rural populations. It is also a means of diffusing some of the "pressure"[65] of Lesotho's precarious political economy: to resolve contradictions of the water-reservoir era, namely that water export generates government revenue but no long-term employment.

3

The Soil Solution

In the Lesotho highlands, winter brings *likupu-kupu:* strong, gusting winds that lash the landscape with bits of sand and grass. *Likupu-kupu* swirled around Masilo and me as we stood at the edge of a rural village, far up the Mokhotlong River Valley. We scrutinized a pile of stones organized in a row that wound around the hillslope and out of sight. Most of the stones were no larger than a tennis ball. In places, they formed discernible piles, but elsewhere along the line they became diffuse and scattered. He kicked a stone and it rolled a few feet downslope. Masilo worked for the Lesotho Ministry of Forestry, Range, and Soil Conservation ("the ministry"), in charge of overseeing what are known as *fato-fato* projects: country-wide, state-funded soil erosion control programs. *Fato-fato* employs rural people for about $4–5 USD/day for a month in groups of around twenty to forty workers to do manual labor planting trees, or building soil conservation works such as gabions, check dams, or silt traps.

We stood over one such silt trap, called a "stoneline" in vernacular English (in Sesotho, *motsele-tsele*), which had been built several years before Masilo came to work for the Mokhotlong District's ministry office. Running perpendicular to the slope, a stoneline is supposed to slow the flow of water over land, accumulate sediment, and eventually provide a platform for revegetation (see fig. 10). Masilo seemed puzzled and ashamed at its state of disrepair—particularly as he was showing me, a foreign researcher, the work that his office does to combat soil erosion. We were there because he had received a call from a local schoolteacher, asking that he get his office to finish construction of a water tank for the school, a project that had stalled long ago. As we walked up to see the tank, the schoolteacher complained also about some stonelines on the hillslope above the school. They were built a few years ago but were now falling down, and she hoped another *fato-fato* project could fix them.

The stonelines were, like most others I would see during my field research in Lesotho, haphazardly constructed and prepared for a modality of rain and

FIGURE 10. Soil conservation structures. Photo by author.

sediment movement that was rare in Lesotho. They would never slow down the channelized runoff that causes the bulk of erosion. The strong, sudden rains common in the country—more common today, as I was told repeatedly—were simply too much for them. Some stonelines that I saw were situated near the top of barren hillslopes, meaning that there wasn't much sediment for them to collect, nor a significant amount of water to slow down. Others that were more substantial seemed to be channelizing runoff and thereby *encouraging* erosion, with signs of gullying at their edges.[1]

This chapter explains how these slipshod soil conservation works are critical parts of Lesotho's water production infrastructure—part of a broader, apartheid-legacy arrangement whereby Lesotho stands as periphery to the South African core. Though they do not prevent soil erosion by and large, they do maintain political quietude in ways that sustain the water economy. To show how this works, I start by presenting the ethnographic puzzle about *fato-fato* that first caught my eye: the programs are objects of ridicule and do little to conserve soil, but they constitute the primary mission of an entire government ministry and are implemented with high levels of success. I then describe ethnographically how one conservation bureaucrat envisions this work by recounting a field visit I took with him in an area where he carries out these programs. In the course of doing so, he asserts his ideas about how water flows over land upon the rural people who work on his crew. Moving back in time, I show how the labor form of *fato-fato* dates to colonial and post-independence times, a long-standing system of distribution that maintains a precarious social contract in the water-reservoir era.[2]

"SEDIMENT TRAPS NEEDED"

I was not alone in my critical assessment of *fato-fato* and its ability to stem erosion. An official, government-sponsored report on the state of the environment in Lesotho determined that *fato-fato* is not simply bad at preventing erosion, but that it is in fact *harmful* to the environment—the word the report used was "catastrophic."[3] The very name, *fato-fato*, which translates literally as "dig-dig," captures the problem well. More specifically this term means "scratching about on the ground like a chicken, aimlessly or pathetically." Before I learned of this pejorative connotation, I had come to know *fato-fato* as the standard term for the programs. But when I would use the term in conversation, I noticed that Basotho sometimes cracked a smile or even started laughing—particularly people from the urban lowlands who didn't actually work on *fato-fato* crews.

I got this reaction, for example, when I presented at a 2014 United Nations–funded sustainable land management conference in the capital, Maseru, organized by the ministry. The audience was made up almost entirely of a professional class of people, like myself: civil servants and NGO workers, many of whom were college-educated and mostly from the urban lowlands. When I used the term *fato-fato* in the course of my presentation, the entire room burst out laughing. Flush with embarrassment, I scrambled to reassure the audience that I was not condemning *fato-fato*; I simply had heard no other term to describe it. The room calmed and I carried on with my presentation. At lunch, I asked a few employees of the ministry what I should call it. They looked at one another, unaware of the program's official name, and then explained that one might call it *ntlafatso ea mobu* or *paballo ea mobu*, which translate to "improvement of the soil" or "protection of the soil." It was only through a concerted Google-search effort that I managed to find the official name: the "Integrated Watershed Management Project." But even Google was inconclusive. There were just a few scattered mentions.

I was puzzled as to why the program would be a joke among these professionals invested in conservation. It's certainly not because soil conservation is unnecessary. As I described in the previous chapter, soil loss is quite a high-stakes problem, and Lesotho has been described as a global soil-erosion hot-spot.[4] World Bank experts have suggested the threat of sedimentation might imperil the country's signature water-export scheme, the Lesotho Highlands Water Project.[5]

It cannot be because *fato-fato* is marginal or somehow insignificant, either. In a country famous for the failure of its development and conservation programs,[6] it is noteworthy that the stated national targets for construction of conservation works are not only met but often exceeded. For example, the targeted 71 kilometers of stonelines in fiscal year 2010–11 was surpassed by 650 percent, after a total of 464 kilometers of lines were built.[7] One report showed that from 2007 to 2012, 366 million Maloti (USD 36 million) were paid to nearly 388,000 workers across the country.[8] Lesotho's total population is just over 2 million.

What is so funny about soil conservation and why would conservation programs be described as aimless or pathetic—even as protecting soil is critical and the programs exceed their goals? I argue that their comic status betrays an uneasy social arrangement between national elites and the rural peasantariat of Lesotho,[9] an arrangement which staunches the human fallout of the water-export economy.

Today, work on *fato-fato* crews is one of the few sources of income other than livestock that is available to people living in rural areas. These slipshod conservation works, in ruins from the start, are part of an infrastructure of water production, not because they channel water well, but because they channel government funds well. That is, they support an economy of distribution in a manner appropriate to the country's cultural and historical context, a fact hinted at by the materiality and temporality of the structures themselves. In literature on the African state, such systems of distribution are often derided as "neopatrimonialism," a perversion and corruption of the state according to some Weberian ideal.[10] In the case of Lesotho, this system should be seen as a modestly successful—though environmentally destructive—effort to keep unemployed rural people from starving.[11] Not only does it reproduce the state and distribute resources, as the anthropology of development has shown,[12] but it ameliorates the contradictions of the water economy.

This arrangement represents what I call the "soil solution," in a pun on the soil science term for the liquid phase of soil, which refers to the mixture of water, organic, and mineral materials in which important soil ecological processes take place. The soil solution as I use it refers to an equally productive set of relationships surrounding soil and water: that is, addressing problems of poverty and geopolitical marginality through performative labor—combatting soil erosion with conservation practices that do not conserve soil.

Lesotho's watersheds have been transformed into what Ashley Carse has called "natural infrastructures" for water production.[13] His account of Panama Canal watersheds illustrates how such infrastructures work. The canal requires a tremendous amount of fresh water to operate, and engineers effectively rendered peasant forests in the upstream catchment as an infrastructure of terrestrial reservoirs that could retain water and release it into the canal's system of locks. An analogous situation prevails in Lesotho, where soil conservation programs are put in place for water production and export. But, in contrast to this Panama case, many soil conservation infrastructures in Lesotho are of such dubious quality that they are ineffective or even harmful, and their failure to stem erosion draws these dam reservoirs into a crisis that imperils the water economy's long-term viability. Oddly, then, Lesotho's water is produced not only by the high-tech work of skilled engineers, but also by low-tech, even haphazard techniques—arranging stones in a line on a hillside. Shoddy soil conservation structures are counterintuitively key to the success of water production.

In chapters 1 and 2, I showed that water's nature is unstable and debated in Lesotho—how volumetric "national water" is confronted by fluvial water in actually existing landscapes. If the fluvial pedagogy described in chapter 2 reconciles the *conceptual discord* between volumetric and fluvial water, teaching rural people to care about fluvial water for the sake of volumetric water commodities, the conservation structures described in this chapter reconcile the *structural discord* of the water-export economy, preventing the complete unraveling of this social order. These structures represent a kind of applied fluvial pedagogy, hitching together a proposition about water's interactions with soil as it flows over landscapes and another about the state's capacity to channel the flows of water commodities toward citizens. Inscribed upon the landscape, *fato-fato* executes a translation, in which the flow of sediments over land is folded into another kind of sediment: a common-sense understanding about political and material orders.[14] The structures at once declare rural mismanagement, environmental crisis, and state efficacy, but also bind elites and nonelites together in an uneasy alliance that enables water production and diminishes anger over entrenched rural poverty and exploitation. In the process, problematic soil sediments are made productive.

In the next section, I return to the 'Muela Reservoir, where sedimentation problems are most pronounced, showing ethnographically how these conservation programs work in practice. As I explained in the previous chapter, one of the few measures taken to monitor rates of sedimentation took place there, when a bathymetric survey was done in 2003 to determine the sediment profile of the reservoir. Done just six years after completion, the reservoir had already become 7 percent filled with sediment. A subsequent survey done in 2019 found that this figure had risen to 12 percent. Tellingly, the "Environmental Management Plan" that was created for the reservoir in 1994 set out only the most general observations and recommendations.[15] A program table outlined the primary environmental challenges facing the 'Muela Dam. Of the three issues listed under the component, "Dam," one was "soil erosion." The "Comment" for that issue was simple: "Sediment traps needed."

LEARNING TO SEE LIKE A CONSERVATION BUREAUCRAT

I met with Tau at nine in the morning at his office in May 2014. Tau worked for the Lesotho Highlands Development Authority (LHDA), the administrative body that built and maintains the LHWP. In charge of administering soil conservation programs in the 'Muela Dam catchment, his office overlooked the dam and reservoir, which sit at a narrow passage of the Nqoe River, itself a small tributary to the

Caledon River fed by runoff from the mountain escarpment that looms over the area, just ten kilometers to the east.

I asked Tau if he thought sedimentation posed a threat to the LHWP. With a serious demeanor, he said: "Yes, there is a lot of silt in the dam." Taking me over to the window, he pointed out the sediment piling at the tail of the reservoir, a lurking brown mass. Further up, he said, the sandy area now partly covered in grass was once part of the reservoir. He explained that there was a plan currently being floated with the Lesotho Highlands Water Commission (i.e., the binational body that oversees the water project) to dredge the area and then dump the sediment onto a small plateau just above the dam reservoir, which will be reinforced with gabions and seeded with grass. (When I visited again in 2019, five years after my conversation with Tau, the commission still had not allocated the money.) But, Tau was quick to add, in order to address land degradation, one must manage it at the source. This is why they are carrying out the Integrative Catchment Management programs, or "ICM," he explained. These ICM programs had been promoted from 2005 to 2010 as a pilot scheme, but the commission had been skeptical about their importance and potential. After the World Bank's Panel of Environmental Experts raised alarm in a 2011 report about the sedimentation problem at 'Muela and other project catchments, he said, they wanted to fund it.[16]

The programs included the promotion of conservation agriculture (or, "no till agriculture"), the creation of grazing associations, and the construction of soil conservation works like gabions and silt traps.

"Have they been successful?" I asked.

He proceeded to list a series of achievements: "Yes. There is improved vegetation, the palatable grass species are coming back. . . . This has a knock-on effect, too," he went on to explain. "When you have good grass, you have better cattle, and then you have healthier cattle for ploughing your fields. Erosion has decreased in these areas."

On further probing, it became clear that he had little data to substantiate those claims. And the grazing associations and conservation agriculture programs had not yet taken root. Instead, the physical conservation structures were his focus. With excitement, he gestured for me to come behind his desk and showed me a long series of pictures on his computer from a quarterly report he was about to submit.

"All over this catchment," he said as he scrolled through the document for me, he and his teams of local workers had built gabions—stones enclosed in rectangular blocks of wire mesh—to reinforce eroded terraces. They built "stonelines" like the ones I visited with Masilo. They built check dams—piles of stones in erosion gullies—to prevent gullies from widening further. They dug trenches perpendicular to the slope called diversion furrows above agricultural fields to divert water quickly toward the river. This work was ongoing, he said.

He logged off his computer, grabbed his keys, and we hopped into his truck so he could show me in person. We parked down by the bridge at the Nqoe River a short way up the valley and headed up the hill toward the worksite. Tau got winded quickly on our way up the hill and told me between breaths that his aim there was to *control* the silt, not *prevent* erosion entirely. The goal should be to reduce the problem, "because to prevent it is very difficult."

As we approached the work area he had brought me to see, he explained that the key reason for building the structures is to reduce the velocity of water, which would otherwise careen downslope, carrying soil along with it. We came upon a large ditch—a diversion furrow about 1m wide and 0.75m deep. The extra dirt had been piled up on the lower side of the furrow, making it appear even more impressive. We walked along the furrow as it wound around the side of the slope to a point where we found five men pick-axing at the leading edge. When finished, it would spill into the small tributary stream before dropping quickly into the Nqoe River and into the reservoir. Some women stood in a line farther up the slope, moving rocks from a pile, person by person, for construction of a stoneline.

Tau paused so that I could speak with the group of workers. Work stopped, and everyone gathered together. It would soon become clear that Tau saw my visit as an opportunity to assert his expertise and a particular view of fluvial water. Over the course of our group conversation, he would repeatedly contest the workers' statements with his own. For example, I asked about the timing and causes of soil erosion—when did it become a problem, and why then? Several of these people claimed that recent changes in the rain toward droughts and violent storms encouraged soil erosion. Others suggested that the presence of the 'Muela Dam had increased land pressure because it had removed land from use. At each turn, Tau countered their points and asserted that soil erosion stemmed from local land use: overstocking, failure to rest pastures adequately, broken land management institutions, and so on. I asked the group whether they thought there were more livestock today than in the past (a contention of Tau's).

A woman raised her hand: "No, there are less today because people sell more to the butcheries than they used to."

Tau stood up to "clarify," as he put it, explaining that people here do not raise livestock to sell for meat and asked everyone to agree with him. A handful nodded or affirmed languidly.

Before returning to my questions, he asked the crowd to agree that the rangelands were not in good shape and that the reason was because people have more animals today than in the past. The crowd sat mostly motionless. Tau's foreman, a local man named Relebohile, then added in English directly to me that only two out of ten people in the area sell meat to the butchery. Tau added that this was because they use livestock instead to "do their cultural things," by which he presumably meant things like payment of bridewealth (*lobola*) or feeding people at funerals.

I decided to solicit the group's opinion on the matter of land condition: Did they think the range was better or worse today than it was when they were growing up? Tau cut in again, in Sesotho. He did a study in 2010 with a specialist who came and they did, "something called 'transects' in order to understand the carrying capacity of the range." They found that there were too many animals in the area, he said. A silence hung over the crowd.

I tried a different tack: "If the range is degraded," I asked, "when did the degradation start?"

A man raised his hand and said, "The problems began when *metsi a lihlaba* arrived," referring to the Lesotho Highlands Development Authority, the parastatal body that administers the dam—and for which Tau works.

Everyone laughed except Tau. He stood up frustrated, yet again. He defended the LHDA amid titters and said that the project only took a small amount of land to construct the dam and that people were compensated for it. Eventually, however, we came upon one point of agreement. When I asked what should be done to stop soil erosion, the consensus was that more conservation structures were needed. Residents of the area completely disagreed with Tau on the causes of erosion, but agreed completely on the cure.

Tau then asked Relebohile, the foreman of his crew, to show me the extent of their work on this particular hillslope. As we walked, I referred to the work as *fato-fato*. He laughed a belly laugh and I asked him if they weren't the same thing, even though the work here was coordinated by the LHDA rather than the government of Lesotho. He proceeded to explain in a somewhat rambling response that the government programs and LHDA programs were slightly different but, yes, this was similar to *fato-fato*. Later, as we headed back to the truck, I asked Tau if he agreed and he smiled. He tentatively agreed, but he wanted to draw one distinction. Whereas the government ministry pays people 48 Maloti per day of work, the LHDA pays 78 Maloti. With a satisfied smile on his face, he did the math for me: they typically hire forty people to do twenty days of work, totaling M1,560/person, meaning that this single project was set to bring M62,400 (USD 6,200) to this community for just one hillslope. As a result of the Lesotho Highlands Water Commission's renewed commitment to tackling erosion in light of the sedimentation at 'Muela, he said that there is a M1.9 million (USD 190,000) budget coming his way for soil conservation.

"I'm the big man around here," he said, quickly adding, "But it's all about protecting the dam."

On our way back to the office, Tau took a detour to show me a number of other structures they had built. We dwelled on them. He wanted to show me the quality of the craftsmanship, their size and number, the sediment trapped behind them, and the signs of erosion farther upslope above them. There were many signs that the problem was continuing despite their construction though, with sediment depositing beneath them as though having overflowed, and small gullies forming along their sides. Many structures I saw had completely filled with sediment, meaning that water would no longer be slowed. In 2019, the conservation bureaucrats who gave me a tour of the catchment showed me gabions that had been built

FIGURE 11. Seeing like a conservation bureaucrat. Photo by author.

just one year prior, but which were already full. They said that additional courses of gabions were needed to raise them higher. Where gullies were forming along the sides, they suggested that stones should be used to plug them. That is, even when the structures achieve their goal of trapping sediment, it is clear they are but temporary interruptions to its flow. While driving, one of them explained half-joking that what was needed was a large weir across the river that might catch all the sediment. Of course, that too would eventually fill.[17]

Rather than suggesting a failure of the structures, for Tau and his colleagues this situation demonstrated the need for more structures. As we drove back, he pointed out the many places he hoped to build them next.

With Tau's help, I began to see the particular fluvial landscape that he saw—to read the landscape as a conservation bureaucrat (see fig. 11). It was almost postapocalyptic, in need of urgent attention, overflowing with malevolent land users, and characterized by not-deep-enough soils over which water coursed freely. Not a fluvial landscape shaped by variable rainfall and *impacted by the arrival of the 'Muela Dam*, as people in the village described it, this was one shaped by irresponsible grazing and agriculture that *impacted the Dam*.

A given hillslope was not merely a hillslope, but one that either did or did not yet feature a conservation structure. For example, as impressive as the diversion furrow he showed me was, he explained, the area it drained was in fact only a very small section of the catchment as a whole. Many more would be needed, he said. So far, his structures have accounted for 45 hectares (ha) of the catchment—out of a total 2,869 ha.

His responsibility was to restore the landscape, and yet it was clear that, for him, a degraded landscape was in some sense a good one—a landscape in need of his solutions. Tau's landscape historiography linked his perceptions of irresponsible rural people to a system of distribution that both enabled water production but which also performed and justified his expertise. It was green imperialism at its core.

Walking with Tau's foreman, Relebohile, another day, I was provided a more distilled version of this attitude. I had asked him whether people living in the 'Muela area were upset about the presence of the LHDA and the 'Muela Dam, which had led to some village resettlements, confiscation (with compensation) of agricultural and grazing land, and surely other disruptions during construction of this massive project.

"Some people were upset," he said, but they didn't have good reason to be, pointing out to me that "people don't realize that the reason they have these *fato-fato* jobs is *because* of the reservoir." Because of the reservoir, he went on to explain, the problem of soil erosion has become more significant and *fato-fato* programs are now needed to remedy it. "Problems are good because they bring opportunities." For example, he said, "the HIV/AIDS epidemic is a job-creator: when the money comes in for aid, someone is given a job to ensure that the money is being spent efficiently. So, people can go on making problems and then benefitting from them."[18]

This techno-optimist vision of the landscape was not merely Tau's or the LHWP's. It also reflected that of the ministry, too. On trips to the field with ministry officials, some of them would make fun of *fato-fato* workers for being lazy as we drove by, sometimes departing from the truck to harass them in person. This, even as they conceded in private that the people are paid poorly and the work is very difficult. They alleged that communities would sometimes destroy *fato-fato* conservation works simply to try to get another *fato-fato* project. Tau told me similarly that local people had been stealing the wire from the gabions for their own, personal use and ruining them. This was antithetical to *fato-fato* as these conservation bureaucrats saw it. *Fato-fato* seeks to "build ownership to the land," as one ministry official put it to me, teaching rural people to value their landscape. In response to rumors of vandalism (or of communities *causing* degradation to solicit a new *fato-fato* project), LHDA and ministry officials threatened to cease *fato-fato* in the area.

Put another way, conservation workers deemed *fato-fato* programs necessary, and yet also wielded them as a tool to manage how rural people used and perceived land—or even how they interacted with powerful state and parastatal institutions around them. What these officials in charge of soil conservation projects did not mention, of course, was implicit in Relobohile's point: that they too were "beneficiaries" of degradation. Their everyday work consisted entirely of carrying out these programs—that is, to look for and find degradation.

Tau's landscape historiography and the state-citizen relationship it afforded were certainly artifacts of his professional circumstance. They made his work sensible and possible. But they also emanated from a prior historical moment in national soil erosion control, to which I turn to now.

A POLITICS OF DISTRIBUTION

"Jonathan Not Happy with British Aid": that was the all-caps headline in *The World* newspaper on October 20, 1966, just a few weeks after Lesotho gained its independence from Britain. Prime minister Leabua Jonathan, the conservative figure who was hand-picked by the British and (initially) friendly with the apartheid regime of Hendrik Verwoerd,[19] demanded a larger aid package than the one being offered by Britain in the weeks following Lesotho's independence. It was "making a mockery of our independence," he was quoted as saying, and threatened to reject it outright.[20] The irony that Lesotho's independence from Britain would be predicated upon an *aid-dependence upon* Britain was surely not lost on Jonathan, the first elected leader of Lesotho after eighty years of British rule. He was a canny politician who excelled at playing regional powers against each other and against his domestic political rivals. For example, Jonathan emphasized that, without increased British aid, Lesotho would be at the mercy of its powerful neighbor South Africa, already by then understood to be a pariah state in the "international community" for its policies of apartheid and its willingness to intervene militarily in regional wars of independence.[21] (In the end, that logic was sound: in 1986, after years of harboring African National Congress activists and refusing to agree to a water-export scheme, he was toppled in a military coup that was likely supported by South Africa.)

Jonathan's success in soliciting aid money came partly from his penchant for political showmanship, as indicated by his very public outrage over the aid package. In the run-up to independence he performed himself as a man of the people and an agitator for the oppressed. On one occasion in 1962, he marched a troop of indigent people through the streets of Maseru down to the British High Commission, demanding that they be given menial jobs such as digging contour furrows to combat soil erosion.[22] It worked.

In the more than two decades of rule afterward, Jonathan maintained his power in large part thanks to efforts like this one, procuring donor aid from foreign entities and then distributing it to communities (mostly those who supported him) as payment for public works programs like road construction, soil conservation, and tree planting.[23]

The programs seamlessly wove together foreign anxiety over soil erosion, the emergent humanitarian aid economy, and his domestic political demands. They also carried forward prior colonial labor forms, like the work parties used in road construction and soil conservation in the colonial era. The annual British colonial reports are full of mentions of these work parties. Heavy rains were continuously washing out sections of road in the territory, frustrating the British colonial officers responsible for ensuring that administration and capital had easy access to the hinterland. The officers hired local people to do this. The report from 1901 read: "Parties of labourers with practical overseers in charge have been employed repairing the roads, but on account of the almost incessant rainfall during the last five months the work has not progressed satisfactorily, and it has been impossible to do more than just keep the roads open for vehicle traffic."[24] Or, in 1933: "In November and December exceptionally heavy rains seriously damaged many of the spruits and donga crossings, and it will be many months before repairs can be completed. Towards the end of the year gangs of famine relief workers helped to maintain the roads and were of considerable assistance in helping to keep them open to traffic."[25]

The work party as an arrangement of labor was not devised by Jonathan, then, but he creatively reworked it and gave it a new name: *letšolo-la-iketsetse*, which translates roughly as "a goal-oriented group that works for itself." In English, it was often referred to as the Food Self-Sufficiency Programme.[26] Jonathan noted these programs repeatedly in his speeches through *Molia*, the state newspaper, as well as in his weekly radio addresses,[27] and used the program as a way to demonstrate his effectiveness as leader to his domestic audience as well as an international donor audience. At that time, payment was made only in food, such as oil and maize-meal. The narrative of "self-help" was strong at that time of African independence movements and giving handouts—especially of cash—was seen as improper.[28]

As John Aerni-Flessner shows,[29] small projects like these constitute some of the earliest forms of "developmentalism" in postindependence Lesotho, every bit as important as the larger projects analyzed by James Ferguson.[30] This is because they reached into even the smallest villages countrywide. The Thaba-Bosiu Rural Development Project (1973–77) is but one example: "Food-Aid labor has been a major factor in accomplishing many of the rock structures and other hand labor conservation measures. Food-Aid laborers were paid 60 cents per day plus food-aid supplies (5-hrs cash labor and 3-hrs food), and the force was changed every 15 days to maximize the total number given a chance to work."[31] As can be seen in this quotation, the goal of increased short-term employment opportunities was key to these projects.[32] In the "Integrated Conservation Development Project Areas" created across Lesotho in the 1970s, Nobe and Seckler explain:

> Over the life of the project, the Conservation Division has supervised up to 2,400 food-aid workers each year who do small but important conservation project work in all districts. Complete reports of accomplishments have not yet been assembled but, generally speaking, much of the work is directed toward repair of damaged existing conservation structures and related measures. No estimates of the value of food-aid labor are available but as of February 1976, 60,000 Rand has been spent on this program.[33]

The opposition Basutoland Congress Party (BCP) derided these programs as mere "political games,"[34] and asserted that people were being forced to work for them by chiefs, conjuring images of colonial times, when despotic chiefs emboldened by British indirect rule (see chapter 4) were accused of abusing their powers to call work parties on their agricultural fields. BCP leaders even went so far as to describe the programs as a form of "slavery."[35] The work was mostly carried out by women whose husbands were away at the mines, and the crews were mocked by the BCP as *khofu tsa matsoele*, or "excavators with breasts." In some cases, BCP activists destroyed these conservation works as political statements against Jonathan's BNP.[36]

Despite BCP disdain, the conservation programs were reborn in more or less the same form under the BCP after they took power in 1993. As a condition of providing financing for construction of the LHWP, the World Bank required the establishment of an entity called the Lesotho Highlands Revenue Fund (LHRF), to be financed by water royalties and used for development projects—to channel water directly into national development. It would ensure that the royalties would go toward "long-term development benefits" for communities through small-scale projects.[37] After widespread misuse of the LHRF by unscrupulous politicians,[38] the Fund was shut down and reconstructed as the Lesotho Fund for Community Development (LFCD). Its organizing principle was that royalties should still be used for various development projects (as with the LHRF), but that people in rural communities should be paid to do the work.[39] The communities were asked to submit proposals for such projects, and those mostly included small irrigation dams and soil conservation works. Depicting them as a thinly veiled attempt at buying the votes of people in mountainous, rural areas, the now-opposition BNP party sarcastically dubbed the programs *fato-fato*,[40] "scratching about on the ground like a chicken." Weathering these criticisms, the program was eventually taken up by the government as a permanent enterprise. Today, *fato-fato* is the primary means by which the government of Lesotho intervenes to rehabilitate or reclaim land. An entire ministry—the Ministry of Forestry, Range, and Soil Conservation—was effectively created for this purpose after the 2007 elections.

For unemployed rural Basotho, the programs certainly do not seem aimless or pathetic as their epithet suggests. I have been to registrations for *fato-fato* projects. People come out in droves, mostly by foot, and some from several kilometers away. The atmosphere resembles a fair, with people standing in long, winding registration lines, others milling about or seated on the ground eating and catching up with one another.

Fato-fato was only a joke in elite crowds and only when it was me, a foreigner, using the term. I regularly heard professionals use the term with other professionals without eliciting any reaction. My outsider status, I think, exposed the uneasiness of the arrangement: Not unlike the white colonial populations in South Africa in the early part of the twentieth century, who feared that soil erosion could lead to rural agricultural collapse, forcing Africans off their land and into white urban

FIGURE 12. *Fato-fato* workers. Photo by author.

spaces,[41] Lesotho's upper classes understood the precariousness of rural society. Whenever I used the term with rural people, there were no titters or smiles. That rural people worked on *fato-fato* crews was not necessarily a sign of desperation, but rather a participation in a longstanding arrangement with their government. It is true that some rural Basotho decline to work on *fato-fato* crews because the of the low pay and low status. One man I knew well who once held a well-paying job in the mines for many years before a serious injury sent him home refused to participate in *fato-fato* for just these reasons. His wife had no such reservations. When I asked her and other rural people if the term *fato-fato* was derogatory, many said no. In spite of the comical image it conjured of a chicken scratching about, the term was only derogatory, they argued, when it was used in a derogatory way—typically by people who don't like the program or don't want to work on *fato-fato* crews. But my friends from the lowlands agreed that people in urban Lesotho often make fun of it. One of them told me that he sometimes referred to then prime minister Thomas Thabane as "Mr. Stoneline" (*Ntate Motsele-tsele*) because of the deep furrows in his forehead and his enthusiasm for *fato-fato*. These *fato-fato* projects, always visible from the roadside, inscribe upon the landscape a (partisan) state-citizen relationship—one hitched to a fluvial imagination, one fit to the economic times (see fig. 12).

Like rural people who work on *fato-fato* crews, conservation bureaucrats in the mountains who administer the programs also seemed to take *fato-fato* seriously. *Fato-fato* was one of the first things that Masilo wanted to show me when

I told him that I was learning about rangeland condition and management in Lesotho. When we arrived at one of these sites, he was excited to impress me with the scope of the operation—how many people were working there, how much money it cost, the extent of the job. Ministry workers were proud of the potential conservation fix, but also of the amounts of money it involved, just like Tau from the LHWP. On one occasion, when I dropped by the ministry office, Masilo told me that they were extremely busy because the ministry was just given a lot of extra money for *fato-fato* (390,600 Maloti, or about USD 39,000), which they were required spend by the end of the following month. The money was initially given to the Ministry of Gender but they weren't spending it, he explained, so the government decided to give it to a ministry "that knows how to spend money." When I asked what they planned to do with it he told me, "the usual": diversion furrows, stonelines, gabions.

Put another way: "Sediment Traps Needed."

CONCLUSION

Water commodities require production. Producing them is about more than the conceptual transformation from a socially embedded and polysemic water to an abstract category fit for exchange, a primary line of critique for scholars of water privatization, as I outlined in chapter 1. It requires the extraction of water from the soils and other landscape media through which it flows. Soil conservation structures in Lesotho are critical to that work, given the country's notoriously erosive soils and the threat they pose to Lesotho's water-export economy. But the structures built for the task are shoddy to the point of being comical. Why? Because soil conservation is a form of governance. It is part of a long-standing system of distribution, a modestly successful—if sometimes environmentally harmful—effort to keep unemployed people from starving, preventing the structural contradictions of Lesotho's position as a water reservoir from exploding.

Fato-fato shows how neither water production nor soil conservation are universal, scientific engineering practices. Instead, they are local, historical negotiations. The landscape practices of water engineers in Lesotho are not their independent creation, but rather co-emerge with global conservation trends toward "integrated" catchment management, as well as national histories of partisan politics and foreign aid. *Fato-fato* derives from colonial-era work parties refashioned by Leabua Jonathan's independence government, which creatively redirected aid money toward Jonathan's political constituents—and which were later refashioned yet again through water royalties earned from the LHWP as a permanent government program.

In spite of the fact that *fato-fato* structures' shortcomings draws the water-export system into a crisis that imperils its long-term viability, these haphazard stonelines are vital to the "real" infrastructures of production—the high-engineering dam walls and tunnels glorified in the LHWP's promotional materials. That *fato-fato* is successful is not to say that it is a comfortable arrangement. The nervous laughs that I got from urban professionals when I used the term *fato-fato* hinted at the discomfort of this uneasy alliance between elites and the rural poor—the tenuousness of the emergent social contract of Lesotho's water-reservoir era. Decrepit, shoddy, and crumbling, stonelines like the one I described at the beginning of this chapter manage to conjure in their very being a sense of both the potency and impotence of the Lesotho government. Not a state in ruins, but under construction, even if built upon the rubble of earlier arrangements.

Scrutinizing the everyday practices of soil conservation in Lesotho shows how important a play of temporalities is to the terrestrial politics of water, as I began to describe in chapter 2. The LHDA is fundamentally interested in building the dams—not in long-term maintenance. There are tremendous political pressures to move dam projects forward, as they include huge amounts of money in contracts for design, construction and other enterprise. The expected useful lifespan of a large dam is only fifty years,[42] which is therefore the temporal horizon used to plan for financial returns.

This temporal arbitrage is useful elsewhere in the LHWP, such as its compensation plan. Many people I spoke with in the Mokhotlong District who would be impacted by the Polihali Dam were concerned about a fifty-year horizon on compensation for lost agricultural fields, trees, or other resources cited for compensation. This issue was a particular focus of activists who were trying to organize for greater compensation, and it regularly came up at meetings that I attended of the main activist group in Mokhotlong, as well as in their discussions with LHWP officials. These people questioned why it was they would be given compensation for fifty years for, say, an agricultural field, when that same field would be passed down through the generations to their children, grandchildren, and beyond. At one meeting organized by the LHDA in Mokhotlong in September 2014, which saw the top brass of the Water Project gathering to listen to community leaders and their concerns about the project (ahead of their trip to an event at Jacob Zuma's Nkandla estate), several people confronted them about this point. Their responses were circuitous but mentioned a precedent in water projects for a fifty-year limit. When I asked a high-ranking LHWP employee how the fifty-year number came about, he seemed reticent to discuss it. Usually cool and cocksure, he fidgeted nervously and told me that it was the standard because that is the expected life of the dam.

Expansive in scope when portrayed as a vehicle for economic production, the project narrows when seen in light of environmental impacts and compensation.[43]

Driving back with Masilo up the Mokhotlong River Valley from the village I described at the beginning of this chapter, we passed by several stonelines that were built in previous years. In the first, one could barely make out the lines, as the rows of rocks were not very tall and perhaps some had fallen downslope. The area looked pretty bad, with just a smattering of grasses and shrubs interspersed in bare soil and exposed rock. The only appreciable difference was that the hillside had distinctive lines across it. Masilo told me that this one had been built in 2008. I asked him and the others in the car if it looked like it was helping, and we all looked over at it without answering. I think it was clear to all of us that it was not. Masilo turned to me and explained that "maybe they need to make it a rested pasture [*leboella*]." Further down the road, we passed by another set of stonelines that Masilo pointed out, noting that "you can see a little difference there" (*phapangyana e teng*). We looked over at it and gave a nod in another moment of silence, all trying to discern the "little difference" Masilo described.

4

Bureaucratic Ecology

Conservation bureaucrats in Lesotho rely on two measures to manage soil erosion: physical structures, which I described in the previous chapter; and social structures, which I describe in this one. Whereas the physical structures are designed to slow the flow of water manually as it courses downslope, social structures such as grazing associations are said to get "to the source," as Tau put it in chapter 3, preventing land degradation that is the cause of accelerated flow in the first place. The management of rangelands in far-away mountain landscapes may at first blush appear tangential to the work of producing water for export to South Africa, but it is central.

Reconciling the contradictions of Lesotho's water-export economy—namely the competing terrestrial demands of water production and livestock production— means that conservation bureaucrats must translate between an ecology and a sociology. This chapter excavates the bureaucratic work done to make that translation.

How does one devise land reforms in which theories of ecological process articulate well with theories of social process? How does one give bureaucratic shape to the spatial and temporal parameters of an ecosystem? For example, what kind of authority best suits these vast and remote rangelands? Should chiefs be in charge of managing grazing as has historically been the case, with their specific set of tools for enforcing rules and resolving disputes, or some other institution? What might be the political ramifications of promoting one or the other? Should some kind of permitting and registration be put in place? Also: How many animals should be allowed to graze in a particular area? Which types, and for how long? What happens if the year is particularly rainy or dry? Questions such as these converge like locusts upon conservation efforts in Lesotho.

The answers supplied to them and the actions that follow point toward a "bureaucratic ecology." By this, I mean the ecological process imagined by bureaucrats and its effects on the landscape. Bureaucrats inherit and reproduce this bureaucratic ecology, but they are not entirely in control of it. They sometimes struggle against it, as do livestock owners. Even livestock and vegetation are subject to its pressures and idiosyncrasies. This work of translation between a human sociology and a more-than-human ecology therefore demonstrates how social processes entwine ecological processes.[1] Commonly understood to occupy sites such as offices and archives, bureaucracy ramifies in ecosystems as human and nonhuman subjects are forced to contend with its incentives, categories, and contradictions.

The conservation bureaucrats I depict below work as rangeland profession-als, seeking to administer the principles of rangeland ecology. This subfield of ecology probes the hazy boundaries of nature and culture in "rangelands," a term that refers to any uncultivated land that supports grazing and browsing animals, whether grasslands, savannas, shrublands, or deserts.[2] Theoreti-cians and practitioners work to discern how best to maintain rangeland health while producing livestock.[3] They address questions about the effects of different management regimes; the relative importance of management versus environ-mental factors such as climate in determining rangeland condition; and what constitutes "good condition" in the first place (e.g., forage abundance, plant spe-cies diversity, etc.).

Below, I describe two, connected efforts to rearrange the spaces and times in which livestock are grazed. In the first, conservation bureaucrats attempted to impose a controversial rotational grazing method devised by Allan Savory called Holistic Resource Management. They hoped this would improve range condi-tion generally, relieving grazing pressure on the alpine wetlands of concern to water export. In the second, they attempted to reclassify the grazing lands around their project so they could increase the fines for those who failed to follow their rules. In both cases, debates about social roles loom: whether the behaviors of herders and chiefs, for example, are fit to this rangeland ecosystem in the water-export era.

Having presented these two episodes, I parse out the historical and cultural circumstances that made them possible. These circumstances also destine present efforts to failure—and future efforts, too. They entail the manipulation of social institutions: for example, the reworking of the chieftaincy and its grazing-land responsibilities during colonial "indirect rule," the introduction of local gov-ernment councils and grazing associations as checks on chiefly power, and the introduction of various other institutions with some mandate for rangeland man-agement. Each institution represents at one and the same time an organic, local social form, a foreign imposition, and a matter of national debate. My story is anchored in a bureaucratic critique, so that is where I'll need to start.

THE LOG BOOKS

Institutions for managing land in Lesotho today are subject to what, in a different context, has been called "projectification"[4]—the execution of social and environmental programs through time-bound, often-foreign-funded initiatives: "projects." A common approach has been to introduce "user associations" (*mekhatlo*), sometimes called "cooperatives," which conjure a sense of community ownership and empowerment. Here's how it works. A development or conservation project alights upon a village, and introduces one of these associations. Not confined to conservation, these cooperatives can work toward a variety of goals: handicraft groups to sell art objects to tourists, youth groups to engage young people on HIV/AIDS education, egg circles for local food access, and so on. People sign up, interested in the opportunities that might come of it. Constitutions are written, modest annual dues are paid, executive committees are established. As the project wends its way toward completion and dissolution at the end of its funding cycle, the association also slowly erodes away.

But it never fully dissolves. It might stop paying its annual registration to the government. Its members might stop paying their annual dues and attending monthly meetings. But a core group of members always remains, enshrined in their log books: the black, hardcover "exercise" books with red binding tape that are ubiquitous in Lesotho, stored and carried in plastic bags, and a requisite for the executive committee members of user associations. The group lies more or less dormant until yet another project comes along. That subsequent project—even sometimes one seemingly unrelated in its goals and scope—will learn of the existing association in the course of "mapping out stakeholders," understanding it to be a relevant constituency or partner. Their project must either be built around the existing user association, supplant it, or, most typically, incorporate it in the name of inclusion. During my time in Lesotho, because I often asked about these associations, I routinely encountered people who were part of associations of one sort or another, particularly because scores were created in the project areas of the Lesotho Highlands Water Project (LHWP) dams.[5] If I asked while at their home, they would often fetch a plastic bag from a chest or cupboard, pull from it a black notebook with red binding, and show me this list of members, a constitution, a government registration. These were invariably codified in proper legal language, with officers, protocols, and purview well defined.

These log books point to the *contingent* power of bureaucracy. Scholars in bureaucracy studies have long described bureaucratic institutions as tending to expand their reach, drawing ever more practices and persons under their jurisdiction: think "mission creep,"[6] or "the iron cage."[7] Virus-like, bureaucracy ensures that social life serves the form of its protocols rather than the substance of its original rationale. But the quality of that bureaucratic reach is neither even nor assured. It's true that bureaucracy can operate as an engine for structural and state violence,[8] but foregrounding only that tendency risks granting it more power than it has.[9] There are lots of times and spaces in which it does *not* operate, or in which it operates only in fits and starts. Bureaucratic power is defined by its patchy and contingent spacetimes: universalizing, but never universal.[10]

Institutions to manage grazing in Lesotho are useful for thinking about these expanding and universalizing qualities of bureaucracy because of their dramatic proliferation in the country over the past half-century or more.[11] At nearly every turn in Lesotho's history, even before the advent of the development and conservation industry, interventions have been made to rationalize and democratize rangeland use.[12] Energized by donor funds and new-fangled bureaucratic forms, these institutions have extended themselves across rangelands, each with their own spatial and temporal protocols, ecological imaginaries, forms of documentation, concepts, stakeholders, and so on. Funding dissipates. The institution recedes. And subsequent rangeland conservation projects must reckon with the institutional architecture of these previous reforms, limited in power but persistent across time—each perched haphazardly upon the ones that came before it.

The interventions into Lesotho's rangelands that I describe in this chapter don't extend the state or a bureaucratic logic further and further into everyday life.[13] Instead, they create a scattered geography of sporadic bureaucratic power that compromises each subsequent intervention. Not an iron cage, nor a labyrinth— bureaucracy is a perilous wasteland of yesterday's discarded plans.[14]

In the course of translating between a sociology and an ecology, then, conservation bureaucrats stumble over this "imperial debris."[15] Like the subjects of their programs, they navigate a landscape cluttered with what the geographer Stephen Turner has described as Lesotho's "gradually evolving, and gradually decaying" institutions for rangeland management.[16]

. . .

During my field research in Lesotho, conservation bureaucrats envisioned "management" as the critical dynamic impacting land condition rather than climate or some nuanced account involving multiple factors. In this, they worked in accordance with received wisdom from the colonial period about rural livestock production and its impacts on land in Africa.[17]

Revisionist work in environmental history and rangeland ecology from the 1980s and 1990s challenged such a view.[18] It argued that arid and semiarid ecosystems in Africa, which feature strong variation in rainfall from year to year, were responsive primarily to climate. Management decisions in such systems had little effect on land condition—whether defined by species richness and diversity, forage abundance, or vegetation structure—because of the overriding importance of rainfall. It is not entirely clear how relevant these findings are for the Lesotho highlands, which features a semihumid climate (i.e., more annual rainfall than a semiarid or arid climate), but its high interannual variability in rainfall suggests that climate is highly determinant. Yet, the possibility that Lesotho's systems are rainfall-dependent was not a notion that was taken up widely among conservation bureaucrats in Lesotho, whether they worked at the ministry, the Lesotho Highlands Water Project, or foreign organizations.[19]

Bureaucrats were not resistant to considering novel ways of envisioning rangeland ecologies, however, so long as management remained at the center. This next section turns to describe how they incorporated a rotational grazing program developed by the controversial Zimbabwean ecologist, Allan Savory. Whereas decades of conservation thought had suggested that overgrazing was rampant on African rangelands, Savory's program instead argued that *undergrazing* was the problem for reasons I explain below.[20] But while Savory's method is typically applied in heavily circumscribed settings with a system of paddocks to promote concentrated grazing, Lesotho's fenceless, extensive rangelands would demand additional measures.

First, they would need to rouse herders from their perceived laziness, encouraging them to herd "actively" rather than "passively," as I show in this next section. Second, they would need to redefine the rangeland space to better control which areas were open to grazing, the point I turn to in the subsequent section.

It would be a tall order. Even despite the urgent need for soil conservation to save the water-export economy, these attempts were unlikely to succeed. Efforts to improve the condition and management of Lesotho's rangelands become ensnared in—and ultimately undone by—the debris of earlier imperial designs. Rather than improve land condition, management reforms make improvement-through-management impossible into the future.

THE SAVORY ROTATIONAL GRAZING SYSTEM

Motebong ha ho lisoe: "At the cattle posts, one does not herd." I first came across this phrase—a Sesotho proverb (*maele*)—in the ethnographic literature: Hugh Ashton's *The Basuto*.[21] It refers literally to the notion that herding is unnecessary at the "cattle posts,"[22] where animals are thought to simply leave the kraal, graze where they please, and get retrieved in the afternoon. More than that, it captures the slow flow of life at *motebong*, the remote cattle posts where herders stay with their herds for months on end. So distant from the village, herders truly live on their own terms there. The proverb's passive construction carries with it a second connotation in an alternative translation: "At the cattle posts, one is not herded."

My next encounter with the proverb came in a conversation with Sepheo, an employee at the Khubelu Sponges Project. This was a conservation scheme initially funded by the German state aid organization (GIZ) and later taken up by the Lesotho government. It was aimed at protecting the LHWP by preserving the wetlands in the highest reaches of the mountains, based on the logic that the wetlands could retain and slowly release water into LHWP reservoirs better if they weren't subject to so much grazing. Improving range condition in general, they felt, would release pressure from the wetlands.

It was early in my field research, and I met Sepheo at his office in Mokhotlong to learn what he knew about wetland degradation—its symptoms, causes, and solutions. He and his organization sought a way to prevent herders from grazing their animals on the wetlands, and he was encountering mostly dead ends. The rangelands are vast; fences are taboo because of widespread and passionate commitment to preserving common land tenure; getting buy-in from chiefs and livestock owners is difficult due to skepticism about reforms; it's even a challenge simply to gather herders together for a workshop, because they can't leave their animals unattended for long.

But in Lesotho's fluvial economy, bringing livestock production into harmony with water production is key, and Sepheo was working extremely hard in my observation to do so. He was taking an intellectual approach, thinking deeply about the ecology and trying to line up all of the human interests and considerations. He related to me what he felt was one of the central challenges to his effort: the fact that herders do not actually "herd" their animals but instead allow them to graze as they please. Laughing, he said in English, "There is this phrase in Sesotho: *motebong ha ho lisoe.*"

For Sepheo, the saying distilled a truth about herders in Lesotho: that they are lazy and mostly just sit around all day playing the *sekhankula* (a makeshift violin) or napping. It was a perception shared by many in Lesotho, in fact. This laziness manifested in a particular spatiality of grazing, with livestock highly dispersed in the pasture, selectively eating the plants they choose. (Readers will recall a story in the introduction about Tankisi discussing this problem.) The challenge of herder laziness needed to be overcome, Sepheo thought, and he had been persuaded in this by a consultant the Sponges Project hired to evaluate rangeland condition and to suggest management options. The project wanted to encourage herders "to work by the signs of the plants," he said. Farmers tend to prioritize livestock over the range, he explained, and the Sponges Project sought to reverse that trend. I half-expected him to lapse into the old complaint about overstocking—that people keep huge herds of livestock simply because it grants them social status. But he surprised me.

While many believe the rangelands to be overgrazed,[23] he said, in fact they are *overrested*. There are a lot of animals, but their selective grazing is the true problem. Rather than being dispersed throughout the pasture, livestock should be herded tightly so that they graze intensively on one small area, eating palatable and unpalatable plants alike before moving to another area. There could be many more animals on the landscape if herders were more active in their herding. A rotational grazing system is crucial to improving rangeland condition, he said.

I remarked that this approach sounded similar to one I had read about, developed by Allan Savory. His face lit up: "Exactly! This one!"

. . .

The Savory Rotational Grazing Method (also called Holistic Resource Management) was proposed by Savory in 1980.[24] Born in 1935 in Zimbabwe—at that time a colonial territory called Southern Rhodesia—he developed his method while working as a colonial conservation officer. The method features multipaddock rotations, where livestock move regularly from one paddock (or, pen) to another, grazing and browsing the vegetation fully before being moved. This forces livestock to eat the unpalatable as well as the palatable vegetation, ensuring that "decreasers"—those palatable, typically perennial grasses that livestock prefer—do not get replaced by "increasers"—the less palatable annual grasses (or shrubs) that increase with heavy grazing.[25] His rationale was to mimic what he saw as the natural grazing and browsing regime of African savannas, whereby large herds of ungulates consumed or trampled most of the vegetation available to them, depositing nutrients through defecation and urination as they moved.

The method was met by excitement in parts of the lay and applied rangelands community, with its spare and compelling ecological rationale. In 2011, Savory gave a TED talk that has been viewed over twelve million times.[26] In the presentation, he described with an evangelical optimism how his method could reverse the trend of desertification in many parts of the world, showing images of brown, barren land alongside others of verdant and lush stands of trees and grasses.[27]

In the *scientific* rangeland ecology community, by contrast, Savory was met with widespread skepticism since his early publications.[28] Some of the most well-respected range ecologists published responses to Savory's TED talk, including one titled, "The Savory Method Can Not Green Deserts or Reverse Climate Change."[29] There, they refute him and contend that his unsubstantiated claims have the potential to undermine the credibility of rangeland professionals at large.

What is more, Savory's system problematically suggests that ecosystems benefit from very intense livestock grazing, when in fact few measures of ecosystem health would be served by it—a possible Trojan horse for ranchers to overturn conservation regulations.[30] Taken independently of empirical data, one might also question its basic logic. If livestock were to consume or trample everything, the exposed and compacted soil could reduce infiltration, encourage runoff and therefore lead to erosion, particularly given the punctuated rainfall regime of Lesotho described in chapter 2. It seems unclear, too, whether nutritious, perennial grasses would be more likely to establish in the fully grazed paddock than the unpalatable annuals and shrubs that typically colonize heavily disturbed sites. Finally, as I'll explain in chapter 6, the Lesotho highlands likely did not feature large herds of grazing ungulates prior to human settlement in line with Savory's theory.

Beyond its lack of supporting evidence and its specious ecological rationale, the method is also impractical in Lesotho. First, it's worth noting that farmers in Lesotho are generally risk-averse, given the absence of credit and high levels of poverty.[31] Second, the method was designed to be used in intensive settings with a costly network of paddock fences—not extensive, open rangelands governed by common tenure. Sepheo recognized the well-known fact that fences are impossible in Lesotho—not only because of the cost, but also because they are seen as hostile to common property arrangements.[32] Paddocks were therefore not an option. According to Lesotho's rangeland commons, no person can be barred from accessing pasture (although there are conventions that practically place limits on use).[33]

To address this problem, the consultant recommended "active herding"—continually encircling the animals so they graze in a tight bunch. This would be a way to mimic the paddocks, they thought.[34] "Active herding" seemed unlikely to me, given the effort this would require of herders. But he had been spending time, he told me, patiently trying to understand how herders move their animals around and what their interests might be. Armed with that information, he thought, he might be able to encourage them to move according to his modified Savory plan.

A less intensive rotational grazing system in fact already exists in Lesotho, and it has been in place since the earliest days of the country, when King Moshoeshoe I established areas for pasture resting (*maboella*) and seasonal grazing in the nineteenth century.[35] As land pressure increased, good forage was found further from villages and increasingly higher in the foothills and highlands. This would eventually manifest in a form of "vertical transhumance," in which livestock were taken to higher-altitude cattle posts for summertime grazing and returned to lower-elevation areas near villages during wintertime. That transhumance pattern was then formalized as the "A-B-C system" after the 1935 Pim Report, which designated soil erosion a national emergency (see chapter 2), and such a system today governs livestock movements countrywide.

The "A" grazing zone corresponds to summer cattle post areas on the high-elevation plateau (>2900masl), open to grazing during the months of January to March; the "B" grazing zone refers to winter cattle posts at a subalpine elevation (2290–2900masl), open to grazing from April to December; the "C" grazing zone corresponds to the areas surrounding villages, where livestock are only permitted while birthing, for ploughing, for milking, or when subsisting on fodder.

The Savory-inspired rotational grazing method proposed by the Sponges Project was built to work within the A-B-C system, with active herding to take place at these various zones. They also considered dividing the winter rangelands into three subsections, across which herders would move every two months. But this revised spatial logic failed to take account of a variety of factors that determine herder movements. For one thing, herders are directed by the owner of the herd they manage. If the livestock owners tell them to stay in the B rangelands (winter cattle posts) throughout the summer months, then they must do so. They are also motivated to move the animals in a way that ensures the animals are well fed, as livestock owners demand this. Within the immediate vicinity of their cattle post, they typically choose between four to five different routes, each of which will allow the herders to easily water the animals once in the morning and the afternoon, and to get livestock to where the forage is good, where the winds are not too strong, and where they can be observed easily. Sometimes, they also try to visit areas near to another herder, where they can sit and talk while keeping the herds separate.[36]

These problems should not obscure an important point: that Sepheo and other conservation bureaucrats at the ministry demonstrated an openness to new forms of ecological theorizing. They saw management as the primary problem facing Lesotho's rangelands—unlike the weather it was something they could control, after all—but were not inflexible as to what form management should take. For all its shortcomings, Savory's grazing program helped them to solve a problem: by suggesting that undergrazing was the problem rather than overgrazing, the flow of water across the landscape could be improved without reducing the number of livestock.[37]

To make it work, they'd need to do more than simply inspire herders to graze actively. They would need to enhance their enforcement of rules against grazing animals in rested pastures, as I describe in this next section. Their thought was to leverage a political distinction that defines Lesotho's dualist system of government. Lesotho has both a chieftaincy and a state government, whereby chiefs bear the responsibilities of "governance" (*puso*) and the state has the responsibilities of "development" (*ntlafatso*). Rangelands typically fall under chiefly control (a matter of "governance"), but bureaucrats hoped to designate pastures where conservation work was taking place as a matter for the state—a "development" area. In redefining grazing reform areas, that is, they hoped to reterritorialize ecological process, extricating it from "governance" and bringing it in line with "development."

THE IMPOUNDMENT

The Sponges Project's vehicle for carrying out this Savory rotational grazing program was a grazing association (*mokhatlo oa phuliso*) that existed in their project area. A grazing association is a "community-based" institution that aims to devolve grazing management from chiefs to "the people," even though chiefs also sit on the associations. They include women and young people, but mostly in my observation consist of adult men. Grazing associations came about in the early 1980s, as the development and conservation industries came into full bloom, and they were propagated across the country.[38] As one early proponent put it, these would "improve range condition and livestock productivity on Lesotho's rangelands by mobilizing collective management of communal grazing areas."[39] Per the design at that time, each grazing association managed a "range management

FIGURE 13. A grazing association meeting. Photo by author.

area" that mostly mapped onto the territory of one of the twenty-two principal chiefs, which I explain below. In addition to controlling the schedule of livestock rotations, associations were supposed to promote improved livestock breeds and encourage owners to sell their animals at livestock auctions.

This particular association targeted by the Sponges Project was only started in 2000 when an international conservation project suggested the idea.[40] The association members couldn't remember the name of that project when I spoke with them in 2014—something about improving the rangelands, one of them said. Membership was substantial at the outset, but declined through the years. The association became moribund.

Then, in 2013, the Sponges Project came to the area and held a public meeting (*pitso*, see fig. 13). They felt compelled to engage the association, given its relevance to their rotational grazing scheme. In their estimation, chiefs were failing at enforcing rules about pasture-resting, and they needed a more engaged set of local partners. Ministry officials and the police were present at the *pitso*. They told livestock owners that they were going to be very serious about impounding livestock found grazing in closed pastures or those without association-issued permits—the livestock would be taken to the chief's corral and the owner would have to pay a fine to get them back. After that meeting, their membership shot to 285, but it fell again to 87 the next year. I asked some of the association members why they thought membership had declined. They explained that people came to think the association wasn't serious. There were some impoundments initially, but then accounts began to circulate of uneven enforcement—that some livestock without permits were not impounded. The association, it seemed to them, was not in charge. People became sour and disregarded the association once again, declining to renew their membership.

I saw one example play out in living color just a few weeks after that conversation. Some cattle were impounded when they passed into the area that was closed to grazing for the Sponges Project and a ministry *fato-fato* program (see chapter 3). I was stunned to learn that the animals belonged to Tankisi, the assistant chair of the grazing association, which was responsible for deciding when to open and close the area. I described Tankisi in the introduction of this book, a rural man who was often called upon by development and conservation bureaucrats seeking participants for their initiatives. It obviously would not play well with the community at large if Tankisi thought he could get away with this on account of his position in the association. Holding him accountable would be important to ensure that others respect the order to close the pasture.

I attended the next monthly meeting of the grazing association, interested to see how they would handle the issue of Tankisi's animals. In its plot and characters, the scene captures the tangled nature of rangeland interventions like the Savory-inspired Sponges Project and their implications for the water-export era. I describe the scene here before breaking down its significance in the following section.

At *moreneng*, the part of the village where the chief lives and where such meetings are held, people milled about as usual. Young men leaned against the stone kraal as they waited to buy or sell animals; men and women sat and stood near the small, two-room building where *lekhotla* (the village court) would be held. Several horses wandered about around the area, grazing on the closely cropped grasses growing around homes. It was sunny, windy, and cold.

Committee members were rolling in slowly. Tankisi had arrived, as had Ntloko, the chair of the grazing association, and a conservation ministry official named Tefo. The councilor was out of town for a professional training and couldn't make it. We waited for the chief. As we waited, I chatted with Ntloko when my friend Motlokoa sauntered over from his home up the hill. Motlokoa had expressed to me his dislike of the grazing association many times before. A somewhat confrontational person, he interrupted our conversation to ask Ntloko a question, rolling a cigarette and peering up periodically at Ntloko: "What's the point of the association? Isn't it true that I can graze anywhere I want there [gesturing toward the mountainsides around us], and nobody can refuse me?"

The rangelands are commonly held and fundamentally under the remit of the chief, he was implying. His tone was characteristically jovial but blunt. Ntloko seemed intimidated and defensive. He couldn't manage to justify the existence of the association with anything more than some reference to how he and the other members are trying to improve the rangeland. Ntloko would tell me later that it's people like Motlokoa who make the grazing association's work difficult by refusing to cooperate.

The meeting began. The association members and the chief lamented the fact that, while this was an executive committee meeting, only three of the seven committee members were present. After a prayer, the meeting started with Ntloko explaining that the main order of business: to tell the public that the area called Moella would be reopened to grazing for one month.[41] This was also where the Sponges Project and another ministry rangeland improvement project were taking place (also where Tankisi's animals were found). People must procure permits to graze there. The only problem, he said, was that they were all out of the permit forms—he asked Tefo, the ministry officer, to get them some.

The chief then interjected with a pointed question, essentially upbraiding the association for failing to prevent people from grazing in the closed area: "What *exactly* is your work up there?"

Ntloko replied that they are trying their best but "the association has fallen apart," he said.

The conversation then turned to Tankisi's impounded animals—although, of course, they had been talking about Tankisi all along. Tefo was particularly hard on Tankisi, who defended himself by claiming that other people's animals were also grazing in the area but not impounded. (This was not true—I was there and did not see any others.) Why, he asked, were only his impounded? Then he quickly followed with the crucial part of his defense. Besides, he said, the animals were not impounded by an order from the chief, so the impoundment was not legitimate.

Tefo countered as though he'd been waiting for just such a moment: they were impounded in an area undergoing a rangeland improvement project, meaning that it was a "development" (*ntlafatso*) area. Therefore, it was legal for them to impound without a chief's order. Not only that, his fine should be much higher because of that *ntlafatso* designation.

The application of the term *ntlafatso* by Tefo was hugely significant. As I briefly noted above, Lesotho has a legal dualist system of government in which a chieftaincy exists alongside the state. The state is locally represented by elected councilors (and administered by the ministries that constitute the civil service). The responsibilities of the chieftaincy and the state are generally distinguished by reference to two terms: *puso*, meaning "governance," is the charge of chiefs; *ntlafatso*, meaning "development" (or "improvement"), is the charge of councilors. One man explained it to me like this: "If there were a project to build a road, for example, then it would be the councilors who manage the process of selecting workers. Chiefs, on the other hand, would sort out any disputes between people about that selection." In short, councilors make improvements, and chiefs keep the peace.

One of the powers of chiefs in grazing management is to close pastures for rest. Conservation bureaucrats at the Sponges Project and in government believed that chiefs too often looked the other way, and also that the current fines for grazing in these areas were too low to deter herders. Recently, they had begun arguing that larger fines could be imposed for impounded livestock in areas designated *ntlafatso*—some fifty times the chiefly amount or more. According to the 1986 Grazing Regulations, fines for impounded livestock had been fixed at M4 for each head of cattle (around 50 US cents at the time of research), and M0.60 for small stock. After three decades of inflation, these fees were becoming meaningless. The Sponges Project and the ministry sought to work around the existing fee schedule by instituting categorical distinctions: fines in *ntlafatso*-designated land would be higher than in *puso*-designated land. Tefo said that Tankisi's fine could be as much as M900 (over USD 100), a big sum of money for him. But this new fee schedule was a recent, ad hoc imposition and was highly controversial. The look on everyone's faces was one of shock and concern.

Tankisi was ultimately scolded by the chief—but not fined. It was confusing to me that the meeting fizzled to an end after so much drama, and I asked Tefo later why Tankisi wasn't fined. He told me with resigned frustration it was clear the chief wanted to avoid it. The chief probably knew that Tankisi couldn't pay the fine without selling off some of his animals. If Tankisi couldn't pay, the chief would've had to send Tankisi to jail, which was simply too drastic a measure.

I'll turn now to peel apart this impoundment scene layer by layer, in the spirit of Max Gluckman,[42] examining what the basic events of this "social situation" reveal about an underlying system of relationships prevailing upon rangeland conservation. The scene may appear mundane at first blush, but its tensions, ambiguities and maneuverings have profound implications for the water economy. They speak to the elaboration over decades of a set of management structures that, since the colonial period, have become increasingly baroque—the proposed solution to which has been more management structures. They go beyond the water-export economy, too, striking at the heart of political authority in Lesotho. Addressing the water project's land problems therefore entails a confrontation with hotly contested questions of political representation and participation, national identity, and more. This is the terrain into which the Savory program and its spatial logics were to be introduced.

PUSO, NTLAFATSO, AND THE PROJECTS

Attempts to square a sociology with an ecology in Lesotho bump up against partisan national politics, their colonial admixtures, and the development-conservation industry. A key to the story is the advent of Lesotho's "legal dualist" system of government in the late nineteenth century,[43] which created an opposition between traditional authorities (i.e., chiefs) and the state or "statutory" government (i.e., elected politicians like local government councilors).[44] The system is a legacy of British colonial rule, but also represents a substantive national debate about how best to carry out the work of government in this constitutional monarchy.

These political systems—the chieftaincy and the state government—are fundamentally different in their structure and legitimacy. The chieftaincy is a hereditary aristocracy: a nested hierarchy that descends from the king of Lesotho (*Motlotlehi*), an influential though mostly powerless figurehead, through to twenty-two principal chiefs (*marena a sehloho*) and a thousand or so ward chiefs (*marena a sebaka*) and headmen (*bo-ramotse*). The state government is elected in a multiparty parliamentary system descending from the prime minister to cabinet ministers, members of parliament, and local government councilors.[45]

Though officially a dual system of government, in practice one form has been privileged over the other at different moments in Lesotho's history, often in relation to issues of land use.[46] Since missionaries and British colonists introduced or imposed European systems of thought and governance into Basotho life, there has never been agreement among Basotho over how (or whether) to incorporate them. In the late nineteenth and early twentieth centuries, the debate cut along class lines and urban-rural lines. Wealthier, urban, western-educated Basotho were much more likely to endorse European systems. Poorer, rural Basotho were more likely to endorse the chieftaincy as a foundation of Basotho culture and thought. But neither institution is purely "foreign" or "indigenous," as I'll show.[47] In the three following subsections, I describe the historical trajectories of these institutions, each in shifting states of growth and decay, so as to explain how they converge upon the Savory-inspired effort to reorganize grazing for the water-export era.

Institution 1: Chiefs (Puso)

The chieftaincy antedates colonialism, but the institution has morphed over time. For example, the British strategically supported the chieftaincy during the colonial period through their policy of "indirect rule." They affirmed chiefs' powers of tribute extraction, such as through *matsema* work parties where commoners were conscripted to work on chiefs' agricultural fields.[48] They also affirmed chiefs' authority to manage land, including the *leboella* system by which chiefs determined how livestock would be rotated to allow for pasture-resting—and by which chiefs received payment for fines when animals were caught grazing in closed pastures.[49] The British eventually even paid them a monthly salary. In return, chiefs helped them to collect taxes and fines, while also disseminating British policy.

The legitimacy of chiefs came under attack in the early twentieth century from two sides: urban, mission-school educated citizens, and a poorer rural citizenry. The urban class established the Basutoland Progressive Association (BPA) in 1907, which spoke out against chiefs. They criticized an increase in the number of chiefs and alleged that chiefs were abusing their power in the issuing of fines, land allocation, the calling of *matsema* work parties, and more. In rural areas, a separate movement of Basotho, also critical of the chieftaincy, called the Lekhotla la Bafo ("Commoners League"), was led by Josiel Lefela. But whereas the BPA pushed for slow reform toward western-style democracy, the Commoners League was radically anticolonial, antimission, and protradition.[50] According to Lefela, the BPA elites had been poisoned by missionary education—they were out of touch with everyday people and the social order that accompanied precolonial political organization. Lefela was also critical, however, of the chieftaincy's capitulation to the colonial authorities, seeking a return to an uncorrupted chieftaincy.

After the soil erosion crisis of the 1920s and 1930s, Alan Pim's 1935 report on land condition (see chapter 2) formalized the concerns of the BPA into concrete recommendations for a reform of the chieftaincy. The number of chiefs had increased dramatically over the previous decades, as the second and third sons of chiefs began settling relatively uninhabited areas in the foothills and highlands—villages where they would become chief. This complicated British efforts to disseminate and enforce centralized rules regarding land use, not to mention to collect taxes. Pim famously stated that, "there are now as many chiefs in Basutoland as there are stars in the heavens."[51] His report recommended a "gazetting" program that would mark an inflection point in the establishment of British indirect rule in Basutoland. According to the program, a significantly reduced number of chiefs— from twenty-five hundred to around twelve hundred—was officially recognized in the government gazette. "Gazetted" chiefs would be constrained in some ways, but newly empowered in others. For example, they were curtailed in their ability to issue some court fines, but because court fines were critical to chiefs' income, the national treasury compensated for this loss by issuing them a monthly salary. Chiefs not gazetted by the administration could not issue fines, solicit *matsema* labor, impound livestock, nor hold courts for serious criminal matters.[52]

This was the status of chiefs at independence from Britain in 1966, when Basotho would make important decisions about how to build a postcolonial democracy: they were seen as emblematic of Basotho culture and they possessed real power, but many corners of society were frustrated with their abuses of authority. The legitimacy and power of *puso* was in question.

Institution 2: Councilors (Ntlafatso)

In advance of 1965 elections to form a postcolonial government, the British promoted a conservative party whose leader appeared most amenable to future cooperation with the British government.[53] The Basotho National Party (BNP) was led by Leabua Jonathan and narrowly won the elections over the Basutoland Congress Party (BCP), which had a more adversarial stance toward the British. The BCP won next election in 1970, but instead of ceding power, Jonathan declared a state of emergency, crafted a new constitution, and purged BCP supporters from government and civil service positions.[54] He would rule until being overthrown in a military coup in 1986.

Jonathan, who was a chief himself, was sympathetic to the chieftaincy, while his opposition was not. His supporters came to be known as the "National" movement, and the opposition was known as the "Congress" movement. The National movement was not only prochieftaincy and represented by the BNP, but also conservative and mostly Catholic. By contrast, the Congress movement was

TABLE 1 A Political Divide in Lesotho's Postcolonial National Politics

National Movement	Congress Movement
Prochieftaincy (*puso*)	Prostatutory government (*ntlafatso*)
Catholic	Protestant
Conservative	Liberal
Represented by the Basotho National Party (BNP)	Represented by Basotho Congress Party (BCP) and its off-shoots

sympathetic to the state government, represented by the BCP, liberal, and mostly Protestant. The National and Congress movements have become scrambled in today's electoral landscape,[55] but still have purchase for Basotho—especially older Basotho—many of whom self-identify as being on one side or the other of the debate.

Embodied in this differing posture toward the chieftaincy and the state government, these "National vs. Congress" party politics helped to install *puso* and *ntlafatso* as reference points for postindependence everyday life (see table 1). When Tefo asserts that Tankisi's livestock were impounded on *ntlafatso*-designated land, wresting it from chiefly control and rendering it a matter of state control, he was calling forward this partisan history.

It must be said that Jonathan supported the chieftaincy strategically, just as did the colonial government. For example, the village development committees (*likomiti tsa ntlafatso*) that he created as local political organizations for the BNP grew to take over certain responsibilities of chiefs, carrying forward his effort to entrench his power through "development," as described by James Ferguson.[56] Immediately after the coup in 1986 these committees were given fuller legal authority, eroding chiefs' power in land and other matters.

When a BCP government came to power in 1993 after seven years of military rule, it built on that architecture and advanced "decentralization" as one of its primary objectives—eroding chiefs' power further by transforming those village development committees into "local government councils" to handle the work of government that the BCP felt chiefs had failed at.[57] Shortly after the election, they began developing councils that were legally established through the Local Government Act of 1997 to work alongside chiefs. The authority and reach of these councils were then extended in 2005 during the first local council elections and again in 2014 with the National Decentralisation Policy,[58] which increased their funding and responsibilities. It is significant, for example, that the councilor could not attend the grazing association meeting about Tankisi's impoundment because he was away at a training. There are few such trainings for chiefs. The process of "decentralization" has not always taken account of chiefs' input, leading to disputes and the perception among them that their power was being "whittled away."[59]

Land has always been at the center of debates about the legitimacy of chiefs and the state government.[60] Common land tenure is regularly described by development projects as one of the primary obstacles to national development,[61] and responsibility for managing land was partially transferred to councilors in 2005. But chiefs have worked to maintain their power of land allocation and rangeland management.[62] This is why Tankisi called upon the "chief's order" to support his case against having his animals impounded. And, any initiative that looks like a threat to the commons will also be received with hostility by livestock owners (e.g., Motlokoa's confrontation with Ntloko), who then reaffirm chiefly control over land.[63] For example, the Lesotho government has for decades (since a USAID-inspired effort) hoped to institute a grazing fee for the use of rangelands, which could be used for rangeland improvement and possibly to lower stocking rates.[64] But the fee has proven a third rail of Lesotho politics. During military rule in 1992, advocates came closest, getting the legal language drawn up and establishing the support of some politicians.[65] Livestock owners have resisted these fees as an assault on the commons and found general sympathy from chiefs (most of whom are also livestock owners).[66] After the government was elected during democratic elections in 1993, the responsible minister dropped the issue.[67]

More than a devolution of authority from chiefs to councilors, then, decentralization has resulted in an interdigitation and confusion of authority. As I've shown above in these dizzying historical movements, many of the rules and concepts that concern pasture management today predate colonial rule but were formalized under the British through their efforts to configure the chieftaincy in their favor, affirming chiefs' power in land management. But chiefs were also undermined along the way after becoming perceived by some everyday Basotho as colonial sympathizers. Chiefs were then further undermined by the efforts of reformers from outside Lesotho and within who were frustrated by their enduring control over rangeland management. The result is that, today, chiefs are on the back foot. They are paid a small monthly stipend, but it is less than councilors receive. Chiefs are often depicted by government bureaucrats I spoke with as important community figures but sometimes unknowledgeable and uneducated, yet councilors are given regular trainings on new legislation or government programs—trainings that take place in hotels in the provincial capital, where participants are well fed.

Institution 3: Projects

Overlaid upon this institutional matrix—the chieftaincy and the state government's local councils—one finds a mosaic of political figures and institutions converging on rangelands with competing mandates, spatial reach, and social theory. Development and conservation organizations have come and gone, leveraging and manipulating these structures. From targeted workshops to multiyear initiatives like the Sponges Project, they endeavor to improve rangelands, whether by educating herders on rangeland management techniques, by proposing new institutions, or by proposing new *coalitions* of existing institutions.[68] Alongside them, civil servants at the Ministry of Agriculture have served as "technical advisors" to chiefs and councilors, being ostensibly trained in the technical skills of rangeland assessment. This, even as the ministry fragmented over the years to cultivate networks of elite patronage, including the Department of Livestock, the Department of Rangeland Resources Management, the Department of Soil Conservation, the Department of Environment, and others, all of which have had something to contribute to rangeland management.

The water-export economy has only intensified this proliferation and fragmentation of rangeland authority. Grazing associations, for example, had been instituted intermittently until, as Stephen Turner puts it, a "more focused rationale" for them emerged with construction of the LHWP, and they were instituted country-wide.[69] Their legitimacy has been in question, however, as was seen when Motlokoa confronted the chair of the association, Ntloko. They lack true legal authority, after all, instead managing pastures *on behalf of* chiefs.

Not only that, but grazing associations have proliferated in such a way that they come into conflict. Associations with distinct territories and responsibilities were created in the 1980s by USAID; in the late 1990s by the Maloti-Drakensberg Transfrontier Project; and in the 2000s by the Lesotho Highlands Water Project. One 2012 report by a sustainable land management project from the United Nations Development Programme proposed to "harmonize" these and other associations into a *new* set of user associations, arguing that, "Poor governance is the root cause of degradation of the range resource complex."[70]

Bureaucratic reforms come to the rescue of bureaucratic reforms.

Recall the impoundment scene once again briefly. The assistant chair of the grazing association, Tankisi, had his livestock impounded in an area managed by that association (on behalf of the chief and councilor). The association was initiated by a foreign conservation effort in the late 1990s, but it went into a dormant state until being resuscitated by a more recent conservation project seeking to protect Lesotho's water economy, the Sponges Project. Bureaucrats at the state government's conservation ministry advocated the Sponges Project's rotational grazing plan, inspired by Allan Savory's controversial theories of rangeland ecological change. To make that grazing plan work, the ministry and the Sponges Project sought to reclassify the pasture where Tankisi's animals were impounded, deeming it a state "development" (*ntlafatso*) area, outside of chiefly control and therefore subject to higher fines. It was a kind of ad hoc attempt at decentralization. Like the conservation bureaucrats, however, Tankisi also sought to creatively use and exploit differences and possibilities in these legal regimes.[71] He appealed to "governance" (*puso*), suggesting that the rangeland space was still under chiefly authority, and the impoundment was unlawful because it didn't result from a chief's order. With the councilor away at a training and just a few grazing association officials attending the meeting, the chief effectively sided with Tankisi, chiding him rather than fining him. Had the councilor been present, things may have gone

differently—they also sit on these associations.[72] The decision likely had consequences for how others would view the threat of impoundment and the authority
of the grazing association. As a high-ranking member of the grazing association,
Tankisi's actions threatened the institution from within, and possibly future institutions, too.

CONCLUSION

Seemingly far away from the action of the water project, meetings and initiatives
like the ones I described above are where the rubber meets the road for water production in Lesotho.[73] There, agencies try to reconcile the contradictions of water
production: that it requires minimal livestock impact on the land, while leaving
livestock production as one of just a few possible livelihoods for people living in
the upstream catchments. And they do so atop the ruins of so many earlier efforts.

Developed while he worked as a colonial conservation officer in Rhodesia, Allan
Savory's simple and compelling ecological story appealed to conservation workers
in the way it privileged *management* as a tool for improving rangeland condition.
It also solved a problem for them. Because the system envisioned *undergrazing*
rather than *overgrazing* as a problem, the presence of humans and their livestock
on the landscape was no longer an issue to be resolved.

Savory's approach acquired a significant following in Southern Africa in spite
of its many problems and its many detractors. His ideas form the basis for several rangeland management consultancies, such as the one hired by the Khubelu
Sponges Project. One long-standing conservation ministry bureaucrat told me
about how he invited Savory to visit the ministry in 1988 and remembered the
visit with fondness, even saving the letter that Savory wrote to him in response.
Savory gave a keynote at the annual meetings of the major wool and mohair growers association in South Africa in 2013, too. In the audience was none other than
the king of Lesotho, Letsie III, an avid sheep farmer himself. Their joint presence
was highlighted in *The Silo-Lisiu*,[74] the dual-language, English-Sesotho livestock
industry magazine sold in the checkout lines (where I found it) at most supermar-
kets in Lesotho.

The intensive form of management required by the Savory system conflicted
with generations of herding practice, however, and was unlikely to succeed in
the upland areas of concern for Lesotho's water production. The ministry officer
Tefo must have known its prospects were grim. Even Sepheo from the Sponges
Project must have known. No doubt, their offices' own spacetimes got in the way—
the spending deadlines and project milestones and reporting cycles critically
configured their work.[75] Like most projects, money needed to be spent during
specific periods, or the project might have been discontinued. Sepheo used some
of the early, exploratory phase funds for a consultancy, just as he was set to explore
the options for rangeland improvement in Lesotho. That costly international

consultant armed with Savory's program helped set their agenda, captivating them with an ecological theory. A path was charted and there was no turning back. Even if the plan later seemed unworkable, there was not room within the project time-line to change course. And anyway, it was the ecological theory that drew Sepheo and his colleagues in. It articulated so well with a social world in which livestock production was critical to rural people, even if that social world would need to be adjusted: herders would need to become more active, and the resting of pastures would need to be enforced through higher fines.

The call for new and improved institutions is loud in Lesotho, as in other postcolonies where land is managed by traditional authorities. The water econ-omy has only amplified them. With rangelands reconfigured as water-production infrastructures, social orders became unfit to the ecological order. Calls for reform partly stem from an influential Euro-American myth of the late twentieth and early twenty-first centuries that institutional reform projects like the ones described above are antidotes to African traditionalism gone wrong. That myth suggests that Lesotho's political institutions, charged with executing postcolonial democratic procedures, are but hollow figures of the real thing—corruption, the tragedy of the commons, and patrimonialism continually undermining efforts at reform.[76] The Sponges Project's attempt to circumvent chiefly authority in impos-ing their conservation program was emblematic of this. Not only were fines in *puso*-designated land too low, they felt, but chiefs too often neglected to enforce them. Yet, the decline of chiefly power in Lesotho is not a story of "modernization" or the withering of tradition. It is one of the endless fragmentation and manip-ulation of Basotho social orders by colonists, development experts, and local politicians—but also of a substantive national debate among Basotho with differ-ing opinions. Basotho society is heterogenous and conflicted, like any society. As Catherine Coquery-Vidrovitch asks: "How far back do we have to go to find the stability alleged to be 'characteristic' of the [African] pre-colonial period?"[77]

It is not a failure of traditional institutions that makes reforms necessary. Instead, it is the failed reforms, programs, and projects strewn across Lesotho's landscapes that—through their partial success—have ensured the need for subse-quent reforms. They also ensure the failure of those subsequent reforms.

Within and beyond these bureaucratic ecologies, herders and livestock owners make a living. I turn to their stories now.

5

Livestock Production

I've shown how conservation bureaucrats are working to slow the flow of water downslope in Lesotho's upland catchments through social reforms to the administration of grazing, but I haven't said much about the livestock themselves—the livestock production that is seen as a problem for water production. In this chapter and the next, I consider the kinds of livestock being raised, the uses to which they are put, and the effects they have on the landscape.

Recall how the 1935 Pim Report that I described in chapter 2 marked a watershed moment in the country's fight against soil erosion. The legacies of that report and its fluvial imagination are still present today as Lesotho works to protect its land for the sake of producing water commodities. The report provided the British colonial administration with an assessment of Basutoland's economic potential, determining that soil erosion was "the most immediately pressing of the many great problems which now confront the Administration."[1] Pim made three primary recommendations, which were implemented soon after the report was published. First, he suggested that soil conservation programs be rolled out across the country, efforts I described in chapter 3. Second, he suggested a reduction in the number of chiefs so as to streamline the administration of the colony, particularly with regard to land management, which I outlined in chapter 4. Finally, this chapter turns to the third recommendation: the construction of bridle paths to link highlands wool producers with lowland markets. That initiative, it turns out, was wildly successful—in ways that threaten water production today. With the decline of Basotho employment in South Africa, labor is no longer exploitable and exportable, encouraging the commodification not only of water by the government but of livestock by ordinary people.[2]

THE OVICAPRINE MYSTIQUE

An older man, perhaps in his sixties, appeared in the doorway of the village court, cutting a silhouette in the bright morning sunlight that poured into the room. As per custom, he leaned his herding stick (*molamu*) against the wall outside and removed his knit hat as he entered. The man greeted the handful of people in the room with a slight bow, a two-handed wave, and a quiet greeting, "Hello everyone" (*Lumelang*), before sitting next to me. Opening up a black plastic bag he was holding on his wrist, he carefully pulled out three small booklets and a folded piece of paper, which he proceeded to unfold and hand to the chief (*morena*). The chief and the secretary (*mongoli*) were seated at the front of the room behind an old, rickety table painted in the turquoise color so often used in Lesotho on doors, window frames, and furniture. It was early in my fieldwork in the rural Lesotho highlands, and I had come to the court to sort through the criticism and praise I had heard about chiefs in their management of grazing land. One of the primary sites where everyday people interact with these figures is the village court, called *lekhotla* in Sesotho—a place people visit to settle disputes, to obtain the chief's stamp and signatures for official documents, or to register their livestock. I arrived first thing in the morning to see it for myself.

When the man returned to his seat, I asked him why he had come to the *lekhotla*. He explained that he was selling two sheep. The small booklets that he carried were livestock registration books distributed by the Ministry of Home Affairs that keep an account of his livestock—their type, sex, and markings—with a stamp and signature from his chief. The paper he handed to the chief was a letter written by the man that requested the transfer of title to the buyer—a young, local man named Tumisang.

The room slowly filled with people, nearly all of whom did just as this man: they entered, handed a letter to the chief, and waited. For each case, the chief read the letter and wrote up a *bewys* (Sesotho: *babeisi*), an Afrikaans word for a title, or proof of ownership. The *bewys* listed the name of the seller and buyer and was carbon-copied in a government-issued receipt book. The secretary signed the *bewys*, updated the buyer's and seller's livestock registration books, and had them place their fingerprints on the carbon copy. There were so many people that the chief and the secretary did their work in batches, taking seven to ten receipts and then calling the parties up two by two to have them affix their fingerprints all at once. The sellers included young men and old men—but also several women. This was surprising, given that women are conventionally known to lack access to livestock property, according to the ethnographic record.[3] The buyers, however, were exclusively men, and mostly young men. I was intrigued. First, given what has been written about the reticence of Basotho to sell livestock, even during punishing droughts,[4] why were all these livestock being bought and sold? Second, how could these young men, almost none of whom had access to formal employment, be purchasing livestock?

I asked which type of animal people were selling, and invariably it was sheep and goats—mostly sheep. At the end of the day, I asked the secretary how many animals were sold. "Forty-seven," he said. I asked him about how many animals were sold each month, and he did some quick math—they go through about one hundred to two hundred receipts each month on average and each sale includes about one to five animals. He thought about it and told me that he estimates about two hundred to three hundred animals are sold every month—mostly sheep and goats—with perhaps four hundred to five hundred being sold during the months of December and January, when school fees must be paid and when the maize harvest is not yet in, as well as April and May, when the animals are fat and fetch a good price. I asked him how these young men could afford the livestock, and he explained that most would not keep the animals. Instead, they would take them in the next few weeks over the border to Qwa-Qwa, the former "Bantustan" for South African Basotho that formed part of apartheid's system of segregation until South African independence, where the livestock would be sold to butcheries. I asked if they were selling the old livestock (*maqheku*), which James Ferguson described as being saleable during his research in the 1980s. No, he said, the livestock being sold are younger animals that will be desirable to butchers.

This economic traffic seemed uncanny in this small, mountain village that was home to just a few thousand people. It's not only men from this village who are trekking these animals to Qwa-Qwa, he added, but from towns all over the northeast highlands. He and I agreed that there must be well over a thousand animals sold in Qwa-Qwa every month.

In the pages below I track down this mystery—why hundreds of livestock are being sold each month between rural villagers with little money in a place where livestock are supposedly not often sold. I draw a contrast between the sale of "small stock" (*likhutšoanyane*) like sheep and goats and the sale of cattle, and consider what they say about how rural people are navigating the water-export era.

A focus on the nature of commodification can illuminate this situation and its implications for the water-export economy, including the ways it shapes the flow of water across the landscape. Conservation workers, development experts, and anthropologists have long scrutinized cattle in Africa for their social function and resistance to commodification. Ironically, water has served the same function in the literature,[5] as described in chapter 1. I argue that sheep and goats are similarly significant—not because of the obstacles they pose to commodification but because of the *ease* with which they are commodified. The charisma of noncapitalist, cattle-mediated social relations in Africa have distracted these experts, blinding them to the livelihood and landscape implications of readily commodified sheep and goats. James Ferguson's concept, the "bovine mystique,"[6] described a set of cultural rules and political contexts that circumscribed the sale of cattle in ways that puzzled development and conservation workers. In dialogue with Ferguson's work, I describe what I call the "ovicaprine mystique," a set of conditions that have enabled a puzzlingly vigorous production and exchange of small stock. Whether partially commodified, as in the case of cattle, or fully commodified, as the case of sheep and goats, commodities are always textured by their dynamic cultural particularity. Even when commodification appears effortless, I argue, it is a contingent achievement, requiring both agency and specific political, environmental, and symbolic conditions.

In Lesotho, sheep and goats have been produced in huge numbers for the better part of a century—specifically, for their wool and mohair sold in global textile markets. Owing to the ingenuity and entrepreneurialism of many rural Basotho, sheep and goats have repeatedly been used as a means of making a living in the seams of an oppressive regional political economy.[7] Ovicaprid production in Lesotho first expanded in the late nineteenth century, when commoner Basotho sought to settle in the country's upper highlands and wrest themselves from the control of the chieftaincy.[8] Over time, as Lesotho was marginalized and transformed from an agricultural center to a labor reserve for South African industry, small stock production became both a retirement strategy for miners returning from South Africa and part of an economic dreamworld into which young men and women imagined themselves.[9] They introduced improved breeds into their herds, and Lesotho became a major producer of wool and mohair, today producing a fifth of the world's mohair—the second largest producer of mohair after South Africa.[10]

Their use is shifting with Lesotho's transformation from labor reserve to water reservoir, and conservation projects to protect water production bump into them around every corner. With the collapse of mining employment for Lesotho citizens in the late 1980s, the entrepreneurial dream in which ovicaprids figured as a source of retirement income dissolved. Instead, they occupy the vanguard of a new entrepreneurial dream—one that was first revealed to me during my visit to the *lekhotla*. Though farmers continue to produce wool and mohair, small stock have shifted from retirement strategy to full-fledged occupation, increasing the pace with which the animals are raised and sold. By integrating mutton breeds into their herds, rural Basotho are developing dual-purpose animals whose wool and mohair clip is sold annually, but can be sold at a moment's notice to South African butcheries. Small stock are newly enrolled as intimate figures in the economic dreamworlds of Basotho eager to find a future in Lesotho's water-export era. In the rubble of old arrangements, new opportunities are found. What has remained the same over time, however, has been the danger and precarity of Basotho's position vis-à-vis South Africa. Like the danger of life on the mines, transporting ovicaprids over the border is a risky proposition.

THE BOVINE MYSTIQUE

As understood by water engineers and conservation bureaucrats described earlier in this book, livestock are a threat to water production. The problem engineers seek to overcome is the specific position of livestock in Basotho society, namely as a noncommodity. In this, they share an interest with anthropologists. Like water, livestock have been central to anthropologists' theorization of the commodity form and its relationship to social structure. Since Melville Herskovits described the "cattle complex" in eastern and southern Africa,[11] anthropologists have drawn attention to cattle's imbrication in a variety of social institutions, including religion, politics, economy, and more,[12] depicted as a Maussian "total social fact,"[13] and a site for exploring how African societies respond to urbanization and cash economies.[14] This imbrication complicates their rendering as straightforward, capitalist commodities for market exchange,[15] making cattle a key site for understanding social and symbolic systems, particularly as relationships to cattle are reworked by shifting political economies.[16]

James Ferguson's work was crucial to this conversation.[17] Debunking the perception among conservation and development experts that cattle were an "obsession" of Basotho seeking social status—an obsession that experts said led to unsustainably large herds and land degradation—he showed instead that cattle ownership needed to be understood with reference to kinship and political economy. Development workers were right, Ferguson explained, that cattle were not treated like an ordinary commodity. They were only commodified according to cultural rules that produced a one-way barrier to sale, what he called the "mystique": cattle could be bought but not sold. As described elsewhere in Southern Africa, as well as in the Sudan, cash was seen as transitory, whereas cattle worked as a "dam" against the flow of cash.[18] Through bridewealth payments known as *lobola* and other livestock leasing arrangements (e.g., *mafisa*), cattle extended social ties through time and space. Moreover, these cattle-keeping practices were not holdovers from a timeless precolonial past. Instead, the rules that governed cattle exchange reflected the politics of the contemporary labor-migration economy. Examining when and why Basotho preferred to sell or keep their animals, Ferguson illustrated how the terms of ownership were contested across gender and generational lines: young men working at the mines saw little benefit from paying *lobola* when compared with older people for whom periodic bridewealth payments were a source of wealth into old age. Miners also sought to purchase cattle as a means of preventing their wives from accessing cash for household goods such as food or clothing. As cash, women were socially able to make claims on wealth—but not as livestock.

When a conservation-development project sought to establish a beef-production industry in the rural areas where many of Lesotho's livestock are located, Ferguson showed, the effort failed because it misunderstood cattle's position within society. Cattle resisted commodification through beef production, not because of an "irrational" obsession with social status as conservation and development experts said, but because of kinship relations and local power dynamics, which themselves were configured by the structural conditions of the regional political economy.

Anthropologists have been less interested in applying this same kind of scrutiny to what I think of as "clean-break commodities": goods that seem to disarticulate easily from social relations and the conditions of their production.[19] Contrast, for example, the attention given to African cattle with the sparse mention of African sheep and goats. Where small stock are discussed, they tend to figure straightforwardly as elements in a livelihood strategy or system of production,[20] rather than a rich cultural domain, as with cattle.[21] This risks forgetting a lesson from the substantivist-formalist debates of the 1970s and 1980s[22]—that economics is not a domain of rational actors but rather of cultural, historical actors. We should not assume that some commodities are more inflected by culture than others. The disenchanted commodity is never as it seems.

If the bovine mystique captures a mystery of *partial* commodification, the ovicaprine mystique captures the mystery of *full* commodification. The commodity is, after all, as Karl Marx said, "a very queer thing, abounding in metaphysical subtleties and theological niceties."[23] Sheep and goats embody the aspirations and anxieties of some rural people I describe in this chapter. Ovicaprids were crucial agents in the settling of the Lesotho highlands, as I show in this next section, and they help shed light on the conservation problems faced by the Lesotho Highlands Water Project today.

SHEEP, GOATS, AND THE SETTLING
OF THE LESOTHO HIGHLANDS

Phase 1: 1700–1900

Sheep and goats—but especially sheep—have been central figures in the settlement and colonization of southern Africa. This is true over the *longue durée* in that ovicaprids enabled the southward colonization of pastoralist people in Africa by "domesticating" the landscape in tsetse zones through the clearing of woody vegetation.[24] For example, fat-tailed sheep were present in indigenous Khoisan herds when the Portuguese and Dutch first came to Southern Africa in the fifteenth century.[25] But it is also true for the colonial period. William Beinart describes the dramatic increase of these animals in South Africa during the eighteenth and nineteenth centuries.[26] Sheep numbered about 1.5 million in the Cape in 1806—mostly the fat-tailed mutton breeds. Wool-producing merino sheep subsequently rose in importance, and their population shot up to 5 million by 1855 and 10 million by 1875 as the textile industry in Britain drove significant demand.[27] This trajectory mimicked Basutoland's, though merino sheep arrived there several decades later.

Until the 1870s, all livestock types in Basutoland were primarily kept in the low-land areas near villages, with very few kept at cattle posts in the colder, expansive highlands. The highlands up to that time were inhabited only by diffuse, highly mobile, and often culturally creolized communities (incorporating San hunger-gatherers), many of whom were involved in or suspected of raiding cattle from lowland communities.[28] Three factors changed that: land pressure in the lowlands, British colonialism, and class dynamics within Basotho society. Land pressure increased with substantial population growth, loss of lowland Basutoland terri-tory to Afrikaner farmers over the eastern border, and the South African Land Act of 1913, which pushed South African Basotho into Basutoland.

By the mid-nineteenth century, white "Voortrekkers" were increasingly settling in areas that are today known as the Free State Province and came into conflict with refugees who began to coalesce into a political group under Moshoeshoe. After severe droughts in the 1860s, those white farmers worked to seize more land at the western end of Basotho territory.[29] With land and population pres-sures brought about by white incursion, and because of an interest on the part of Basotho aristocrats in protecting their large herds from potential cattle raids by whites and other African groups, the first wave of semipermanent or permanent settling of the highlands for residence and pasture came in the 1870s. The colonial government at the time exercised little control over this process,[30] a point that worried colonial administrators, particularly with respect to their concerns about unregulated population growth and land degradation.[31] During this initial period, however, the settlers were mostly herders in the employ of an aristocratic class that sought to render itself less vulnerable to the effects of wars with white settlers and other African groups.

What were initially highland cattle posts would later morph into permanent villages. Around the turn of the twentieth century, and in the aftermath of a rin-derpest epidemic that killed over 95 percent of cattle herds in Southern Africa,[32] Basotho and the British colonial administration came to recognize that the high-lands were some of the best sheep-producing areas in the region, albeit for short summer seasons. The British began promoting wool and mohair production through the issuing of licenses to white traders for the establishment of moun-tain trading posts where wool and mohair could be legally exchanged,[33] and later through the construction of bridle paths to facilitate its transport to markets in South Africa. Judith Kimble reports that between 1893 and 1908, Basutoland wool exports grew by 380 percent in weight and 480 percent in value, increasingly from mountain areas.[34] Mohair exports also ballooned by nearly 3,000 percent in weight and value, though they started from much lower levels. In 1923, a wool export duty was introduced, indicating the importance of that growing industry to colonial profits,[35] and the Prevention of Scab Act was passed to make dipping compulsory throughout the country.[36] The transition to wool production not only led to range-land degradation, which I discuss in the following chapter. It also led to nutritional deficiencies among families in the highlands who substituted dairy cows for sheep, contributing to a serious outbreak of pellagra, the skin condition caused by a lack of vitamin B3.[37]

The highlands became much more important to wool export production than the lowland areas ever were.[38] The elevated importance of the cattle post areas prompted the Basotho aristocracy to assert its control over those lands around that time.[39] But chiefs struggled to control highland settlement, as commoner livestock owners established highland cattle posts that helped them circumvent chiefly authority over grazing land. Struggles between those two groups were evident from the early twentieth century onward, as I described in chapter 4.[40] Cattle remained at that time tightly tied to the "tributary mode of production,"[41] a system in which subjects are promised security and prosperity in return for tribute payments of cattle and labor to the chief, the standard-bearer of a tributary class.[42] Small stock, however, were not under such tight control. Because they could remain for much of the year in the higher, colder reaches of the mountains, they did not conflict with chief-controlled cattle pastures in the lowlands or the lower-lying areas of the highlands.

Phase 2: 1900–85

Commoner Basotho exploited that opportunity, and numbers of small stock in Lesotho surged from 1.5 million in 1900 to 3 million in 1930.[43] Serious anxiety emerged at that time surrounding the ecological effects of sheep in both Lesotho and South Africa, including claims that they were leading to shifts in vegetation, soil erosion, and compaction, and even that they were encouraging generalized desiccation—a decrease in rainfall and in the capacity of soils to retain moisture.[44] After dramatic droughts in the early 1930s, when all livestock types plummeted, herds recovered over the next decade, and highland cattle posts rose "exponentially" between the 1930s and 1980s, though total herd size has not returned to 1930 levels again.[45]

Over time, as sheep and goat production became central to rural livelihoods, Basotho have become skillful fiber producers. However, Basotho had not always been interested in wool- and mohair-producing varieties. Back in the 1830s, when the missionary Thomas Arbousset accompanied King Moshoeshoe I to his cattle post in the highlands, Arbousset described indigenous fat-tailed breeds being given preference over European wool breeds, the former of which he saw taken into a covered kraal during inclement weather and fed hand-picked forage.[46] But by the 1940s, the anthropologist Hugh Ashton reported that Basotho were more interested in improved sheep and goat varieties than improved cattle. This he ascribed to the heightened social role played by cattle, in contrast to sheep and goats, from which a "considerable cash income is derived from the export of wool and mohair."[47] By the time Ashton was writing in the 1960s, the poor-quality fleeces of earlier times had been "almost completely submerged through the introduction of merino sheep and angora goats."[48] Contrast Arbousset's account with one from my own research in 2014, when I came upon two herders while hiking through the upland cattle post areas one day. One of them was seated on the ground with a sheep reclining comfortably between his splayed legs. The sheep was an adolescent and it seemed perfectly at ease, so much so that at first, I thought it might be ill. The herder was picking burs called *bohome* (*Xanthium spinosum*) from the sheep's wool.[49] It was such a tender scene, speaking to the intimacy of herders and their animals, the duties of a herder to maintain the quality of a sheep's wool by keeping it well fed and free of burs, and the value of wool.[50]

The upswing in small-stock production and the transition from fat-tailed mutton to merino wool and angora mohair varieties was a response to the punishing poverty of Lesotho's labor-reserve era. As I noted earlier in this book, Basutoland in the late nineteenth century was dubbed "the granary of the Free State,"[51] for its prodigious agricultural production, but it would be slowly drawn into becoming a labor reserve for the mining industry through colonial and South African policies. At any given moment since the early twentieth century, tens of thousands of Basotho miners worked in South Africa, returning to Lesotho after retirement or injury.[52] Because of apartheid-era laws prohibiting miners' families from immigrating to South Africa, and partly because of Basotho desires to remain in their own country, mining labor was in some sense an entrepreneurial activity: a means of acquiring money to invest in a future by varied means, including through bridewealth payments, education for children, a sturdy home, a taxi or clothing business—and a herd of animals. The herd would pay out over time, with cattle producing milk and plow-strength, and sheep and goats producing wool and mohair for slaughter and cash. It is likely that the commodification of small stock acted as a buffer to the monetization of cattle during the labor-reserve era, injecting much-needed cash into rural households where the social ties that prevented cattle sale continued to matter a great deal. That is, the hypercommodification of small stock I call "the ovicaprine mystique" made the bovine mystique possible.

Phase 3: 1985–Present

Beginning in the mid- to late 1980s, as opportunities for Basotho in the mines dwindled, this economic dreamworld was no longer tenable. As in former Bantustans, the monetization of rural economies, the HIV/AIDS pandemic, and enduring poverty have ramified in people's relationships to gender, kinship, livestock, and political authority in Lesotho, in many ways sharpening class and gender identities.[53] In the post–labor reserve era, raising sheep and goats has gone from a retirement activity to an occupation. In one of the rare successes of foreign and domestic development work, wool and mohair growers associations were created across the country that organized production, further improved animal breeds for wool and mohair quality, and cut out middlemen to secure favorable prices for farmers' clip. In 2001, they were federated as the Lesotho National Wool and

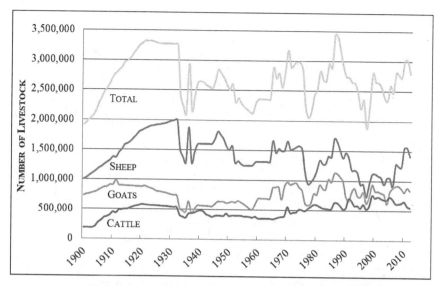

FIGURE 14. Livestock statistics, 1900–2013. Source: Lesotho Bureau of Statistics and Swallow and Brokken (1987).

Mohair Growers Association. Revenues from wool production in 2014–15 were M195 million (USD 19.5 million), while mohair generated an additional M57 million (USD 5.7 million),[54] a form of foreign revenue that primarily accrues to ordinary people in contrast to water export, which must "trickle down" through government programs like *fato-fato* (see chapter 3).[55]

Livestock registration statistics for the village I described at the outset of this chapter certainly reflect an emphasis on small stock. Sheep and goats together accounted for 80–90 percent of the total herd every year between 2001, when records were first kept for the area, and 2014. Sheep alone accounted for 60–70 percent of the total herd, with goats accounting for another 20–25 percent. Tregurtha states that the average herd size in the mountains is fifty,[56] but that 50 percent of owners own less than forty head of small stock, meaning that most of the production is by smallholders. I was regularly told that today there are more *barui*, livestock owners with large herds, than in earlier generations. Then, however, *barui* might own eight hundred or many more head of livestock, whereas today a large herd is typically closer to three hundred (see fig. 14).

Mokhotlong District, where my research was sited and where the Polihali Dam is sited, produces the most wool of any of the ten districts in Lesotho, with over 19 percent of the total clip (roughly 680,000kg of a total 3,600,00kg) from 18 percent of the total herd.[57] The district produced over 86,000kg of mohair or 21 percent of the total clip and the most goats. In the village where I conducted interviews, the chief's livestock registry showed that between 80–90 percent of the livestock were sheep or goats, with cattle, donkeys, and horses making up the remainder. The

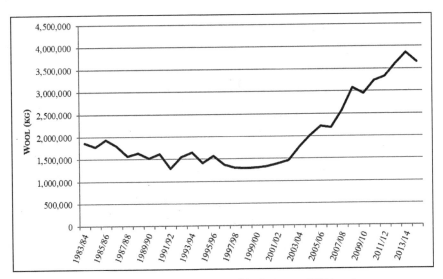

FIGURE 15. Wool (kg) sold through Lesotho's woolsheds. Source: BKB (2015).

amount and the quality of wool has consistently increased over the past decade, thanks partly to the Wool and Mohair Growers Association, a network that now includes 37,500 farmers in ninety-eight local cooperatives across Lesotho and registered in 2001.[58] Each cooperative has its own woolshed where sheep and goats are shorn, and all sell their clip to BKB,[59] a major wool and mohair processing company in Port Elizabeth that sells fiber by auction to global textile manufacturers.[60] After selling the wool to the woolshed, farmers wait as much as one year before receiving their check (see fig. 15).

However, as I began to see at the village court described at the opening of this chapter, rural Basotho are seeking new forms of entrepreneurial diversification. While wool and mohair continue to be produced, a new market has been found for mutton, allowing for the quick sale of small stock to young men who traffic them illicitly over the border to South Africa. After my visit to the village court, I asked the secretary whether this was a recent phenomenon. He told me that for a long time—fifty years or more—people from Mokhotlong had been taking wool to Qwa-Qwa for sale, but not the animals themselves. In fact, in the 1950s, there was a woolshed at Letšeng on the high plateau, along the road from Mokhotlong to the lowlands, sited specifically so that animals could be shorn near their cattle posts and their wool taken immediately to Qwa-Qwa by horse or donkey—on the same paths used today.

"When did the sale in sheep and goats increase?" I asked.

"It began in the late 1980s," the secretary explained, "because of 'the changes' [liphethoho]." He said that at that time mineworkers were losing their jobs and they began to think about how else they could feed their families. "They asked themselves, 'What am I going to do?'" So, they started to sell animals at butcheries in Qwa-Qwa, where the animals fetched a high price.

Lesotho's structural position vis-à-vis South Africa has shaped the ways that rural Basotho relate to livestock, including both cattle that resist commodification and ovicaprids that do not. Small stock are objects both of long-standing interest (see fig. 14) and of recent innovation in Lesotho, becoming different kinds of commodities at different historical moments. In the following section, I give a fuller account of the ovicaprine mystique and its relationship to the bovine mystique from the perspective of livestock owners.

"SHEEP ARE OUR MINES!"

In a footnote, Ferguson suggested that all grazing domestic animals were probably governed by similar rules of exchange as cattle, although he conceded that more research on the point was needed.[61] As a result, he used the term *livestock* to refer to all grazing stock types. But including sheep and goats in this category of "livestock" obscures important differences. This is especially so because these differences may have amplified since Ferguson's writing.[62] For example, sheep and goats can be sold much more easily than cattle, making them desirable, as I was consistently told.[63] Herders who work for one year tending someone else's livestock are typically paid either twelve small stock or one cow. I would often ask herders whether they preferred to be paid in sheep and goats or in cattle. Without exception, I was told sheep and goats. When asked why, they responded like one young man named Likhang: "Sheep? They're money" (*Linku? Ke chelete*), he said, swiping his fingers over an open palm in the vernacular sign for money. Cattle are major investments. If you have an emergency, you can sell a sheep or goat—but you cannot sell part of a cow. So, in contrast to cattle, with their "barriers to sale,"[64] small stock are always ready for sale. They're not sold carelessly, of course, but are saleable whenever one needs the cash for food, medicines for their animals, school uniforms for their children, or other household items. This held generally, whether I was speaking with owners of small or large herds, and whether the owners were young or old.[65] As one elderly man put it with an apt regional metaphor, "Sheep are our mines!" (*Nku ke maene ea rona!*).

Ferguson described how he presented men with a hypothetical situation: If someone offered them one ox or the cash equivalent, which would they choose? The men always chose cash, which could be converted into cattle, whereas the reverse was not true. If they owned a cow, they would never sell it, even under dire circumstances, because of its potential future value. When I presented men with the same scenario for sheep and goats during research in 2014 and 2016, men largely opted for sheep over cash. I posed the question to a middle-aged man whom I picked up on the high plateau while driving to Mokhotlong. He was not particularly interested in livestock and owned just a few sheep and a few cows.

He didn't want his children to be *barui* (wealthy in livestock) either, because he'd rather they go to school than become herders. But when I asked him whether hypothetically he'd choose a sheep or R750 in cash (the price he quoted me for one sheep), he opted for the sheep because "small stock are a business—you make money off of them."[66] I then asked him the same question about whether he would choose a cow or R4,000 (the going rate). He reported that he would take the money rather than the cow, but not because he could use the money to buy a cow, as told to Ferguson, but because he wanted an animal that he could sell easily. "A cow is difficult to sell—and it takes a long time to grow." During that time, he said, it might die. Sheep and goats, on the other hand, sell easily and multiply rapidly. Their easy commodification made them desirable.

When I asked which animals women preferred, they, like the men, told me that the cattle are important for plowing, but that the small stock are important because of their easy commodification and their rapid multiplication. When I asked men about whether *they* or their wives made decisions about when to sell sheep, most told me it was them—not their wives. But some men explained that they would sell when they understood that their wives needed things around the house.

Women I spoke with mostly suggested that they chose to sell sheep and goats in concert with their husbands, although some said that they were more firmly in control. "No! *I tell him* [when we need to sell]!" one woman said. To be sure, sheep, goats, and larger stock are primarily the domain of men in rural Lesotho. Many livestock, particularly the small stock, are kept at distant cattle posts over which women have no direct control. But none of the people I spoke with described a situation for sheep and goats quite like that outlined by Ferguson for cattle— that is, as a special domain of property and a dam against the flow of cash. And because small stock are so easily sold, women are certainly able to make more claims upon them. In my visits to the *lekhotla*, I saw numerous women selling small stock themselves. I was told by men and women, in fact, that it had long been the case that men working in South Africa would sometimes instruct the chief of their village to allow their wife to sell sheep as she saw fit. I could not discern how this may have changed with the decline of mining employment, but it seems clear that women have long had greater access to ovicaprids than cattle.

Perhaps more striking to me than the fact that people liked the flexibility of small stock was how confident they were that a market for sheep and goats existed. After all, just as conservation workers told Ferguson, they told me that a big problem facing livestock owners was poor market access. As indicated above, conservation and development workers described by Ferguson sought to resolve Lesotho's land-degradation problems through the development of a beef-production industry. They believed that rangeland degradation—seen as pervasive and potentially catastrophic—could only be resolved by extricating cattle from the shackles of cultural tradition and placing them under the control of the "invisible hand" of the market.[67] It was by similar logic that the British colonial resident commissioner Godfrey Lagden in 1898 suggested that more Basotho men must work in the mines or face the threat of overstocking.[68] These notions endures today. A World Bank report on Lesotho from 2010, for example, advocated "livestock development projects involving pricing policies, trek route construction, new slaughter facilities, [and the] purchasing of livestock in the field [for] reduced numbers of livestock on the range and reduced grazing pressure."[69] It explained that Lesotho should enter into "international trade agreements such as the Lome IV Convention ('Beef Protocol Agreement') which allows for sales of beef to the European Union at above world market levels."[70] In my conversations with government and conservation officials in Lesotho, too, the issue of Basotho valuing cattle for their conferral of social status came up on numerous occasions when I asked them if and why they thought rangelands were degraded. Conservation bureaucrats believed that livestock owners cared more about the size of their herd than they did about the quality of the animals.[71]

All this emphasis on markets, yet livestock owners were insistent to me that they could sell ovicaprids anytime they wanted.[72]

I saw conservation bureaucrats struggle with this issue—their insistence on improving market access when markets exist—at a meeting for the Khubelu Sponges Project in Mokhotlong. The meeting gathered together "project stakeholders" for updates on progress and challenges. Ministry representatives were there, as well as chiefs, councilors, and others. The first thing discussed was an issue raised by a Ministry of Commerce representative regarding the cross-border sale of animals.[73] The ministry wanted animals to be sold *inside* the country,[74] he explained, so it staged auctions across the district—but livestock owners did not show up.[75] They were "afraid," he said, to bring their animals because they feared the bidding could yield a low price, preferring instead to take their animals over the border to Underberg, Qwa-Qwa, or even as far as Vanderbijlpark near Johannesburg.

Another ministry representative chimed in to sympathize with the livestock owners. A sheep in Mokhotlong might fetch R600, but at Vanderbijlpark, the animal would sell for as much as R2,000, she said—obviously, people are going to take their animals where they can get the best price. Everyone nodded in agreement. Even the term for auction—*fantisi*—would dissuade sellers, another person pointed out. It derives from a former trading post named Fantasy, but in common parlance it is used to refer to selling something very cheaply. *Ke fantisa nku ea ka* would translate to, "I'm selling my sheep for cheap."

Sepheo, the director of the Sponges Project became frustrated and referred everyone to the law. He said that it was important to focus on the fact that this is an "illegal act" (*tlholo ea molao*) to take animals across the border without the proper permits. They could not simply accept that this was the way it was.

. . .

The fact that ovicaprids can be sold easily does not mean that small-stock entrepreneurialism is as desirable as, say, a living wage. Few herders would pass up a job at the mines. But whereas they used to tend their father's livestock as boys, head to the mines as young men, and return to Lesotho in retirement to live off of the herd they acquired through mining wages, mining work is scarce and herding has become a full-time occupation. The mining economy was one fraught with risk and violence—from thieves in South Africa's cities to police harassment to the occupational hazards of working underground. The livestock economy presents a new set of dangers, as I describe in the next section.

JOURNEYS TO QWA-QWA

Thapelo and his friend Khutliso were heading to a horse race that Thapelo's uncle would be participating in, and they invited me along. On our way there, Thapelo told me that he planned to head to Qwa-Qwa the following morning, taking twelve sheep with him. What Thapelo referred to as "Qwa-Qwa" technically does not exist. That is the name of the apartheid Bantustan created on Lesotho's northern border, an impoverished "ethnic homeland" that was designated for South African Basotho who were not in possession of a permit to work in that country's segregated white cities and towns. Qwa-Qwa was dissolved as a legal entity with the end of apartheid, but it remains a poor and densely populated area featuring a large town, Phuthaditjhaba. With a population of fifty-five thousand people, Phuthaditjhaba is, like other former Bantustan capitals, a conspicuous urban center in the middle of an otherwise rural landscape. Most of the land surrounding it, however, belongs not to smallholders but to large agricultural companies or individuals. Few of those enterprises raise meat for the town's butcheries, meaning a market opportunity exists for people like Thapelo. He can sell his small stock there for around twice the going rate in Lesotho. (Sheep are mostly desired in Qwa-Qwa, but further to the east, where amaZulu people predominate, I was told that goat meat is preferred.)

Like those purchasing livestock at the *lekhotla* I described at the beginning of this chapter, many young men in the Mokhotlong area make a living in this way, buying animals with whatever money they have or can borrow and selling them in Qwa-Qwa. But it is no easy task. The trip there is arduous and dangerous. After paying a truck to drop him and his animals off on the high plateau along the road between Mokhotlong and Butha-Buthe, Thapelo will set out at a quick pace north. From noon, when he begins the hike, he will drive the animals through the day and through the night, arriving before dawn at the edge of the escarpment that marks the border with South Africa. From there, he will descend about four thousand feet into Phuthaditjhaba, whose nighttime lights illuminate the trail. There is a border gate along the footpath and 4x4 road at the base of the mountains, which Thapelo will need to avoid; as for most other herders, neither Thapelo nor his animals have the proper documents to enter South Africa, which are difficult and expensive to acquire. Over the course of the next few days, he will stay with friends and bring his animals to one of the main kraals in the town, where buyers from local butcheries come. When all or most of his sheep have been sold, he will return home by the same path, cash in hand.

Thapelo explained this all with an air of satisfaction—a kind of masculine pride. With a wife and a young baby, he was eager to reinvest his profits in more sheep that he can sell in Qwa-Qwa. Thapelo had sought work in South Africa without success and was disinclined to continue working at the cattle post as he had for several years prior, given how little herders are paid.

I asked Khutliso if he drove animals to Qwa-Qwa, too. I half-suspected not. Whereas Thapelo was stocky and confident, Khutliso had a small frame and disarmingly kind eyes. He used to do it, he told me, flashing a nervous smile and bowing his head down. But he doesn't anymore. He explained on my prodding that, after having made the trip a few times, he had a bad experience. Three years ago, he and his childhood friend Relebohile were held up at gunpoint and robbed of their entire flock—about thirty animals. Two armed men stopped them at daybreak, just as they reached the escarpment. Worried that he and Relebohile would head to the police after having seen their faces, the two men took Khutliso and Relebohile to a cove, beat them up, and tied them together. After several hours, during which time Khutliso assumed they were trying to make a plan, the men decided to shoot them. With Khutliso watching, the men put the gun to Relebohile's head and pulled the trigger—the gun jammed. They stabbed Khutliso in the stomach, immobilizing him, and then stabbed his friend repeatedly. Khutliso pulled up his shirt and showed me a one-inch scar on the side of his abdomen. While the men prepared a fire that Khutliso believed would be used to burn the bodies, Khutliso managed to free himself of the rope around his hands and feet. He ran away, hobbling with his stomach wound as fast as he could back to the road through the day and into the night. There, he managed to catch a lift with a passing car back to the clinic at Mapholaneng. He will never take animals to Qwa-Qwa again, he told me.

Shocked by the sadness and violence of the story, I asked Thapelo if he wasn't scared about his impending trip. He replied, "It's just that the money bites, it bites" (*Feela he chelete ea loma, ea loma*).

LEKALAPENSE: WEIGHING WOOL AND MUTTON IN THE WATER RESERVOIR

Fiber production has been heavily emphasized in Lesotho over the second half of the twentieth century—not only by British colonists, but by rural Basotho and the Lesotho National Wool and Mohair Growers Association—yielding a national flock of fiber-producing ovicaprids. Consider the use of the term *lekalapense* in Sesotho. The term is a Sesotho-fied version of the Afrikaans word, *kaalpens*, which means bare (*kaal*) stomach (*pens*), or "no wool on the stomach." The term refers to the Dohne Merino sheep, a breed of merino from Germany with a wide, short tail, produced for its meat instead of its wool. However, the term is used in a derogatory way to refer to any sheep with poor wool quality by wool farmers and employees at the woolsheds, where sheep and goats are shorn. At Growers Association woolsheds, it was explained to me that a *lekalapense* would be expelled because it threatened to diminish the quality of the clip as a whole. A *lekalapense*, I was told by several livestock owners, is "a bad breed among a good breed." In fact, the word has been recontextualized to apply to people, connoting a polluted, outsider status. In such cases, it is extremely derogatory, and one man even told me that "someone would kill you if you called them *lekalapense*."

One evening, as I walked along a road after finishing some interviews with livestock owners, I bumped into a friend of mine—a young and energetic man named Lesuhla. He flagged me down as I walked along the road past his village, eager to show me his new ram. He had told me about it once before, so I was interested to see what he was so excited about. He said that it was a "German" type, meaning that it is fat, but produces only mediocre wool. A young herder who saw us looking at the animal walked over to get a look. He was clearly impressed, and pulled out a cell phone to snap a photo. Lesuhla was excited about the ram because it embodied a grand plan, which he then described to me in impressive detail.

Lesuhla had thirty-four sheep at the time, he explained, five of which he would take to Qwa-Qwa in the coming week. He planned to mate his ram with the remaining sheep, all of which were wool sheep that produce "medium-fine" grade wool.[76] The offspring would be sheep that produce a lot of wool but which would also get fat and fetch a good price at the butcheries. Standing up and gesturing to the agricultural fields outside his home, he said he planned to plant oats (*habore*) as fodder for his sheep. Then he swept his hand over to some more agricultural fields in the distance up the hillside from us. There, he would plant two specific varieties of maize that he would mill for the animals. He would bring back a select group of sheep from the cattle post and fatten them up with the maize before taking them to Qwa-Qwa. In addition, he planned to breed his ram with other people's stock, the privilege for which they would pay him. He joked that he already had a list of people eager to breed with his *lekalapense* (see fig. 16).

He would repeat that cycle and each time reinvest the money to multiply his herd. In the longer term, he hoped to build a brick house and, later, to open up a clothing store in a nearby town.

Lesuhla talked about these plans with excitement. They were so close at hand that it was clear he thought about them regularly. This is only the tip of the iceberg, he explained. He wanted to increase his production by quite a lot. I asked him if he wasn't scared of the thieves that I had heard about. He nodded his head deeply. One time, his entire herd was stolen by three men armed with guns. He and a friend were making the trip with a herd of ninety sheep when they were

FIGURE 16. A *lekalapense*. Photo by author.

stopped. But he seemed pleased that I had asked. He had already agreed with four other men and women to form a kind of cooperative. They would pay annual dues to be members, and these dues would go toward paying the men who herd the animals to Qwa-Qwa, as well as toward purchasing medicines and fodder for their animals. Members would be obliged to direct part of their profits toward purchasing more animals, and every time animals were taken to Qwa-Qwa the herd would be comprised of a number of each of their animals. This way, if the animals were lost to theft, the effects on each individual would be minimized.

Lesuhla and his collaborators were refining an approach to the contingent economy of mutton and wool. The *lekalapense* was just the latest development in a long-standing relationship between Basotho and small stock. Selling these animals in Qwa-Qwa, he and others like him make life possible in post-labor-reserve Lesotho, subtending the water economy through an ovicaprine arbitrage that plays upon differences in market prices for marginal gains.[77] By developing a hybrid line of sheep that produce wool but that are also desirable to butcheries, they both interrupt and extend the government's efforts to capitalize on Lesotho's highland pastures through wool and mohair production. This is not an unambiguously positive development, however. In hedging against the risk and violence of this illicit trade, his venture shows that new livestock entrepreneurship could be as dangerous as life on the mines.

CONCLUSION

Moving further upstream from the sedimentation problems in Lesotho's dam reservoirs, we see how the livelihoods and dreams of rural people come to matter to the LHWP's conservation of catchment landscapes.

Herders and livestock owners are forced to negotiate the spacetimes created by the bureaucratic ecologies of conservation workers that I described in the previous chapter, even as they work to circumvent them. Ovicaprid commodification by rural livestock owners shows how they do so. Conservationists' and anthropologists' emphasis on cattle as recalcitrant commodities has obscured the importance of ovicaprids to culture, economy, and ecology. Small stock have grossly outnumbered cattle for decades in Lesotho, partly prompting the settlement of the highlands and enabling rural Basotho to navigate life in eras of labor export and of water export. Repeatedly, conservation programs proposed cattle commodification to reduce land degradation through the guidance of the market's invisible hand. Yet, ovicaprid numbers have been high precisely because they were skillfully commodified. Whereas conservation bureaucrats believe that market-based livestock production could alleviate overstocking and land degradation, Basotho eagerness to produce ovicaprids for global markets is itself a cause of degradation, as I explain in chapter 6—a product of commodified small stock, not uncommodified cattle.

Like the bovine mystique—the cultural particularity of cattle that determines how they can be bought and sold—the ovicaprine mystique has also been misunderstood. The fluid nature of the exchange relations rural Basotho have with ovicaprids expresses the historicity of these livestock, and it is a reminder that commodity status is not binary but dynamic. Charismatic, recalcitrant commodities do not show us the ultimate limits of commodification but rather expose that unique set of conditions necessary to any act of commodification.

Ovicaprids became clean-break commodities because they grow quickly and in marginal areas; because of a historical process through which bridle paths, woolsheds, and breeding practices were established for their production; and because of shifting political-economic conditions that have made demands of entrepreneurial diversification on Basotho to survive and thrive. In the process of commodification, Basotho projected themselves into that context as agents, expressing particular kinds of economic fantasy. Their dreams arose in response to the slow violence of decades of political-economic marginalization against which sheep and goats had been a lifeline. Small stock in Lesotho became different kinds of clean-break commodities during different historical moments. Once a means to circumvent chiefs in the early colonial period, they morphed into a slow retirement commodity, ameliorating the punishing conditions of the labor-reserve era and allowing young Basotho to envision themselves as (masculine) entrepreneurs in a dreamworld of accumulation verging on the "self-devouring growth" of beef export industries in Botswana.[78] In the water-reservoir era, ovicaprids have transformed again into a primary occupation, even a get-rich-quick dream.

In each case, Basotho worked within the rubble of old arrangements, creatively reorganizing existing practices to make a living in the seams of empire. But the smuggling of small stock to butcheries in the former South African Bantustan of Qwa-Qwa is dangerous, illustrating the violence and risk that continue to characterize Basotho relationships with South Africa. Whereas Lesotho was once forced into acting as a reproductive community for mines in South Africa, producing young men for the market, today Basotho produce fiber for the global textiles industry and meat for the South African proletariat.

6

Negative Ecology

Let us follow the gaze of water engineers and conservation bureaucrats further into the upstream catchment. In the course of producing water for export, it is not enough to merely trap water behind dam walls and redirect it through a network of tunnels and canals. Engineers must contend with the landscapes from which this water issues. The foregoing chapters have shown how, in response to piles of sediment accumulating in dam reservoirs that threaten the water economy, engineers and conservation bureaucrats moved to build physical conservation works that might slow the passage of water downslope. Hoping to get "to the source" of the problem, they moved further upstream, reworking social forms. They reintroduced grazing associations to change how livestock are managed, and they encouraged rural Basotho to commodify their livestock as a way of bringing herd size into line with the market's "invisible hand." They narrowed in on the practices of herders and the preferences of livestock in the cattle post areas of the high mountains. They sought to establish a fluvial imaginary that might help rural people interpret patterns in the landscape in relation to water's flow. They envisioned land degradation—and therefore soil erosion—as being encoded in the presence of dwarf shrubs, but that code was being deciphered in a variety of other ways. Shrubs were seen by some as an effect of climate changes rather than grazing; by others, as a *cause* of poor water flow rather than mere symbols of it; still others saw them as soil-stabilizing agents that *prevent* erosion.

Reading and interpreting the landscape is crucial in the water-export era, clearly. Recall one specific example of landscape exegesis from chapter 4. The Sponges Project, the conservation initiative seeking to protect Lesotho's alpine wetlands for water production, bucked a long-standing trend by suggesting that pastures might not be overgrazed but rather *undergrazed*. To prevent undergrazing, however, herders would need to herd "actively," encircling livestock to encourage them to eat all of the vegetation—not simply the ones they preferred. According to this fluvial imaginary, the selective grazing of livestock that were too dispersed in the pasture expressed itself in the encroachment of shrubs, the decline of rangeland condition, pressure on the alpine wetlands, and ultimately the aggressive flow of water over land that caused soil erosion. But promoting active herding was a challenge, we learned, because they felt herders were too lazy. After all, at the cattle post, one does not herd (*Motebong ha ho lisoe*).

I present an alternative interpretation of landscape patterns in the pages below, one informed by herder perspectives, by an ecological sensibility for the ways a plant community responds to grazing, as well as by a historical sensibility for the structural forces that configure herder interactions with the landscape. I show that the degradation that concerns conservation bureaucrats largely owes to the presence of sheep—the impact of their grazing, the timing of their arrival in the highlands, and the pasture fires that are set for their benefit. Yet, diagnosing this problem as "overgrazing" or "mismanagement" occludes some of the most important factors. These include the labor- and water-export economies, with the opportunities and limitations they have presented to rural people; the changes in the rains in recent decades; and the construction of roads and bridle paths (initially for wool production) that facilitated channelized water flow and the proliferation of encroaching and invasive plants. To the extent that degradation stems from human practices, it should be seen as a function of marginalization at multiple scales: of Lesotho within South Africa, of the highlands within Lesotho, but also and especially of herders within Lesotho society.

Herders are positioned at the center of Basotho cultural imaginaries, yet at the periphery of its social and economic systems. Livestock owners have managed to increase production over the past century in spite of declining rangeland condition by improving their sheep and goat breeds and by importing or planting fodder, as referenced in the previous chapter. But they have also benefited from the labor and expertise of herders who engineer forage in landscapes colonized by shrubs and plagued by drought. Not waiting for conservation projects to improve their fortunes, herders have taken matters into their own hands: they burn the range, drawing young, nitrogen-rich grasses out of the soil; and they introduce molasses and salt to compel their stock to eat unpalatable plants. Burning risks serious soil erosion, but one is not herded at the cattle post. The sense of freedom herders experience there makes the difficult work of herding worthwhile, but it also means that efforts to change their behavior will falter. The molasses, called *nyopo-nyopo*, in fact addresses the problem identified as herder laziness in the push for "active herding," as we will see. Like *fato-fato* and sheep commodification, these medicinal and pasture management practices sustain water export by deferring the unraveling of Lesotho's precarious social contract. Life in the highlands is on shakier ground than ever, even as these mountains serve as a staging ground for the production of lucrative water commodities.

Marginality isn't just a characteristic of these systems; it is an organizing principle of them—the marginality of Lesotho in a system of water production, and the marginality of herders in a system of livestock production.[1] Generating water commodities for South Africa depends on and depletes Lesotho's ecosystems, yet these spaces are invisible to water users in Johannesburg. Invisible, that is, until the problem of soil erosion brings them into center view. The production of livestock for Basotho livelihoods depends on herder labor and hardship, yet they are displaced from the center of social life—at least until soil erosion brings them into center view.

Looking upon these rangelands brought into view by erosion is like looking at a photographic negative, where the trick of producing the photograph becomes clear. An inversion of shades and colors makes reproduction of the image possible. The Lesotho highlands are the photographic negative of South African industry. Lesotho is more than a "shadow" of South Africa, another metaphor used to describe the relationship between places connected across geographic distance through economic networks.[2] It is not simply an *effect* of South Africa. Instead, Lesotho and South Africa coproduce one another. In this way, I have come to think of Lesotho's rangelands as a "negative ecology." In the glimmer of a fountain in Johannesburg's Sandton City Mall, a shrub-encroached pasture in Lesotho. In a gullied alpine wetland, a tactical security guard vehicle in Westcliff.

Envisioning Lesotho's ecosystems as a constituent but unseen part of South African industry (and vice versa)—as expressing something about that industry—also points toward a potential empirical strategy for a critical ecological science, making visible factors that are usually excluded from the frame of mainstream, positivist ecology, such as race, political economy, and history. Their invisibility, I would argue, is a product of the divide between humanities and the natural sciences, and it undermines our ability to respond to our planet's environmental crisis. A negative ecology calls for an account of these factors, but not only as a political economic backdrop, as is typical within ecological science or human ecology. These factors should be understood as ecological variables themselves. Rates of livestock grazing, for example, are typically reduced to a universal variable—"grazing density" or "grazing intensity," depending on the question being asked. These are then measured by quantitative means or classed on a qualitative scale, such as by dung count or scheduled observations. These variables are useful abstractions, notably because they make statistical inference possible, but they bracket important questions, such as why those animals are there and not others, at what point in history they arrived, why they graze at a given density or intensity, and so on.

Are Lesotho's transitions from agricultural producer to labor reserve and from labor reserve to water reservoir simply a backdrop? Or are such changes constitutive of these rangeland patterns, insinuated into the assembly of this ecological community? Does it matter that young, poor, male herders graze the animals, or is the measure of "grazing density" all we need to know? Just as postcolonial theory helped to provincialize the universal categories of western thought,[3] we should provincialize the universal presumptions of ecological variables. To this end, negative ecology might be a useful, critical-scientific practice fit to the Anthropocene.

This chapter, then, presents an interpretation of ecological patterns in this specific landscape, but also an argument about how to interpret such patterns in general. Making this argument raises complex debates about interdisciplinary genre, empiricism, and theory. I don't resolve those byzantine problems here, but rather call out from inside their darkened passageways.

ON DEGRADATION

In the introduction to this book, I described a visit to the cattle post of a man named Tankisi, a skilled negotiator of the water economy's terrestrial politics. Tankisi understood the costs and benefits of different landscape interpretations, sensing the possibilities afforded by rangeland rules or institutions that coalesced around these interpretations. He endorsed the plans of conservation projects, even as he disregarded them where necessary. On our hike up the mountainside that day into those vast, common-property pastures, we passed by some agricultural fields which he had ploughed that year for the first time. This was odd. Planting crops in the cattle post areas is forbidden—not by law, but by a widely held understanding of the threat it poses. Livestock are not as closely watched at the cattle post as they are near the villages, so inevitably some will end up grazing in his fields. Tankisi would be within his rights to impound those animals, and the owner of the livestock would have to pay a fine. Conflict is imminent. In fact, Tankisi told me that complaints had already come to him through the chief.

I asked what he had planted. I assumed he would say wheat, which is sometimes grown at high elevation. Instead, he said, *habore*, a fodder grass. I was incredulous—Tankisi was cultivating grass in a grassland pasture. More than that, he had taken commonly held rangelands and privatized them by ploughing. In a sense, he was "dividing the commons."[4]

Had Tankisi planted wheat, this all might have seemed less shocking— ploughing "marginal" land is somewhat common, even though rarely is it quite so marginal as this. But fodder grass? It meant that Tankisi had effectively lost faith that the rangeland could naturally produce enough forage for his animals, and that he felt compelled to hedge his bets by purchasing grass seed, laboring to plough, plant, weed, and harvest—all the while working to protect it from other people's wandering livestock and risking conflict with his neighbors. He showed me a wire laying on the ground at his cattle post that he had been using to prevent his own sheep from heading to these *habore* plots at night.

A generation of scholars in political ecology and environmental history taught us to be wary of expert accounts of land degradation.[5] They detailed Malthusian subtexts in complaints about rural land use and in the market triumphalism of "development."[6] They documented how conservation projects sometimes disenfranchised rural, indigenous, and otherwise marginalized people for the sake of eco-tourism, soil conservation, or biodiversity, questioning *for whom* nature was being conserved.[7] These conservation projects, they showed, demonstrate an implicit (and sometimes explicit) belief among colonists, conservationists, and development workers that rural people are simply incapable of managing their "natural resources."

I came to this project expecting to refute the notion that Lesotho's rangelands were "degraded," partly out of this suspicion and partly owing to the fact that Basotho livestock farmers appear to be so productive. If their land is degraded, how could they consistently export such an incredible amount of wool and mohair? But degradation was too widely agreed upon, and my observations of distressed landscapes were too numerous. Tankisi, for example, was not alone in ploughing his way out of a dependence upon the annual whims of rangeland forage. I met others doing the same.

But what is meant when people—me, conservation bureaucrats, herders, others—talk about "rangeland degradation?" In the ecological science literature, it can refer to a wide variety of changes, including declines in species diversity or richness, soil compaction, and other changes. There is no direct Sesotho translation for a term so semantically freighted as "degradation," and in my conversations with conservation bureaucrats and water engineers, they typically used the English term to reference three things: soil erosion, shrub encroachment, or the decline of forage abundance. But in other moments, they were referring to increases in bare soil, diminished water-retention capacity, or several of these connotations in combination. Descriptions of decline by herders, livestock owners, and others in the rural Mokhotlong District usually employed the Sesotho term *ho fokola* (to be weak, barren, or to falter). That term is a catch-all for "poor condition," but the specific condition to which herders and livestock owners referred was typically a lack of forage grass, rather than soil erosion or shrub encroachment. They emphasized that there were more livestock owners with large herds (*barui*) today than in the past, and that this put pressure on the range. But they also typically referenced the changing nature of rains. In response to the question, "How are the rangelands?" a common response was something like: "Hey, they are in poor condition. There is no rain, no grass." Slippage between these different significations—by ecologists, bureaucrats, and herders—interrupts any consensus regarding interpretations of rangeland condition and solutions for their improvement, inciting disorientation in historiography of the landscape.

My attempt here is to sort through that disorientation, first by drawing attention to these different connotations as I have just done here and elsewhere in this book. Second, I hope to recognize the environmental impacts of rural livestock production, but to resituate these impacts at an appropriate scale so as to rethink how agency and responsibility are assigned for rangeland degradation.[8] In this, I affirm the fundamental truth of Piers Blaikie's insights about the influence of "non-place-based" factors in shaping land condition.[9] Problems of scale are crucial to understanding soil erosion, Blaikie explained. While the immediate cause of an erosion gully might be livestock overgrazing, this disturbance of the soil only makes sense when understood in reference to the broader political economic forces that circumscribed people's choices about how and where to graze their animals in the first place: for example, the settler colonialism through which Lesotho lost significant territory; the country's domestic politics of land use and management; the strategic firming up of Lesotho's borders to regulate the flow of itinerant migrant laborers; the climatic changes that are making crop and livestock production more difficult; among others. Naming "overgrazing" as the cause of land degradation is to exclude all of that from view. Rural livestock production pushes against the limits of Lesotho's rangelands, but this strain is not strictly a function of management decisions, as I described in chapter 4: how many animals to graze, where, and for how long. It is one of marginalization, or the situating of Lesotho on an economic periphery. And, as I'll show below, also of the peripheral status of herders within Lesotho society.

So, let's follow the gaze of water engineers and conservation bureaucrats into the cattle post areas of the upstream catchment, the geographical margins that herders occupy. Before turning to hear from herders, I need to conjure the scene, to depict what it feels like to move through these cattle post landscapes. I need to give a rendering of the ecological patterns that are of such concern in Lesotho's water-export era, and which are subject to these diverging interpretations: by engineers and conservation bureaucrats, by herders and livestock owners, and by me.

PATTERNS IN THE LANDSCAPE

I took a walk in the highland cattle post areas—"the source" of the water-export economy's sedimentation problem as Tau had explained it to me in chapter 3. It was a bright April morning when I got off the bus near the top of the pass at Motšerimeli. I got lots of quizzical looks. The only people who visit cattle posts are herders and livestock owners, and they typically go by foot, by horse, or by donkey. There, a solitary herder, sometimes two, will stay for most of the year in a small, dilapidated rondavel with a stone kraal. Dogs stand guard.

I hiked up a spur that jutted out southward from the valley head. Trees are essentially absent in the highlands, and views from the ridgeline are majestic. From valley bottoms, they can be claustrophobic, the slopes are so steep.

At the base of the valley head was an alpine wetland in a state of decay. Hooves had punctured the plush, grass surface. Ice rats (Otomys sloggetti) scurried between

FIGURE 17. Wetland featuring active erosion, the mass wasting of clods of peat. Shrubs grow at its edges. Photo by author.

burrows at the edges. Thick clods of grass-covered soil hung from the wetland banks above a stream, with piles of the dark peat accumulating above the water's edge. It was clear that the stream was not a stream so much as it was a gully cut into the peat. Despite the clear effects of trampling, the road was in large part to blame for the degradation of this particular wetland. The specific name for the spot where the wetland was situated was "Hoekong." The Afrikaans word, *hoek*, in the name describes the spot well. The road is truly like a hook or corner, curving sharply as it switches back toward the plateau. Roads, which channelize water and thereby encourage erosion,[10] have damaged many of these wetlands near the roadside, an accompaniment to the livestock impacts (see fig. 17).

I walked up the spur toward the ridge. Cresting it, I sat for a moment to look out over the area. The rangelands can appear monotonous from afar, but in fact there is tremendous variation. The palette and structure of the landscape express a multispecies politics and history.

A narrow band of open stream ran up the centerline of the valley below. Dark, organic, nutrient-rich soils, formed by the deposition of soil, plant materials, and livestock excreta emanated two to three meters out from the river. Rising steeply from the river was a shrubby zone, whose species composition varies by aspect. Those facing south were dominated by *Helichrysum trilineatum*, which favors the cold, moist, and slightly more acidic, mineral soils formed by that solar and temperature regime. Those facing north were dominated by *Chrysocoma ciliata*, which favors relative warmth and soils that are drier, with a lower organic matter

FIGURE 18. Cairn demarcating between the "A" and "B" rangelands, with cattle post in the distance. Photo by author.

content. Bushy patches of silvery blue *Inulanthera thodei* were situated in sheltered valley nooks, where occasional piles of scree could be seen. The largest, oldest, and healthiest shrubs were limited to the lower reaches of the valley, growing smaller and less dense toward the upper reaches. There, they become interspersed with smaller forbs, smaller tussock grasses, and the characteristic *Merxmuellera* tussocks spiking outward, a bunch grass whose high silica and lignin content makes it shine in the sun—good for grass-craft objects like hats and trivets, but poor for forage. A steep, grass-dominant zone at the upper limits reached around the valley and gave way at the top to bare rock and gravel where vegetation thins into the scraggly shrubs and herbs. There, annual grasses like *Aristida spp.* were interspersed. Brown bands of exposed basalt rock bending back from a spur speak to their continual exposure by runoff, trampling animals, and gravity.

A handful of cattle posts—some in use, some abandoned—were within view from the ridgeline (see fig. 18). Noticeable as a blotch of bare earth surrounded by the vibrant green of grasses thriving in the high-nitrogen soils where livestock urinate and defecate, they are not situated arbitrarily throughout the landscape, but are always within a short distance of a stream or spring, often perched on a spur. They are mostly found on the warmer, north-facing slopes, and sometimes two or three are grouped beside each other—the benefits being companionship and better security against thieves; the costs being increased grazing pressure in the immediate vicinity, the transmission of diseases, and the hassles of separating herds when animals mix.

At finer scales, other colors come into view. On the ridge, where I sat, the uncanny yellow ray florets of *Euryops decumbens* splayed out from a bright, yellow disk, all set against its scraggling, brown branches; the silvery green basal rosette leaves of small *Helichrysum* species erupted seemingly against all odds from dry, mineral soils; a mottled-brown lizard darted underneath a rock ledge. Mineral sediments as well as organic plant matter are continually added to the soils on the slopes below, accumulating in a colluvial pan where the wetlands form. A distinct set of plant species grow on the wetlands. Their long root systems can reach several feet into the soil profile, which become visible when erosion gullies expose them. The relative absence of air in the pores between waterlogged soil particles create conditions that prevent decomposition, meaning that organic matter accumulates and accumulates.

I spotted an area in the distance that clearly had been burned within the last year or two, with a distinctly green zone filled with grasses and fewer of the dark green shrubs. The burn must have been managed, as it ended abruptly in a more-or-less straight line. It resembled another pasture that had been burned during my field research. That was September 2014, and when I hiked through it in the month afterward, I found that almost none of the vegetation had visibly survived, with some rather large shrubs leaving behind only devegetated stems; a very sparse cover of grasses and forbs had begun to establish. When I visited the site again in February 2016, the place had already seen a significant amount of regrowth. Plenty of dwarf shrubs had begun to regrow from root stock at the base of those same scorched stems, suggesting that pasture burning, a commonly used management tool across the globe to control shrubs, probably does little to diminish the abundance of these populations, even though it would prevent them from growing to their full height at maturity.

Looking out across these open highland vistas, one feels as distant as can be from city life, or even from village life. It is so quiet, the insects are loud. Bucolic though these rangelands may seem, they hum with the bustle of the city.

NEGATIVE ECOLOGY

From the ridgeline, I saw a herder walking down toward the wetland. I decided to go speak with him. As I approached from a few hundred meters away, he started singing loudly and did not respond to the greeting that I yelled out to him. He clearly did not want to speak to me—it was impossible that he did not hear or see me. Declining a greeting is unheard-of in Lesotho, an extraordinary breach of etiquette that I don't recall ever experiencing in my years there, where greetings are an entire domain of social life.

As I walked past his flock, I noticed several sheep had been carefully adorned with ephemera: old plastic bags of various colors; flags that reached one to two feet into the air; pom-poms of nylon string hanging from their foreheads; bits of material tied to dangling strings as tassels; and even a reflector vest from the mines or construction work.

After walking back up on the ridge to look out over the next valley head, I sat on another rock and rested. I could see a herd of about forty sheep, thirty goats, and eight cattle—but I strained for some time to find the herder. I have often found my sense of distance is compromised in the mountains. The field of view can be disorienting. When I noticed him—a gray spot on the landscape—he may have been a kilometer away, but perhaps closer. I called out to him in the manner custom to the rangelands, with drawn out enunciation and ostentatious masculinity: *Ntaaaaaateee, keaaaa tla hee, kea u lumeliiiiiiisa!* (Hey, I'm coming over to greet you!). He hollered something back—most of it was indecipherable to me, but it included an affirmation.

The herder was an older man, which was unusual. Most herders in the cattle post areas range between fourteen and twenty years old.[11] They were not always so young, but the migrant labor economy prompted a pattern in which, while older men were away working in the mines, their male children took their place at the cattle posts. When arriving at working age, those young men would head to the mines and younger ones would take over at *motebong*.

We walked toward each other across the wide valley, and he corraled some of his sheep and goats together as he went, whistling and shouting, throwing an arm into the air. He picked up a rock and threw it sidearm at a sheep in the distance. With the astonishing accuracy possessed by every herder I've met, the rock landed just on the far side of the sheep, nudging it away from the perimeter of the herd.

He wore typical herding clothes: tattered pants, gumboots, a shirt, and a gray blanket. As he threw stones to draw other animals back into the herd, his blanket rose at the arm and got caught by the wind, which blew it back along with the rest of the blanket beneath his waist. His balaclava was stretched and sagging beneath his chin to frame his entire face, yet he nevertheless had a habit of pulling it down from time to time as he spoke. His blanket was, like most herders' blankets at the cattle post, old and torn. He carried a herder's stick (*molamu*), as all herders do. His black boots had patches at the stress points—the toe crease and other spots along the sole. His socks were the typical stockings, bunched up at the top of the boots where, in place of elastic, they were fastened with a string just above his calf.

His name was Mothusi. I told him I hoped to talk with him about herding and rangeland condition, and we sat down in a grassy patch, surrounded by small *Helichrysum trilineatum* shrubs. It was not so windy on this side of the valley, relatively speaking. I was surprised to learn that he was from a very distant village in Thaba-Tseka District, and had only been herding at this cattle post for one season, working for a man from Tlokoeng. Like many herders, including younger ones, he was an itinerant laborer, moving periodically from one cattle post to another—a year here, two years there—but he had come farther than usual. Many herders I met were from the most rural of villages, but hired by wealthier livestock owners from towns in Mokhotlong District, like Mapholaneng or Tlokoeng.

Mothusi was clearly extremely poor. He told me he had no animals of his own, having lost most of his small herd over the previous few years to drought, theft, and sale. He was fifty years old, meaning that he grew up at a time when mining employment was relatively abundant and nearly a rite of passage for young men across Lesotho. Yet he never did work in the mines. I was surprised. Did he not want to work there, I asked?

He had wanted to, he said, but after having done some "piece jobs" in South Africa while looking for stable work, he was robbed at knife point and decided to come back to Lesotho where he worked as a builder. He and his wife were not able to conceive children. She had died a few years earlier. With no construction work in Thaba-Tseka, no support from children, and a diminishing herd of sheep and goats, he decided to return to herding at the cattle post, as in his youth.

Mothusi's twelve months of work at *motebong* would be compensated with livestock, just as it is for every herder I've met: either twelve small stock (sheep, goats, or a combination of the two) or one head of cattle. Herders have been paid the same amount for at least fifty years, as was confirmed to me by men in their sixties and seventies. During my many conversations with herders, some told me of their dreams to get a job in the mines, even despite the odds against landing one. Quite a few wore a hardhat as though they already did. Others sought a life as a farmer, building up a herd, selling an animal when cash was needed, trafficking sheep to butcheries over the border in Qwa-Qwa, selling the wool and mohair from small stock, and eventually hiring a herder to keep their animals at the cattle post when their herd grew large enough to pay one.

Mothusi and the man who declined to greet me hint at the heterogeneity within herder social worlds. Yet, both capture a sense of herders' peripheral position within Lesotho, and of Lesotho's position within Southern Africa, including the region's material culture, its violence, and its opportunities. Just as men like them were drawn into South Africa's mining industry, while also being expelled to its margins—the "disjunctive inclusion" to which Achille Mbembe refers[12]—so, too, for herders within Lesotho society, as I'll show in the next sections. This position is encoded in traces in the land, the spacetimes of the pasture.[13] Lesotho has been transformed off-site by South African industry and the social worlds that coalesced around it.

THE SPACETIMES OF FREEDOM

Livestock production is not simply a "livelihood strategy." It is a social and cultural practice, contested along lines of gender, class, and generation in Lesotho.[14] The herders (*balisana*) who labor to produce livestock work within a world that is both firmly *inside* the Basotho cultural mainstream and at its farthest edges.[15] Some of the most charismatic figures in Lesotho society, herders are often depicted as iconic of Sesotho culture. As with the "national water" I described in chapter 1, herders are nearly certain to appear on any given tourist brochure for the country and promotional materials for the Lesotho Highlands Water Project.[16] A 2014 feature-length film about life in Lesotho, *The Forgotten Kingdom*,[17] drew upon this figure when it included a young herder character that operated as both a jester and a sage, guiding the protagonist through remote parts of the country and helping him to overcome his personal struggle.

The herder attire—a gray blanket, balaclava, herding stick, and gumboots—is emblazoned across Lesotho's cultural landscape. The immensely popular "famo" musicians regularly use the attire to assert their cultural roots, though few of them these days would have been resident at a cattle post—they are typically lowlands-born Basotho.[18] Herders do work that is critical to the Basotho household, caring for the animals that plough agricultural fields, provide families with milk, and produce wool for cash. And, they do so under serious physical duress. At *motebong*, herders' diets consist almost entirely of maizemeal (*papa*), with wild greens (*meroho*) only when in season; they live under threat of lightning strikes and livestock thieves; jackals lurk behind shrubs and prey on their lambs; they endure rain and snow; and they care for animals twenty-four hours a day, seven days a week. There are no weekends at *motebong*.

Despite this embrace of the cultural symbols associated with herding and the centrality of herding to Basotho livelihoods, herders are largely seen and treated as outcasts in everyday life (see fig. 19). When in town, they cut an awkward and edgy figure. They do not small-talk well—including with other Basotho—and often wear their balaclava over their face, even when inappropriate. Many are illiterate, having been prevented from attending school because of their herding duties, and they are often portrayed by adults as being rude, disrespectful, and sometimes even dangerous.

I asked three young men working at neighboring cattle posts in Mokhotlong District whether they enjoyed staying at *motebong*. It was the late winter and the sun had only recently risen over the ridgeline. The winds had already started gusting. The day would be like many others: they would eat a breakfast of maizemeal and head out with their herd of sheep, goats, and cattle to the pasture near the seep at the head of the valley. They would sit and chat, play a game called *moraba-raba*, take a nap. After midday, when the animals seemed content and the herders became hungry, they would drive the animals back to the kraal and settle down for a maizemeal supper. In the morning, they would wake to do it over again.

As we stood, the brown earth stretched out around us, up and downhill. On account of their being, as they put it, too "lazy" (*botsoa*) to fetch water down the hill, they ate the remnants from last night's maizemeal for breakfast instead of making a fresh pot. All three responded emphatically to my question: yes, they like working at *motebong*. Why?

"Because we do what we want. We are independent. There isn't anyone who can tell us what to do out here."

FIGURE 19. Herders at the cattle post. Photo by author.

"Who tells you what to do when you're in the village?" I asked.

One responded: "*All* the adults—people like Motlokoa." Motlokoa was the chief's uncle and more than a little imposing. They mentioned Motlokoa because they knew he was a friend of mine, but the herders were referring to *all* adults (*batho ba baholo*).

Their response struck me. This was clearly a lonely and difficult life—and, to be sure, they would take other, good-paying work if they could find it. But the cattle post areas were spaces of freedom for them. They were spaces of independence and of responsibility on one's own terms, even if also of marginalization.[19]

It would be forty-five minutes before we left to take the animals to pasture. As we stood chatting, one of them leaned against the doorway opening to the rondavel. Unlike most cattle post rondavels, theirs had a corrugated metal roof instead of a thatched one. Large rocks lined the roof, holding it in place to withstand the strong winds that could easily blow it away. As he leaned, some of the rocks began to give way and several large ones came crashing down, knocking over the three-legged cooking pot containing the maizemeal before rolling downhill. The largest of them rolled five hundred meters or more down the slope as we watched in silence. Everyone burst out laughing. These were young men living on their own, free to be absurd and reckless. I scanned the horizon—nobody for miles.

ENGINEERING FORAGE

Rangelands are degraded. The rains are changing, and changing for the worse. Forage is insufficient, shrubs are encroaching, wetlands are gullied and dying.

It begs the question: how is it that Basotho are producing wool, mohair, and mutton in such great quantities? I presented one reason in the previous chapter, which is that breeding and veterinary care have both improved tremendously over the past century.[20] This means that the amount and quality of wool or mohair per animal is far higher than it once was. I also showed how Tankisi and Lesuhla (see chapter 5) were planting fodder to supplement the rangeland forage. Another reason, however, is that herders are forage engineers. They use medicines to transform vegetation from unpalatable to palatable. They set fires to draw nitrogen-rich grasses out of the soil.

Inside any cattle post rondavel, spare as can be—just a three-legged pot, a sack of maizemeal, a few boxes of matches, and one to two beds made of stone platforms covered with shrubs for padding—one can almost always find a small jug of *nyopo-nyopo* and a bag of salt. *Nyopo-nyopo* is molasses infused with other substances or medicines (*meriana*). When speaking with herders, I would ask what they used these for, and herders would explain that it was "so the animals will be able to eat and drink water" (*hore li khona ho ja, hore li noe metsi*). I often thought to myself: why wouldn't an animal know how to eat when it was hungry or drink when it was thirsty? Further questioning only elicited similar answers.

Back at Tankisi's cattle post, shortly after he had told me the "joke" about how livestock selectively graze, described in the introduction of this book, I came to a realization: salt and *nyopo-nyopo* were strategies for keeping animals alive in a degraded rangeland. He had carried on from that joke to explain that sheep have good memories. When forage is low, he said they will leave the herd, sometimes even at night, to go find forage they recall from another day—particularly during lean winters when forage is poor everywhere else. He pointed way down the valley toward the road, from which we had just hiked. He said that sheep might head all the way down there in search of forage, and that herders must be vigilant.

I asked, "What can herders do to prevent that when forage is low?" It seemed to me that would be a constant problem during droughts and the dry winter months.

"They give them *nyopo-nyopo* and salt, so the animals will be able to eat."

I had been doing this research for many years by this time, but it only occurred to me in this conversation with Tankisi that herders use these supplements to entice their livestock to eat plants they would otherwise avoid: unpalatable plants, like shrubs, annual grasses, or grasses that were simply past their nutritious prime. Herders use it most commonly in the winter, from June to October or November. In the summer, from January to April, no *nyopo-nyopo* is needed because they find all the nutrients (*matsoai*) they need from the grasses they eat. One herder told me that he would scatter it in a circle in the morning outside the cattle post: only salt in the summer, once per week; salt with *nyopo-nyopo* in the winter, three times a week. The livestock eat it with glee.

More than that, Tankisi said, herders use the supplements to get their animals to come back on their own to the kraal. In these unfenced cattle post areas, after all, one does not herd. *Motebong ha ho lisoe*. I chuckled to myself after this because, whereas conservation bureaucrats promoted the Savory rotational grazing method I described in chapter 4, including fencing or "active herding" to delimit the spaces in which livestock graze and circumvent the problem that livestock graze selectively on palatable forage, herders have developed an alternative solution to these problems. They use *nyopo-nyopo* to configure livestock movements and entice them to eat unpalatable plants.

A second way that herders engineer forage is by setting fires to elicit grasses from the soil. Herders are famous for setting rangeland fires, and these are prohibited by law because they are widely seen as encouraging soil erosion. The fires rid the range of the old leaves from *Festuca caprina*, for example, a perennial, fire-adapted bunchgrass that produces a tremendous amount of dense leaf growth, which, if not eaten, can accumulate and discourage additional growth. Burning the rangeland can remove these accumulated moribund, high-carbon leaves and stimulate the growth of new, nitrogen-rich shoots (*thoko*). Sheep—especially lambs—love these new shoots. This is a common practice worldwide, but in Lesotho it is condemned for its effects on soil stability. If the range is not given sufficient time to rest before livestock are introduced, or if heavy rains come before vegetation has regrown sufficiently, then the land is exposed and incapable of retaining its top layer of soil.

Engineering forage has consequences beyond increasing soil erosion. I had often been struck in my conversations with women about changes in the landscape that, rather than decry the proliferation of shrubs as men did, they complained that there were no longer *enough* shrubs. Women and girls are tasked with collecting shrubs for cooking fuel in village areas, and there are few good stands of shrubs near highland villages. While shrubs may be proliferating in the cattle post areas, then, they have diminished in the areas surrounding villages, where they are needed as fuel. This, many women told me, was because of herder pasture fires that had eliminated the large shrubs that are useful for cooking. It wasn't that there were no shrubs near villages, but rather that the shrubs were small and worthless. After all, fires do not remove shrubs completely. Many of the most invasive shrubs are fire-tolerant, able to regrow from basal meristems at the soil surface, as I described earlier.

If fires are harmful, causing soil erosion and ruining fuel sources, I would ask, "Well, then why do herders continue to do it?" With remarkable regularity, a wide diversity of Basotho women and men in the highlands would respond by saying that herders are *setoutu*. *Setoutu* is a Sesotho word that could be roughly translated as "stupidity," but that specifically connotes carelessness and irresponsibility: the stupidity, perhaps, of young men. As one person put it, someone would be described as *setoutu* when they know something is wrong but they do it anyway.

Herders are largely aware of the link between pasture burning and soil erosion in my experience. Because it is illegal and taboo, however, it was difficult to tell if they believed it was true, much less for them to confide in me about whether they or nearby herders do it. But soil erosion is not their concern. Engineering forage to feed to their flock is what matters. Herders and their livestock are agents of degradation, but they are better thought of as "making do" in degraded landscapes—a product of their structural position as central to rural livelihoods and national identity yet also on the periphery. Their peripheral position within society, however, means that measures taken to change their behaviors, whether by conservation bureaucrats or ordinary Basotho, are unlikely to reach them. Herder freedom at the cattle post means that they are unbound by obligations to those in town. Their translation of herding work as freedom makes herding valuable and worthwhile to herders, but it also draws them out of social control. It is yet another impediment to addressing erosion.

. . .

Having reached the next, penultimate section of this last chapter, I'm now in a position to assemble a landscape history informed by the foregoing pages and chapters. It is a landscape history based on a reading of my ethnographic and ecological data, archival sources, and ecological theory. In it, I traverse the different senses of degradation, including declines in biodiversity, the encroachment of shrubs, and soil erosion.

I have shown throughout this book that the search for South Africa's water security has interpellated theorists of water's flow across the landscape, an incitement to the fluvial imagination. A proliferation of discourse on the topic has generated disorientation as to the nature of water—its meaning and materiality. I've tried to document that disorientation, sounding its depths for all its implicit significations. More than simply amplifying the disorientation, however, my hope here is also to clarify it, reorienting us with an alternative landscape historiography.

SHOCK TROOPS OF EMPIRE—AND SURVIVAL

In the previous chapter, I showed that development and conservation experts have sought at least since the 1980s to commodify cattle as a way of improving land condition in Lesotho. They argued that the cultural status of cattle in Basotho society incentivizes the acquisition of more cattle than the landscape can accommodate. Such a narrative ignores the fact that sheep and goats have been earnestly commodified for global textile markets for over a century. Small stock have heavily outnumbered cattle for decades, and their numbers have been high *precisely because they were linked into global textile markets.*

In an important sense, small stock instigated the settlement of the highlands in the first place. Sheep have been like "shock troops" of empire,[21] turbo-charged by colonial efforts to promote wool production. Yet they have also served as tools for survival, enabling rural people to navigate the historical moment, be it during the labor-reserve era or the water-reservoir era. These two related processes—of extraction and of survival—have catalyzed rangeland changes.

Sheep are known to be a particularly destructive animal,[22] including by many people in rural Lesotho. A herder named Lumisang explained to me that "sheep spoil the range the most because of how they eat [so close to ground]," making a pinching motion with one hand into the palm of the other. When I suggested that, perhaps cattle also have a big impact on account of being so heavy and trampling vegetation, he and the herder he was with both stopped me before I could finish: "No, no. Cattle don't trample, they eat just fine." They conceded that cattle consume more forage than small stock, and that cattle trampling is a problem in the wetland areas, where they can puncture holes in the peat and encourage erosion. But they were otherwise insistent that sheep were the type of livestock affecting the rangelands most. In effect, where there was concern among rural Basotho during my field research regarding grazing-induced land degradation, it was primarily with small stock—not with cattle. Once, a councilor told me and my friend from the ministry that in the area under his jurisdiction, small stock are fined more severely than large stock. For each cow, horse, donkey, or mule impounded for grazing in closed pastures, the owner is fined 20 Maloti. For each sheep and goat, they pay 50 Maloti. When asked to explain why they charged more for small stock—the official regulations fine more for cattle (M4/animal) than sheep and goats (M0.60/animal)—the councilor said it was because small stock destroy the range more than the large stock.

The relative importance of livestock to vegetation changes is variable across ecosystems, as I noted in chapter 4. Particularly in arid and semi-arid systems, precipitation is often so variable from year to year that it is the primary determinant of vegetation and other aspects of land condition. The Lesotho highlands have high interannual rainfall variation, suggesting this possibility. However, the total annual rainfall is higher than in a semi-arid zone and Lesotho's climate is considered temperate, suggesting otherwise. Beyond parsing the relative influence of livestock grazing versus climate, however, it is hard to argue that livestock are benign figures in Lesotho's highland pastures, or that herder alteration of the landscape, such as pasture-burning is harmless.

The historical absence of heavy, sustained grazing in the highlands is significant, too. Prior to the introduction of sheep in the highlands, this territory was not accustomed to intensive grazing. Ungulate herbivores were present in the highlands in prehistory as seen through archaeological study and some early historical records, but probably in much smaller numbers than domestic livestock of today.[23] Unsurprisingly, the higher reaches of the mountains were home to fewer mammalian herbivores in terms of diversity and population size—the relative lack of woody plants, for example, would have limited the number of browsers.[24] And they probably migrated into the highlands in the summer rather than residing year-round. These naturally occurring large herbivores and their carnivore predators were likely exterminated by 1900 as livestock took their place.[25] Gray rhebok (*Pelea capreolus*) and mountain reedbok (*Redunca fulvorufula*) can be found today, but in small numbers and only in the most remote reaches. Like them, domestic livestock initially grazed the highlands during the summer only, and remnants of that system of vertical transhumance endure in the A-B-C system, as I described in chapter 4. Since the mid-twentieth century, however, many areas have come to be occupied year-round.[26]

Rangeland ecologists have shown clearly that the evolutionary history of a plant community shapes the magnitude of livestock impacts (e.g., on species richness, species diversity, community structure and other factors).[27] In a pasture that has been historically only lightly grazed (or browsed), for example, a steep increase in grazing will have a substantially greater impact than if the pasture had a long history of intensive grazing. The reason is that the vegetation in lightly grazed pastures is not adapted to endure the impact of livestock, which includes not only defoliation but also trampling. Their tolerance threshold for recovering from this disturbance is lower and, as a result, more susceptible to shifts in vegetation (see fig. 20).[28]

The late nineteenth-century introduction of sheep into pastures that had not experienced significant grazing pressures almost certainly led to heavy losses of species richness and diversity and triggered localized shifts from grassland and grassland-shrub mosaics to shrubland. The loss of browsing animals would've also allowed shrubs to spread unchecked. If the transition were reversible, it is prevented today by a combination of grazing and periodic drought,[29] both of which disfavor herbs and favor shrubs. Soon after the highlands were settled for small stock pasture in the late nineteenth century, colonial administrators would be sounding the alarm about overgrazing and other land degradation stemming from agriculture in the highlands. One described pastures "invaded by inedible weeds," presumably referring to burweed, which spoiled the wool and mohair clip, and the dwarf shrub *Chrysocoma ciliata*, which was known to crowd out grasses.[30] Basotho, too, were complaining about the situation, such as in a 1912 letter published in the newspaper *Leselinyana la Lesotho*, titled "Makhulo a Felile" (The Pastures Are Finished).[31] In 1947, the British closed off approximately fourteen hundred square miles of mountain rangeland cattle post areas in Mokhotlong and Qacha's Nek Districts, where the *Chrysocoma ciliata* invasion was said to be most severe,[32] though it is unlikely that Basotho adhered to that closure.[33]

Just as British colonial concerns about degradation flared, however, they were building roads and bridle paths to encourage wool production for colonial tax rev-

FIGURE 20. A negative ecology. Photo by author.

enues. These pathways accelerated wool production in the early to mid-twentieth century, built to ferry wool from the highlands to the markets beyond. They also created a regularly disturbed pathway for shrub encroachment and the channelization of water.[34] It is clear to any observer that certain shrub species like *C. ciliata* thrive along the heavily disturbed roadsides and bridle paths. *C. ciliata* has long been present in the highlands,[35] but it and others that similarly like disturbance have expanded their ranges and population sizes thanks to livestock grazing, drought, and these roads and paths.[36] Ecologists and botanists have suggested that today's invasive weeds were confined to valley coves and Cave Sandstone overhangs where animals were sheltered in the early days of highlands grazing of the late nineteenth and early twentieth centuries before expanding into grass-dominated areas by moving along pathways such as livestock trails.[37]

· · ·

Negative ecologies raise profound empirical problems, as well as ethico-political ones: how do we assign responsibility for environmental degradation when drivers of environmental change can be so multifarious, indirect, or occluded? At heart, however, this is consistent with a basic question in ecological science, namely: how can one discern the factors that give rise to ecological patterns when a landscape presents itself as fully formed? My contention is merely that the factors available for consideration within ecology are often too narrowly conceived to meaningfully interpret these patterns.

Shrub encroachment, degraded wetlands, and denuded hillslopes are the by-products of a system of livestock production in Lesotho. Yet, that system is itself a by-product of the water-export economy—and the labor-export economy upon which it was built. As Raymond Williams has shown,[38] the by-products of a system are truly its products. Abiotic factors such as climate are profoundly important in determining the condition of land in Lesotho. But to the extent that livestock contribute to the production of landscape patterns there, these patterns express the pressures of a regional political economy, as well as of the aspirations and marginalization of herders who work within it. Living in post-labor-reserve Lesotho, herders not only produce livestock, but also the conditions that promote soil erosion. While those responsible for establishing Lesotho's export economies—of labor and of water—seek to engineer storage, herders are compelled to engineer forage. They are not the sole cause of erosion, but their position within Lesotho society encourages it, a situation that illustrates how identity can be empirically valuable for seeing ecological process. Their sense of freedom at the cattle post makes their work worthwhile, but this independence also delinks them from even the most well-thought-out rangeland management program.

I've offered an alternative interpretation of the shrub-encroached and eroded landscapes of the highlands to the one put forward by conservation bureaucrats. Whereas they saw an overly dispersed herd and a lazy herder leading to shrub encroachment, declines in good forage grass, and wetland degradation, I've shown that the evolutionary history of grazing in the highlands, the timing of livestock introductions, marginalization, and the wildly successful colonial efforts to promote wool production are central factors in shaping land condition. Herders are well aware of how livestock preferences shape livestock movements, and about the preponderance of unpalatable forage. Rather than taking up "active herding," though, herders elect to stimulate livestock appetites with *nyopo-nyopo* and to draw young grass shoots from the ground with pasture fires.

Conclusion

How could it be that a multi-billion-dollar dam project crucial to the regional economy was sited in a country with a global reputation as a soil erosion hotspot? How could it be that so little was done to understand the threat of sedimentation, much less address it? I kept asking myself these questions over the course of my research. Surely, I thought, I was missing something; some piece of information or rationale.

On one hand, South Africa's desperation is clear. Perhaps this explains things, I considered. The geographic fact that the country's commercial and industrial hub was built upon the arid Witwatersrand gold reefs puts the country in a tight spot. Its poor planning is also clear. Rather than taking steps to cut demand, such as fixing leaky urban water infrastructure, cutting subsidies to major industrial consumers, or otherwise controlling consumption of water, municipalities and water management bodies there (as elsewhere) work with a myopic supply-side economics: get more water and business will follow.[1]

Yet, it's not simply a matter of the fact that "decision makers" failed to gather all the right information to arrive at a sound policy. This would presume that large dam projects like the Lesotho Highlands Water Project result from a deliberative process with a coherence of purpose—as though landfills were built for their methane. Or, perhaps better put, a large dam project is like a fresh carcass on the roadside, hit by a reckless driver: a throng converges upon the scene to pick it clean. These projects are a feeding frenzy for industry and politicians. International consultancies, construction syndicates, law firms, distribution companies, and others thrive on them. They carry prestige for domestic politicians who use them to demonstrate development, to generate jobs, and to cultivate their connections with business.[2]

Enthusiasm for large dams had diminished somewhat as a result of five decades of intense international activism, but we currently live amid a global boom in dam construction.[3] Engineering experts from countries without any more good rivers to dam, such as the United States, Canada, France, and more recently China, fan out across the globe to push their wares.[4] As of 2020, over fifty-eight thousand large dams—that is, a dam wall with a height of 15m or more, or which has a reservoir volume of more than 3 million m3—have been built around the world.[5] This, even though large dams on average overrun their budgets by 96 percent and their construction schedules by 46 percent.[6]

That kind of calculation excludes so many other costs, too. Dams and their associated infrastructure, such as roads and power lines, have displaced millions of people worldwide. They are often presented as "development projects" by governments and other proponents, but there are few benefits for displaced "development refugees."[7] Resettlement disrupts communities and kinship networks, forces people to find alternative livelihoods, and creates tension in receiving communities.[8] Compensation schemes for resettlement are often inadequate and tend to presume that resettled people can move easily from one livelihood into another; those living downstream are neglected even more so.[9]

It is not only humans that suffer, of course. Up- and downstream from dams, biodiverse riparian areas are either inundated with water or starved of it. Inside the reservoir, a novel ecosystem forms in the transition from river to lake. Decomposing organic material off-gasses CO_2.[10] Diminished flows of water and sediments downstream make life impossible for many plants and animals; stagnant pools breed bacteria and water-borne disease; delta floodplains subside, coasts erode.[11] The sediments trapped behind the dam wall, such a problem for the dam, are a source of life-giving nutrients downstream. Not only are flows reduced below the dam, but they are often regularized in ways that are fundamentally different from a naturally flowing river, which experiences fluctuations throughout the year, with surges from storm waters, and so on.[12] While some dam projects put in place "instream flow requirements," which are management regimes based on the minimum specific ecological requirements of the downstream community, none were developed for the Katse Dam.[13] Ecological and social consequences were quite obviously an afterthought.[14] Only a few, vague provisions were made in the LHWP Treaty for such impacts in contrast to the long, detailed financial and engineering sections. An environmental impact assessment wasn't even done. Only in 2004 was an instream flows program drawn up and put in place (without data on the predam ecosystem).

As these problems pile up, as sediment accumulates in reservoirs and water flows to Johannesburg, I wonder: at what cost will the contradictions between storage and extraction in this repurposed labor reserve be reconciled?

At the leading edge of global natural resource politics, Lesotho offers a cautionary tale about the technological promise of engineering water transfers from one river basin to another in the Anthropocene. More broadly, it calls into question beliefs about human dominion over the natural world, including those that continue to influence the humanities,[15] while also showing natural scientists why power and critique are vital to the project of understanding and preserving our environment.

Humans are thought of as the preeminent "niche-constructors," referring to the practice of cultivating the conditions that will maximize an organism's potential for reproduction[16]—like beavers that build dams to create safe habitats for themselves. As outlined by G. Evelyn Hutchinson, a niche is an "n-dimensional hypervolume," in which any number of limit conditions for a species' survival could be identified.[17] Niche construction, then, is the process of remaking environments into one's own image: humans bring environments into conformity with the human hypervolume. Humans under the spell of (or at the mercy of) the expansionist logics of imperialism and capitalism impose this environmental model across the globe—pushing and pushing until the system falters. Geoengineering projects like the LHWP then promise to put things back into alignment.

The innovation of the Anthropocene concept,[18] however, has been to show how this sign of human power and supposed mastery is also a source of human peril. Human niche construction entails species-threatening human niche destruction.[19] The dam-building feeding frenzy looks an awful lot like niche-construction-destruction: servicing "human needs" in general through reckless projects that are in fact fueled by racial capitalism—designed for a specific set of humans rather than humans in general. This is not a "human" niche so much as it is an imperial one.

Scrutinizing the aesthetics and politics of Lesotho's water-export economy, we can see not only the material labor but the interpretive labor required to stave off the contradictions of niche construction-destruction. The water economy has incited a profusion of discourse about the environment in relation to water's flow across the landscape: theorists of fluvial water and historiographers of the landscape have been called into action. To paraphrase Emily Martin's writing on human reproduction discourses,[20] however, in debating the problem of sedimentation in Lesotho we learn about more than simply the flow of water over land; we learn to inhabit fluvial imaginaries with all the cultural and political content that comes with them: of allegations of rural mismanagement, of aspirations for better futures, of state power, of partisan politics, and more. Water's very nature as a landscape feature has come under scrutiny, and this spasm of theory stems from the economy's central contradictions, namely that it demands storage but also extraction; that it demands minimal impact by livestock while leaving livestock production as one of the only ways to make a living.

As "water silos" or "water factories,"[21] Lesotho's mountain rangelands have been converted into "natural infrastructure" for South African industry.[22] The transformation of Lesotho into a water storage tank is not an innovation but rather a variation on a theme, however, having long served as South Africa's labor reserve. That history is instructive, as it reveals the forms of social, symbolic, and ecological engineering required to make storage possible. Elites work to promote the notion that water abundance is an inherent feature of the nation-state of Lesotho and part of a Sotho cultural lexicon—a kind of water I call "national water." But national water is unfamiliar to most people in Lesotho, given that its homogeneous spatial and temporal framing contradicts everyday realities. Rather than a property of the nation as a whole, Lesotho's water is more commonly understood as patchy, erratic, and destructive. Indeed, this destructive water is now imperiling the water economy. The volumetric water of the reservoir is confronted by the fluvial water upstream from it. As during Lesotho's labor-reserve era, the omissions and contradictions of these storage infrastructures threaten the system itself. Water is a gift that destroys.

In spite of Lesotho's global reputation as a soil-erosion hotspot, the LHWP ignored the issue of sedimentation for those critical years when the project was being made into law. As the problem of sedimentation inevitably surfaced again, old discourses about the impact of rural land use on water's flow across the landscape have seen a renaissance. Rural people are said to need a better sense of fluvial water, which would help them understand soil erosion while also investing in them a concern for water as a national good. In the meantime, soil conservation works, such as gabions, check dams, and silt traps, are being constructed to address the problem directly. The conservation efforts are both a failure and a success. Often poorly constructed, unable to stop sediment, sometimes even worsening erosion, and falling apart from the start, the structures are crucial components to water production. This is because they serve a parallel goal: namely, to redistribute a small portion of national wealth to an impoverished, voting public in rural areas through labor-based welfare programs. Providing meager employment to rural people who have few other opportunities, they defer the social unrest that might otherwise accompany Lesotho's precarious economic position.

While those conservation structures are presented as evidence that government agencies are fighting soil erosion, the full extent of erosion—and the effectiveness of conservation works in preventing it—goes largely unmeasured. In place of measurement, indicators of land degradation are used by conservation workers to identify soil erosion, including dwarf shrubs. Shrubs do not always co-occur with or promote erosion (and likely even prevent it), but they have come to represent land degradation and desertification in the flesh through a crude equation: more shrubs equal more soil erosion and less water.

Beyond educating rural people about fluvial water and building conservation works that will slow its flow, bureaucrats from the Lesotho government and foreign NGOs seek to engineer social forms that might protect Lesotho's water resources. But they cannot extricate their efforts from the history of which they are part. The many interventions that have been made into land management, including indirect rule, postcolonial efforts to undo the effects of indirect rule, development and conservation projects, and grazing associations are seen as getting to "the source" of the problem: inadequate grazing institutions. In fact, they complicate rather than streamline rangeland management, undermining rangeland institutions into the future, each subverting the ones that come after it.

Stopping erosion might be impossible, anyway, given the scale of the problem and the nature of rains, soils, and topography in Lesotho. Conservation measures would need to overcome the fundamental, structural causes of land degradation: the abiotic properties of Lesotho's natural environment (e.g., its steep slopes and erratic climate) and the forces that push people into livestock production. Additional pressure has been put on the rangelands in recent years with the decline of the labor-migration economy, when sheep and goat production went from a retirement strategy to a primary livelihood. Increasingly unpredictable rains make this even more acute.

Revisionist environmental histories in Africa taught us to be skeptical of claims about land degradation, but livestock can have dramatic impacts on environments, even if these effects might be modulated by environmental variables. The notion that Lesotho's landscapes are in poor condition is not particularly disputed, even if definitions of "poor condition" vary. Stocking levels and land use should be understood not as an indigenous tradition that is misidentified as harmful, but rather a result of a century of pressures from Southern African racial capitalism. Basotho living in the highlands are not a benign indigenous population "in tune with" their natural environment, even though certainly they know more about how to manage their land responsibly than elites from the lowlands or foreign NGOs with little understanding of the highlands' history or ecology. Rural Basotho form part of a peasantariat that is forced to occupy a harsh territory, which "scratches about on the land."[23] Blaming herders and livestock owners for degradation makes little sense, then, in a context where "non-place-based" factors yield only the narrowest range of livelihood options.

Conservation bureaucrats and water engineers ultimately must learn Blaikie's lesson when they are led further and further into the upstream catchment in their efforts to produce water commodities, concerning themselves with the micropractices of herders and livestock far away from the urban center. They are led from the reservoirs to the eroding slopes above the reservoirs, to the alpine wetlands above the slopes, to the political institutions that manage grazing, to the ideas of herders that graze the animals, and to the forage preferences of sheep. Each step upstream takes them further from the South African core, and yet in a sense each points back toward it.

Across Lesotho's transition from labor reserve to water reservoir, the politics of land use and degradation have remained more or less in place. Nonsustainable multispecies livelihoods, a tenuous politics of distribution, land degradation, and soil conservation are architectural features of a regional political economy: the (by-)products of Lesotho's historical experience as an apartheid storage reserve. Water production is fundamentally a racial project, then, even as it masquerades as economic exchange. Before water flows through tunnels and pipes into South

Africa's wealthy gated homes and through prepaid water meters in impoverished townships, it carves paths through the soils upstream, entraining sediment from headwaters to reservoir. The Lesotho Highlands Water Project "might bury itself in a few decades,"[24] along with millions of South Africans who depend upon it. All buried by the sediment of a system of storage and extraction. Water is a gift that destroys.

NOTES

INTRODUCTION

1. See Waters et al. (2016). The ecologist Yadvinder Malhi (2017) has suggested that the magnitude of changes in the Earth system might be high enough for the Anthropocene to be upgraded to a period (the Anthropogene) or even an era (the Anthropozoic).

2. Thank you to Laura Ogden for helping me to articulate this point.

3. Green (2020); Muller (2018).

4. GreenCape (2017); Gauteng City Region Observatory (2019). On the history of water administration in the region, see Tempelhoff (2003). On the threats posed to Johannesburg and the Gauteng region, see Kings et al. (2015); Kings (2015); and Hosken, Smillie, and Goba (2016). On Johannesburg's "world city" aspirations, see Nastar (2014).

5. Niang et al. (2014).

6. LHWP (1981, 4–4).

7. Dubow (1992); Erasmus (2008); Posel (2001); Bowker and Star (1999).

8. On sovereignty, see Folch (2019); Cattelino (2008); and Rutherford (2012) for excellent anthropological accounts. The nation-states of South Africa and Lesotho loom large in this book in ways that risk what Kathryn Furlong (2006) calls the "territorial trap" in thinking about transboundary water issues. I hope it will become clear over the course of the chapters below that connections across (and dependencies between) these sovereign territories matter as much to my story as the divisions that separate them.

9. Adams (1993); Geisler (2015).

10. Kaika (2006); Folch (2019). On oil, another object of natural resource modernity, see Apter (2005); Rogers (2015); Appel (2019); Mitchell (2011).

11. Isaacman and Isaacman (2013); Mitchell (2002); see also Hecht (2012) on mining.

12. Wolpe (1972); Magubane (1979); Mbembe (2008).

13. Schmidt (2017); Alatout (2009); Hastrup and Hastrup (2017); Mehta (2001).

14. See the important work by von Schnitzler (2016); Anand (2017); Folch (2019); Ballestero (2019b); Bakker (2003); Andersen (2016); Hayat (2020); and Barnes (2015).

15. Hitchcock et al. (2011, 22, 16). See also Lewis et al. (2015); Hirst (1995); Makara (2013); Turpie et al. (2021); Chatanga and Seleteng-Kose (2021); Bega (2021); Zunckel (2003).

16. Kabi (2017).

17. Creamer (2016). Delays on the next phase of the LHWP (i.e., the construction of Polihali Dam), which is a decade behind schedule, have already prompted some alarm. Demand is projected to outstrip supply before water from Polihali arrives in 2027, as Mike Muller (2020) explains. See also Gauteng City Region Observatory (2019).

18. The engineer was technically an employee of the Lesotho Highlands Development Authority (LHDA), the administrative body charged with carrying out the LHWP. Where possible, I've tried to diminish the number of acronyms used in this book for the sake of outside readers.

19. See Appel (2019). In this, I sympathize with Polanyi's (1944) account of "fictitious commodities" like labor, land, and money, but I aim to push it further. Polanyi's distinction is useful for showing how some commodities require underwriting from the state, and water seems like a useful addition to his list. Yet, as will become clear in my discussion of water (and livestock), a much broader range of work is required to achieve commodity status, suggesting the need for a rich, multifactorial conception rather than a binary one (i.e., "real" or "fictitious").

20. See Robinson (2000); Mbembe (2008, 2017); Magubane (1979); Wolpe (1972). See also Hecht (2018); Yusoff (2018); Wynter (2003).

21. One of four provinces in the Union of South Africa. At independence in 1994, the Transvaal was split between the provinces of Gauteng, Mpumalanga, Limpopo, and North West.

22. Pretoria is the former name for the City of Tshwane.

23. Tempelhoff (2003). On water connections across urban and rural spaces on the African continent, see Showers (2002).

24. Ashpole (2004).

25. Thabane (2006).

26. Coplan and Quinlan (1997). John Aerni-Flessner (n.d.) also shows that pressures within Lesotho to reclaim the disputed "conquered territories" from South Africa obstructed attempts to strike a deal.

27. Beresford and Pitso (1986); Meissner and Turton (2003). In the year before the coup, South Africa had imposed a blockade on the Lesotho border to punish Lesotho for harboring African National Congress (ANC) activists and invited the future coup leader General Metsing Lekhanya to visit Cape Town for the purpose of discussing "political and economic matters," as it was described in the press (Xinhua General Overseas News Service [1986]).

28. *Basotho* is the plural form of *mosotho*, referring to people of Sotho descent and ethnicity. The word Basotho is pronounced "bah-*soo*-too" (similarly for "moh-*soo*-too" and "leh-*soo*-too"). Basotho people reside in Lesotho and South Africa (especially in the Free State and Gauteng Provinces). The overwhelming majority of Lesotho's citizens and residents identify as Basotho. However, many citizens of Lesotho reside in South Africa. The total de jure population of Lesotho is 2 million (Lesotho Bureau of Statistics [2016]), with several hundred thousand of them residing in South Africa at any given moment. Based on data describing the primary language spoken in the household, 4.4 million Basotho reside

in South Africa (Statistics South Africa 2020). In this book, I specify "South African Basotho" when referring to the latter.

29. Murray (1981); Maloka (2004).

30. Wallerstein (2004).

31. Wolpe (1972); Magubane (1979); Murray (1981).

32. Ferguson (2006).

33. Mensah and Naidoo (2011, 1021).

34. Crush et al. (2021, 130).

35. Murray (1981).

36. Showers (2005); Driver (1999). The similarities with a contemporaneous case described by Richard White (1983) by the U.S. government on Diné land are striking. Incidentally, the two cases involve some of the same figures, such as Hugh H. Bennett, the first head of the U.S. Soil Conservation Service.

37. Driver (1999, 12).

38. Driver (1999, 16).

39. Tempelhoff (2003).

40. Carse (2015); Schnitzler (2016); Folch (2019); Melly (2017); Anand (2017); Anand, Gupta, and Appel (2018).

41. See Polanyi (1944) and O'Connor (1988) on the contradictions of capitalism in regard to the environment.

42. See Evans (1997) on the bureaucratic administration of apartheid, and Swanson (1968) and Davenport (1969) on the history and evolution of apartheid racial urbanism. On the effects of labor migration on kinship in Lesotho, see Murray (1981) and Block and McGrath (2019). For a related example from Zambia, see Ferguson (1999), which also provides important review of the scholarly debates across Southern Africa.

43. The bulk of my field research took place over twelve months in 2014. During that time, I stayed mostly in Mokhotlong town, but also spent several months in Butha-Buthe near the 'Muela Dam. Additionally, I made short, periodic stays in a mountain village on the main road between Mokhotlong and the lowlands, in Roma, and in Maseru. Prior to that, I did one month of preliminary research in Maseru, Katse, and Mokhotlong in August 2011 and another in August 2013. I did two follow-up research trips in Maseru and Mokhotlong in February 2016 and January 2019. My methods were broadly ethnographic, observational, and participatory, but I also spent time in archives in Roma and Morija, and conducted ecological surveys in Mokhotlong. I did field research alone primarily, except for the January 2019 trip, when I collaborated with Meredith Root-Bernstein and hired Sefiri Seepheephe as a research assistant. We were also periodically assisted by Tšepo Selomo on that trip. I hired Moretloa Polaki to assist with botanical surveys in 2014 and 2016. The interviews and conversations were all conducted in Sesotho unless the people I spoke with preferred English.

44. On "interpellation," see Althusser (1971).

45. I use the somewhat awkward term *conservation bureaucrat* to refer to any person who works in conservation, whether for nonprofit organizations or consultancies (domestic and foreign), government ministries, or the Lesotho Highlands Water Project. I prefer the term to *conservation official*, which connotes state authority, as well as to *conservation worker*, which to my mind does not adequately capture the fundamentally bureaucratic nature of these various conservation activities.

46. The Sesotho term *motebong* is translated as "cattle post" in vernacular English, and I retain that translation here. Yet, all types of livestock are kept there and the Sesotho term does not reference cattle.

47. Stoler (2013).

48. On the affect and materiality of water, see Bachelard (1983); Neimanis (2017); Illich (1985); Raffles (2002).

49. Many but by no means all of these people were men. This is because of the gender composition of these industries, but also because of my own gender position as a man. This shapes much of what I say in the pages below.

50. The crisis of infrastructural breakdown is a crisis of interpretation. Relatedly, Atsuro Morita (2017) has shown that it is precisely in moments of infrastructural collapse that multispecies relations become evident. Thank you to Pierre du Plessis for pointing this out to me. Stefan Helmreich (2011) has also shown, however, that water can operate as a "theory machine" for understanding social life.

51. Also see Raffles (2002) on his concept of "fluvial intimacy" and its inspiration from Gaston Bachelard's (1983) work. In the case of "fluvial imagination" and "fluvial economy," which I develop here, I'm hoping to leverage and sharpen Raffles's interest in the historicity of human engagements with water (as opposed to Bachelard's pursuit of an essential water—one that he describes as "matter" prior to "form") by putting even greater emphasis on the political economic contexts of fluvial thinking and action. In this, I am in dialogue with scholars writing in critical physical geography, including socio-geomorphology. See the important work of Lave, Biermann, and Lane (2018); Lave (2012); Ashmore (2015); Blue and Brierley (2016); and Wilcock, Brierley, and Howitt (2013).

52. In this, I am excluding the sale of bottled water such as luxury mineral waters, such as Perrier, Evian, and others. For an economist's take on the history and likelihood of water export ventures, see Dore (2005).

53. Williams (2005).

54. Tsing (2000, 338).

55. Grove (1996).

56. This might also be thought of in terms of capitalism's impairment of the "conditions of production" (Polanyi [1944]), or what O'Connor (1988) described as the second contradiction of capital.

57. Gay (1984).

58. Appel (2019); Tsing (2009, 2015).

59. Showers (2005:1).

60. See Driver (1999); Showers (2005; 2006); Büscher (2013).

61. Ferguson (1994).

62. Chakela (1981); Showers (2005).

63. Hirst (1995); Khaba and Griffiths (2017); see chapter 2.

64. The wetlands include both bogs and fens, meaning that some are primarily fed by rainfall (bogs) while others are fed by both groundwater and runoff (fens).

65. Preez and Brown (2011); van Zinderen-Bakker and Werger (1974); Jacot-Guillarmod (1962); Chatanga and Sieben (2019); Chatanga and Seleteng-Kose (2021).

66. The notion that the wetlands act as "sponges" is a metaphor not uncommon to Southern African conservation. As William Beinart (1984, 56) points out, forestry scientists such as F.E. Kanthack in the Cape in the first decades of the twentieth century asserted

the importance of forests as sponges that can retain precipitation in the soil and slowly release it. The botanist Amy Jacot-Guillarmod (1962) also referred to Lesotho's wetlands as "sponges."

67. At an earlier stage, the project was called, "Protection of the Orange-Senqu Water Sources—SPONGE—Project."

68. The firm's website (GOPA [n.d.]) states the following: "Despite the importance of the high mountain wetlands as local and regional water source, they continue to be degraded, mainly because of uncontrolled livestock grazing and trampling, infrastructure development, siltation and erosion, encroachment by cultivation and overexploitation of resources."

69. Marneweck and Grundling (1999). A report prepared for the Millennium Challenge Account's National Wetlands Conservation Strategy found that wetlands account for some 22 percent of GDP and 30 percent of total employment either directly or indirectly (Mott MacDonald 2013), a finding of questionable value given the ambiguities surrounding such a calculation, except in testifying to anxieties about the problem.

70. Mokotjomela, Schwaibold, and Pillay (2009); Nüsser and Grab (2002); Grab and Deschamps (2004).

71. GOPA (n.d.); ORASECOM and Lesotho Department of Water Affairs (2018).

72. Here, I am indebted to Antina von Schnitzler's (2016) work on the South African state's pedagogical efforts to cultivate a neoliberal water sensibility among its citizens.

73. Very sensibly, environmental conservation of the wetlands often leverages this geopolitics and the economic logics of GDP. See the political ecologist Bram Büscher's (2013) work for a discussion of a transfrontier conservation area between Lesotho and South Africa, justified on such grounds. Also see Chatanga and Sieben (2019) or Chatanga and Seleteng-Kose (2021) for examples from ecology.

74. Unsurprisingly, there is also disagreement among scientists as to the rates of soil erosion in any given context, as well as to its causes and cures. See Blaikie (1985); Trimble and Crosson (2000); Stocking (1995); Kiage (2013).

75. The highlands at that time were sites of profound anxiety for colonists as well as African groups fearful of cattle raids that were launched from the highlands especially by San people living there. See King (2019).

76. Here, I'm inspired by Ogden (2011); Tsing (2015); Caple (2017).

77. See Lave, Biermann, and Lane (2018); Tsing et al. (2016); Hoag and Svenning (2017); Caple (2017); Plessis (2022).

78. See the debate about whether there is "ecology" in "political ecology," catalyzed by Vayda and Walters (1999); cf. Walker (2005). On the problems of sociobiology (and its cousins), see Sahlins (1976).

79. Behnke, Scoones, and Kerven (1993); Showers (2005); Fairhead and Leach (1996); Mavhunga (2014).

80. Tsing (2015); Mathews (2018); Caple (2017); Raffles (2002); Plessis (2022).

81. Tsing (2015); Caple (2017).

82. See Hoag (forthcoming) for an elaboration on this point. On the "laws" of ecology, see Lawton (1999); Linquist et al. (2016). Here, I'm also inspired by the geomorphologist Peter Ashmore's (2015) call for "sociogeomorphology" that could account for the contingent and historical factors that affect river morphology.

83. Tsing (2015); Mathews (2018); Tsing, Mathews, and Bubandt (2019); Caple (2017); Swanson (2017); Choy et al. (2009). I envision this as a way of building "alliances with our

disciplinary rivals" to advance a "kinky empiricism," as Danilyn Rutherford (2018, 163–64) puts it.

84. Malhi (2017); Waters et al. (2016); Davis, Faurby, and Svenning (2018).

85. See Caple (2017) for an important statement of this point.

86. On the challenges posed by critique, see Latour (2004).

87. Satsuka (2015); Ballestero (2019b); Morton (2017); Moore (2019); Petryna (2018); Messeri (2016); Stoetzer (2018); Haraway (1989, 2008).

88. See Fuentes (2010) and Hoag (forthcoming) for more on this subject.

89. Crucially, this graduate work was supported by Jens-Christian Svenning and the Aarhus University Research on the Anthropocene (AURA) project, led by Anna Tsing and Nils Bubandt.

90. See Stoler (2009) and King (2019) on the anxieties of colonial states. On those of White settler colonists in Africa, see Hughes (2010).

91. Blaikie (1985).

92. Many thanks to Andrea Ballestero for drawing my attention to this.

1. WATER PRODUCTION

1. Mokuku (2004, 106).

2. The LHWP Treaty established several parastatal bodies. The LHDA builds and maintains the project within the country of Lesotho, whereas the Trans-Caledon Tunnel Authority (TCTA) builds and maintains project infrastructure within South Africa. The Lesotho Highlands Water Commission (LHWC) is a bilateral body with Lesotho and South African government representation that oversees the Treaty implementation as a whole. For ease of reference, I gloss these institutional differences as "the LHWP" wherever reasonably possible.

3. Hoag (2014b).

4. LHDA (2014) and LHDA (n.d.b).

5. Government of Lesotho (n.d.b).

6. Bond (2002); Bakker (2003); Schnitzler (2016).

7. See Ballestero (2019b).

8. Mauss (2016, 58); Orlove and Caton (2010); see also Strang (2004).

9. In this, it is like other "recalcitrant commodities" (see chapter 5), such as African cattle (Ferguson [1994]; Comaroff and Comaroff [1990]); intimacy (Constable [2009]); the body (Sharp [2000]); or land, labor, and money (Polanyi [1944]). But see Ballestero (2019b) and Andersen (2019) on why a commons/commodity binary is sometimes insufficient to describe the variety of possibilities and limitations presented by a given water law.

10. Linton (2010).

11. Bond (2002); Ruiters and McDonald (2004); Schnitzler (2016).

12. See Mukwada (2022); Niang et al. (2014).

13. Ferguson (2006). See Folch (2019) for a resonant case in Paraguay, but focused on hydroelectricity rather than water export. As Rutherford (2012) points out, however, sovereignty is always contingent upon relationships of interdependence, audience, and recognition.

14. Schnitzler (2016); see also Ballestero (2019b).

15. King (2019).

16. A "catchment" or "watershed" refers to the geographic space defined by a river basin into which water drains. "Watershed management" is a practice of using this geographic unit as the basis for land-use decisions. In doing so, it emphasizes the interconnection between various parts of the watershed, but also eliminates attention to factors outside the watershed that might impact what happens inside. See Blaikie (1985) for an understanding of this problem. For a critical review of watershed management and its origins, see Schmidt (2017).

17. This is true for ordinary conversation, though geographers typically describe four regions: the highlands, the lowlands, the foothills, and the Senqu Valley.

18. Though much flatter and lower in elevation than the highlands, the lowlands are actually quite high, being an extension of the South African Highveld plateau. As bioregions, Rutherford, Mucina, and Powrie (2006) define the highlands and the lowlands respectively as "Drakensberg grassland" and "mesic highveld grassland." Lesotho famously has the highest low-point of any country, never dropping below a thousand meters above sea level.

19. See Knight and Grab (2015) for a fantastic overview of the geological and geomorphological processes that shaped these mountain chains, including the processes' legacy in contemporary landscapes and the importance of highlands conservation.

20. On the debated historiography of the so-called *Mfecane* or "time of troubles" (Sesotho, *lifaqane*), see Hamilton (1995).

21. Moodie (1975); Etherington (2001).

22. The missionaries codified the Sesotho language in grammars, advised Basotho on diplomatic matters, and documented their cultural practices in ethnographic monographs and histories (Casalis [1965 (1861)]; Ellenberger [1912])—while also seeking to eliminate cultural practices they deemed antithetical to Christian teaching.

23. Correspondence chronicled in Germond (1967, 459). Also see Murray (1981).

24. Eldredge (1993); Mothibe and Ntabeni (2002).

25. See Lelimo (1998); Coplan (2000, 2001).

26. Murray (1981); Maloka (2004).

27. Sanders (2010).

28. The action helped ensure Basutoland would not be later incorporated into the Union of South Africa, preserving its enclave status into the future. Basutoland was a protectorate of the British Crown, like Swaziland (now eSwatini) and Bechuanaland (now Botswana). The Cape Colony was also a holding of the British Crown. Though it was "owned" by the British Crown, the Cape was technically a separate political entity. The Crown had in fact given the Cape Colony charge of Basutoland in 1871, but the Cape returned it to the Crown after the Gun War. Had Basutoland been administered by the Cape Colony in 1910 when South Africa's four territories (Cape, Orange Free State, Natal, Transvaal) became unified, Basutoland may have become a Union province.

29. The Cape Colony first imposed this tax, but it was later doubled after Basutoland was restored as a holding of the British Crown. See Kimble (1999, 50); see also Maloka (2004). For a fantastic and comprehensive account of foreign efforts to undermine commerce in Basutoland and Lesotho (and Basotho efforts to succeed in spite of them), see Maliehe (2021).

30. Chiefs would later be drawn upon for tax collection by the British through the system of "indirect rule," ensuring that even people living in rural areas would need to work in the mines. See Kimble (1999, 28).

31. This is sometimes referred to as the Stallard Doctrine. See Evans (1997), Swanson (1968), and Davenport (1969).

32. Wolpe (1972); see also Magubane (1979), Murray (1981) and Mbembe (2008) for related accounts.

33. Marx (1990).

34. Murray (1981).

35. See Ferguson (2006, 2015).

36. Mensah and Naidoo (2011, 1021); Crush et al. (2021, 130).

37. Crush et al. (2010, 12).

38. Crush et al. (2017, 10). Since then the total number of Basotho mineworkers on contract in South African mines has dropped by more than half. There were 54,749 mineworkers from Lesotho on contract in South Africa in 2003, gradually dropping to 19,410 in 2018 according to data in Crush et al. (2021, 130). Those data show similar declines for other countries in the region.

39. Because of an increase in wages for workers with one of those rare mining jobs, Lesotho continues to have one of the highest remittance rates in the world (29 percent) as a percentage of GDP (Mohapatra, Ratha, and Silwal [2011]). But a smaller number of families are receiving remittances, meaning that the distribution of wealth in Lesotho has grown starker, particularly in rural areas. After independence, the Gini coefficient, used to describe national wealth inequality on a scale from 0 (completely equal) to 1 (completely unequal), rose from 0.23 in rural areas in 1967/69 to 0.55 in rural areas in 1993 (World Bank [1995]). These numbers have improved somewhat, with the coefficient across the country falling to 0.40–0.45 by 2017 thanks to improved social safety nets (World Bank [2019]). Crushing rates of unemployment persist, however, with rates of 56.3 percent in rural areas and 36.8 percent in urban areas according to the Lesotho Bureau of Statistics (2016).

40. Bond and Ndlovu (2010). The government of Lesotho (LMS [2017]) reports that water is the country's largest source of non-tax revenue. Receipts from water constitute some 10 percent of non-tax government revenues according to OECD (2021) data. Royalties are calculated by reference to a Water Royalties Manual that accompanied the 1986 Treaty as an appendix. The formula for calculation takes account of the amount that would have been paid to construct a separate water transfer scheme sited in the Free State Province of South Africa, which would have involved a pump transfer up from the lower elevation areas.

41. LHDA (2021). Between the fiscal years 2014–15 and 2018–19, the project brought in around 700–900 million Maloti per year (LHDA [2019, 29]).

42. Hoover (2001); Thamae and Pottinger (2006); Sello (2020). Corruption dogged the first phase of the project. In 2002, a lawsuit was successfully brought against a number of contractors from France, Canada, and Germany, finding them guilty of bribery, and leading to the imprisonment of the former CEO of the LHDA, Masupha Sole. Sole was released from prison just after the agreement between South Africa and Lesotho was reached for Phase II, and he was hired as a high-ranking technical advisor to the Lesotho Highlands Water Commission, an extremely powerful position in the organizational hierarchy Tlali [2012]).

43. Rosenberg (2004, 176–77).

44. Hoover (2001); Lundahl and Petersson (1991).

45. Bond (2002); Thamae and Pottinger (2006); Hitchcock (2015).

46. The reservoir from Katse Dam inundated 925 ha of arable cropland and 3,000 ha of grazing land. Lesotho has an estimated 300,000 ha of arable land, or somewhere between

10 and 13 percent of its total land area. See Lundahl, McCarthy, and Petersson (2003, 104); Mokuku (2004).

47. See Sello (2020); Hoover (2001); Thamae and Pottinger (2006); Hitchcock (2015); Braun (2010, 2020).

48. See Bond and Ndlovu (2010); Bond (2002); Ruiters and McDonald (2004); Schnitzler (2016). Securing Lesotho's water has dovetailed with a service privatization agenda in South Africa, as those authors show, and partly triggered the widespread "service delivery protests" that took place across South Africa over the past decade.

49. Technically, the municipal water board that provisions Gauteng, Rand Water, purchases the water from the Trans-Caledon Tunnel Authority (TCTA), the body that finances LHWP construction from the South Africa side. (Lesotho and South Africa were responsible for separate components of the LHWP, according to the treaty.) One senior LHWP official explained to me that, because Lesotho's water has such a high purity quality, it is useful for residential consumption but rather expensive. Farmers do not need such a degree of purity and elect for cheaper water where possible, for example. But many industrial consumers in Gauteng such as mining companies require high purity, and they opt for Vaal Reservoir water (40 percent of which comes from Lesotho) despite its high costs.

50. GreenCape (2017). Also see Gauteng City Region Observatory (2019).

51. LHDA (2014).

52. In such an arrangement, water passes through turbines to generate electricity during peak usage hours when rates are high, and is pumped back up to the storage reservoir during low-usage hours when rates are low.

53. For example, see Smith (2010).

54. Ntaote (2010); see Caromba (2017).

55. Most Basotho I spoke with, however, are conflicted, desiring access to South African jobs but reticent about other aspects, including legalized abortion, South African criminal syndicates, or private land ownership.

56. The undermining of Lesotho's economic policy has created political instability that affects South Africa, too. Without the ability to propose distinct visions for Lesotho's economy, Lesotho's electoral democracy has become dominated by a politics of charisma, with parties fracturing into ever-smaller units headed by a politician with a following (Fogelman [2017]). On the specter of "development" in Lesotho's post-independence period, see Ferguson (1994) and Aerni-Flessner (2018). On the undermining of Basotho commerce, see Maliehe (2021).

57. Johnston (1996); see also Cobbe (1980).

58. Aerni-Flessner (n.d.) shows how the issue of Lesotho's sovereignty and its boundaries was very much in play throughout the planning and negotiations for a water project in or adjacent to Lesotho.

59. Goodspeed (1988).

60. As cited in McAuslan (1987, 46–47).

61. Moshoeshoe II (1988). This reputation for water abundance endures. More recently, after a 2015 memorandum of understanding was signed to explore the feasibility of water transfer from Lesotho to Botswana, that country's minister of mineral, energy and water resources, Onkodame Kitso Mokaila, was quoted as saying, "You can put a dam anywhere in the country and you will get water" (African News Agency [2018]).

62. Government of Lesotho (n.d.a).

63. LHWP (1981, Section 4-4).

64. See Alatout (2009), who shows how abundance is neglected in literature on resource conflict and how it can be mobilized politically.

65. For example, a conservation bureaucrat told me of a rumor he'd heard that the United States and Chinese were becoming interested in an effort to export water somehow from Lesotho to their countries. On rumor and fantasy in the production of mining and oil, see Tsing (2005); Coronil (1997); Taussig (1997).

66. Mokuku (2004, 105).

67. Maloti-Drakensberg Transfrontier Project (n.d., 5). See Büscher (2013). These rainfall figures are contested, with estimates in peer-reviewed literature ranging from 750mm per annum (Nel and Sumner [2008]) to 1600mm per annum (Sene et al. [1998]).

68. See Kamara et al. (2019); Nel and Sumner (2008); Sene et al. (1998); Nash and Grab (2010).

69. The Katse Reservoir level dropped extremely close to minimum operating levels in 2017 (Molapo [2018]). In 2020, Mohale dipped to 4 percent of its operating level and Katse to 25 percent, based on data posted on the website of the South African Department of Water and Sanitation: www.dwa.gov.za/Hydrology/Weekly/ProvinceWeek.aspx?region=L (accessed April 13, 2022).

70. Thamae and Pottinger (2006); Mokhethi and Kabi (2021).

71. Thamae and Pottinger (2006).

72. Bell and Haskins (1997).

73. Lesotho Bureau of Statistics (2013b, 12). According to WaterAid (Burgess 2016), 18.2 percent of Lesotho's population lacks access to safe water.

74. Workman (2013).

75. *Mahlopha-a-senya* are things that do good and evil at the same time. "A gift that destroys" is the translation that I was given most commonly, but a literal translation might be rendered as, "Things that [or people who] adorn something with beautiful things while at the same time destroying [or ruining] them." I've heard the proverb stated alternatively as *Pula ke mahlopha-a-senya*, or "Rain is a gift that destroys."

76. *Pula ea sekhoohola* is another term for this type of thunderstorm.

77. Also see Mukwada (2022).

78. I thank the Lesotho Meteorological Society staff for these figures and insights. Also see Nash and Grab (2010), which analyzes drought occurrence during the period 1824–1900. The authors show that single-year and multi-year drought was a regular occurrence—sometimes overlapping with ENSO events—at decadal or shorter time-scales.

79. Tsing (2005).

80. See Schmidt (2017); Ballestero (2019a, 2019b).

81. See Ballestero (2019a) and Helmreich (2007, 2011, 2014) for insight into water modalities and categories.

82. Kabi (2017).

2. THE SOIL PROBLEM

1. McCully (2001, 107).

2. Showers (2005).

3. I thank Elisa Kim for bringing volumetric thinking to my attention.

4. Keck and Lakoff (2013); Lakoff (2016).

5. This is also how the 'Muela Dam is described in project literature. It has two stated purposes: "to balance transfer flows through the hydropower station [and] to provide the required tailwater levels and head for transfer through the delivery tunnel to South Africa" (Arthur, Wagner, and Hein [1997, 48]).

6. On ethnogeomorphology and sociogeomorphology, see Wilcock Brierley, and Howitt (2013); and Ashmore (2015).

7. For example, see Jacks and Whyte (1939).

8. For example, see Carlson (1913).

9. See Driver (1999).

10. See Holleman (2018) and Lyons (2020) for important work on the way soil science expertise travels to rural areas.

11. Beinart (1989); Dodson (2005); Rocheleau, Steinberg, and Benjamin (1995). See also Zee (2017) for a similar case in China. For authoritative recent accounts of the racial, colonial, and economic influences on dryland and rangeland science, see Davis (2016); Sayre (2017).

12. See Etherington (2001) on the problems of "Great Trek" historiography.

13. Interestingly, it was not the first time that an equivalence between good rainfall and moral rectitude had been established in Lesotho, but this time the order had been reversed. Scottish missionaries who visited the Lesotho highlands in the late nineteenth century were rapt by the lush landscapes of the high Drakensberg in northern Lesotho, envisioning desiccated landscapes elsewhere in Southern Africa as examples of the punishment meted by God upon godless people (Grove [1989]).

14. Driver (1999); Thabane (2006); Jacks and Whyte (1939, 274).

15. Pim (1935, 5). Pim's report made three key recommendations, which went into effect almost immediately and which organize the next three chapters of this book: the institution of soil conservation programs (chapter 3); a reduction in the number of chiefs (chapter 4); and the construction of bridle paths to link highlands wool production with lowland markets (chapter 5).

16. As quoted in Jacks and Whyte (1939, 21).

17. Jacks and Whyte (1939, 249).

18. See Dodson (2005) on Bennett's tour of Southern Africa. On his role in the U.S. Dust Bowl crisis, see Holleman (2018). Bennett was a key player in the horrific stock reduction program in Diné territory, partly motivated by fears of dam reservoir sedimentation as described by Richard White (1983; also see Weisiger [2011]).

19. Nobe and Seckler (1979); Showers (2005).

20. McCully (2001); World Commission on Dams (2000). The capture of sediment also has consequences in the downstream catchment, where mineral and organic materials sustain ecosystem function.

21. See Driver (1999).

22. Schmitz and Rooyani (1987). See Showers (2005).

23. Schmitz and Rooyani (1987, 126).

24. E.g., Jehanno et al. (1987).

25. Nobe and Seckler (1979, 56).

26. Schmitz and Rooyani (1987, 98).

27. Knight and Grab (2021).

28. Bell and Haskins (1997).

29. Chakela, Molapo, and Putsoane (1989, 2).

30. Chakela and Stocking (1988, 187). Makara's (2013) analysis of the Phase 2 Polihali Dam catchment draws a similar conclusion.

31. Chakela (1981, 144).

32. LHDA (1981, 5, § 6.2.5).

33. My repeated efforts to acquire internal materials from the LHDA were unsuccessful.

34. Smith et al. (2000).

35. Chakela, Molapo, and Putsoane (1989).

36. Kirsch (2014); Li (2009).

37. Jehanno et al. (1987).

38. Hirst (1995).

39. Hirst (1995, 1).

40. Hirst (1995, 2).

41. Hirst (1995, 6).

42. Hirst (1995, 6).

43. As Scott (1998) and others (e.g., Mathews [2011], Mosse [2005]) have shown, the strategic ignorance of complexity is often leveraged by powerful institutions, even thought it might have serious consequences. See Whitington (2019) for an analogous case in the "production of uncertainty" surrounding environmental sustainability in Lao hydropower operations.

44. Hirst (1995); Hitchcock et al. (2011); Makara (2013); Smith et al. (2000); Horta (1995).

45. Smith et al. (2000, 64). The same rush to construction might take place with Phase 2's Polihali Dam. 'Mamabitsa Makara (2013) concluded that, while sediment loads in the upper Senqu River catchment are lower than in its other major tributaries within Lesotho, such as the Makhaleng and Caledon Rivers, the high erosivity factors in the upper Senqu in Mokhotlong District lead more often to landslides. Makara states that "dramatic measures" (2013, 40) must be taken to remedy the situation, and that the Polihali Dam is likely to silt up before its sister dams at Katse and Mohale. Makara's soil loss estimates were derived by using the Revised Universal Soil Loss Equation (RUSLE) and generally agree with observed estimates from sediment stations. They show a significant increase in overall sediment loads for Lesotho from 1986 to 2009 (Makara [2013, v]). This is also remarkable given that the RUSLE is a fundamentally uniformitarian conception of soil loss, presuming even and steady soil losses across the landscape without accounting for the impact of the major rainfall events that cause most of the soil erosion. In Lesotho, such storms are common, as I've noted.

46. World Commission on Dams (2000, 75, 139).

47. Scudder (2006); World Commission on Dams (2000); Khagram (2004); Isaacman and Isaacman (2013).

48. According to an LHDA water engineer with whom I spoke, the sediment found there mostly derives from the 'Muela catchment, but that water transferred from Katse does sometimes have a fair amount of sediment in it when there are heavy rains. The passage of water with that level of turbidity through the water turbines, he said, does not affect hydropower generation.

49. ICM is a variation on Integrated Water Resources Management (IWRM), a globalized water paradigm whose assumptions and intellectual history are outlined in depth by Jeremy Schmidt (2017). See also Mehta, Derman, and Manzungu (2017) for a look at how IWRM has been taken up in Eastern and Southern Africa.

50. Schnitzler (2016). On the pedagogy of natural resource stewardship also see Carse (2015) and Mrázek (2002). On national pedagogy more broadly see Bhabha (1990).

51. Driver (1999); Beinart (2008).

52. In the literature and in conversations with conservation bureaucrats, pastures are said to recover from *C. ciliata* infestation soon after they have been rested, with the desirable forage grass, *Themeda triandra* outcompeting the shrubs for resources. The literature sometimes cites colonial experiments at Thaba-Putsoa and Thaba-Tšoeu that indicated a return to *T. triandra* could be achieved by simple exclosure and rotational grazing. A colonial report, for example, reports that this transition was achieved in just twelve years at Thaba-Putsoa, an area that was previously "covered with *Chrysocoma*" (Basutoland [1948, 44]). See also Jacot-Guillarmod (1971, 45). Establishing exclusion plots is extremely difficult in Lesotho because of fierce commitments to common rangeland use (e.g., see Ferguson [1994]). These shrubs have allelopathic properties (Squires and Trollope [1979]) that aid its survival and spread, and they can cause fatal illness in lambs (Van der Vyver et al. [1985]).

53. Many of the dwarf shrubs that are linked to overgrazing in Lesotho, including *Chrysocoma ciliata*, are sometimes described as invasive, when in fact they are encroaching. This means that they are native to the landscape, but have expanded their range and/or population size. See Fitchett et al. (2017). See chapter 6 for more on that history.

54. See Hoag (forthcoming) for a deeper look at the ecology and significations of the dwarf shrub.

55. Basutoland (1948, 16).

56. Convention on Biological Diversity (1995, 6).

57. LHDA (1981, 2–3 to 2–4). Also see Jacot-Guillarmod (1971, 45).

58. Hoag and Svenning (n.d.). Exclusion plots, which would help show whether shrubs increase with grazing, are very difficult to establish in Lesotho. One of the few places where such an exclusion plot exists is the Letšeng Diamond Mine. The fenceline features a grass-dominated pasture on the inside and a shrub-dominated one on the other. Though no work has been done to assess differences in sediment transport inside and outside the fenced area, it is quite clear from that site that shrubs respond positively to grazing.

59. See West (2006) on the convergence of these two industries. Also see Moore (2019); Hughes (2006).

60. After all, state officials do not stand in direct and unambiguous opposition to "the public." For example, see Li (2007); Lyons (2020); Anders (2010); Ballestero (2019b).

61. Hummocks, sometimes called *thúfur*, are small, undulating mounds that form in wetlands through frost heave.

62. See Ballestero (2019b) and Schnitzler (2016) for examples of other such devices.

63. Thank you to Nikhil Anand for sharpening this point for me.

64. On the downstream impacts of dams, see McCully (2001); Syvitski et al. (2009); Showers (2009).

65. Anand (2017).

3. THE SOIL SOLUTION

1. That erosion control measures would encourage rather than prevent erosion should not surprise us, given Kate Showers's (2005) work showing exactly that.

2. See Anand (2017) for a similar case in India.

3. Mokuku (2004, 14).

4. Jacks and Whyte (1939); Chakela, Molapo, and Putsoane (1989).

5. Hitchcock et al. (2011).

6. Colin Murray (1981, 19) explained that "the history of development projects in Lesotho is one of almost unremitting failure to achieve their objectives." Also see Ferguson (1994).

7. Lesotho Bureau of Statistics (2013a, 4).

8. Tennyson (2012). See Baviskar (2004) for similar work programs in another former British colony.

9. On the role of humor, the state, and civil society, see the review by Petrovic (2018); also see Obadare (2016).

10. Weber (1978); e.g., Médard (1982); Chabal and Daloz (1999).

11. On the politics of distribution, see Ferguson (2015) and Anand (2017).

12. See Mosse (2003, 2013); Ferguson (1994); Li (2007).

13. Carse (2015).

14. Gramsci (1971); see also Chu (2014).

15. LHDA (n.d.a); see "Table 3.2, Summary of Environmental Issues."

16. Hitchcock et al. (2011).

17. The final stop was the "tail" of the reservoir, the pile of sediment at the reservoir's mouth that Tau pointed out to me five years earlier. They left it for last for effect. Both lamented the size of the pile of sediment, and indeed it was quite a bit larger than when I saw it in 2014. Not only was it advancing farther downstream, but the amount of sediment above the water seemed higher and flush with grass. It was even supporting a robust community of birds and insects and grasses. One conservation bureaucrat said that "this part of the dam is almost useless." They said that four years ago when they first came here, this was merely a brown mass underneath the water.

18. Lesotho has one of the highest prevalence rates of HIV in the world. See Block and McGrath (2019) and Kenworthy (2017) for ethnographic accounts of the epidemic and its treatment in Lesotho.

19. Khaketla (1972); Coplan and Quinlan (1997). See also Aerni-Flessner (2018) for a fantastic narrative of political dynamics in Lesotho across the colonial and postcolonial periods.

20. Aerni-Flessner (2018) shows that the idea of "independence" was closely entwined with the idea of "development."

21. See Khaketla (1972).

22. Khaketla (1972, 28).

23. See Aerni-Flessner (2018).

24. Basutoland (1900–1901, 18).

25. Basutoland (1933, 20).

26. See Aerni-Flessner (2018).

27. For example, *Molia* 2 (103) (Government of Lesotho [1970a]) and 2 (119) (Government of Lesotho [1970b]).

28. Again, see Aerni-Flessner (2018). The development industry has long followed this logic, as described by Ferguson (1994, 2015).

29. Aerni-Flessner (2018).

30. Ferguson (1994).

31. Nobe and Seckler (1979, 86).

32. Nobe and Seckler (1979, 101).

33. Nobe and Seckler (1979, 143).

34. This is how the former BCP politician Ntsukunyane Mphanya described them to me in a 2014 interview.

35. Mphanya (2009).

36. One example of this involves the Lesotho Woodlots Project, a tree-planting initiative in which eucalyptus, poplar, and black wattle trees were planted in small, conspicuous woodlots across the country. Driving with a friend named Ntšoeu in 2014, I asked about the stands of eucalyptus I had long noticed at the base of Moteng Pass. He told me they were most definitely "Leabua plantations," based on the age and size of the trees. Ntšoeu went on to explain that, in the early days of Leabua Jonathan's administration, an incredible number of poplars and other trees were planted along the main highway linking Maseru to Butha-Buthe (the A1). Jonathan had hoped for the highway to resemble a tree-lined boulevard one might find in Europe. Many of these trees are still standing today, he said, but only in small patches. Some of the trees had been felled over the years to widen the road, but in some cases the gaps are due to BCP activism. In those areas where there was strong BCP support, many of the trees were uprooted, so that the places that trees line the road are BNP strongholds. The landscape was scrawled with political statements and histories. Ntšoeu was a member of the All Basotho Convention party, which drew much support at the time from the BNP wing, and our drive took place on a Sunday, when political parties often hold rallies. When we passed by people wearing the yellow colors of that party, Ntšoeu would open his window and yell out in solidarity. Incidentally, the three places this happened were all tree-lined. See Ferguson (1994) for other examples of "development" project vandalism during Jonathan's time in power. On afforestation programs during the colonial period, see Showers (2006).

37. Lundahl and Petersson (1991, 364–65).

38. Monyane (2005); Rosenberg (2004). See Ferguson (1994) for an analogous situation involving the BNP and a Canadian development project.

39. World Bank (1991). Yet another fund was created with the rollout of Phase 1B, the Phase which included the construction of Mohale Dam. This fund, called the Community Development Support Project (CDSP), would be out of reach of the politicians. Its goal was, "to put in place the physical and managerial capacity for Lesotho to transform its principal natural resource of abundance—water—into export revenues that can be applied to poverty reduction and economic stability" (World Bank [2010, x]). But the World Bank's assessment of the CDSP's success was stark: "[W]hile LHWP-1B generated revenues that could have been used for poverty alleviation, CDSP's fund failed to use those royalties for this purpose" (World Bank [2010, ix–x]).

40. Monyane (2005); Pule (1999).

41. Across Southern Africa, land improvement schemes were implemented in the early twentieth century (Beinart [1984, 1989]), partly in response to concerns about the effects of the migration economy on the African family. Because migrants could not migrate with

their families, these conservationists worried that migrants would have no opportunities to make a living "back home" in the native reserves.

42. American Rivers, Friends of the Earth, and Trout Unlimited (1999).

43. The LHDA also seeks narrowness with respect to other potentially unruly concepts, such as kinship. One LHDA official raised the issue of compensation to heirs (*mojalefa*) and sought to define rather narrowly, according to the terms of private property and the LHDA policy, what constituted a "family." Understanding that the issue could be contentious and the importance of establishing the LHDA's definition, he repeated multiple times the phrase *Leloko ha se lelapa* ("Custom is not family"). Fluvial theory is social theory: like *fato-fato*, the assertion of these kinship temporalities subtends water production, tying up its loose ends.

4. BUREAUCRATIC ECOLOGY

1. It shows that ecologies are not closed systems but rather open-ended ones with variable stability, open not only to material effects but to semiosis (Kohn [2013]).

2. Holechek, Pieper, and Herbel (2011, 1).

3. Rangelands are no longer defined by the presence of livestock, as they once were. Livestock production is nevertheless a very common concern within the field. For a thorough account of the history of rangeland science in the United States, see Sayre (2017).

4. Lynteris (2014); on the related syndrome, "projectitis," see Barnes (2014). Ferguson (1994) described this proliferation of projects in Lesotho in the early 1980s.

5. As a Peace Corps Volunteer from 2003 to 2005, in fact, I was charged with assisting two such cooperatives in the Katse project areas.

6. Lederman (2006).

7. Weber (1978).

8. Arendt (2006); Gupta (2012).

9. In this, I'm inspired by J.K. Gibson-Graham's (2006) writing on the nontotalizing character of capitalism.

10. The picture that emerges in critical scholarly literature on conservation is typically one of power and capability. However, conservation bureaucrats and water engineers are not necessarily skillful and successful at imposing their interpretations or plans upon rural people—their efforts are sometimes haphazard, fragmented, contested, or co-opted (e.g., see Beinart, Brown, and Guilfoyle [2009]; Scott [1998]; Mathews [2011]; Li [2007]). The same was true for the "experts" of the colonial period, as McCracken (1982) shows.

11. See Rohde et al. (2006).

12. Bainbridge, Motsamai, and Weaver (1991); Quinlan (1995); Ferguson (1994, 2006); Nüsser (2002); Rohde et al. (2006). Regarding land use and tenure more broadly, see Pule and Thabane (2004) for a fantastic account of the history of calls for land tenure reform in Lesotho, and Fogelman (2017) and Fogelman and Bassett (2017) for important work on the impacts of recent reforms. See King (2019) for a masterful analysis of the early-colonial manifestation of anxiety surrounding political order and disorder in Lesotho.

13. Ferguson (1994).

14. Here, I am indebted to Elaine Gan (personal communication) for her discussion of technology in this light—as a junkyard of failures rather than an ever-improving domain

of mechanical action. In this, I turn my attention from a retrospective assessment of failed bureaucratic projects to a prospective assessment of their effects on future bureaucratic interventions. On prospection, see Miyazaki (2004); Hoag (2014a).

15. Stoler (2013).

16. Turner (2004, 177).

17. As the literature on the everyday life of the state has shown, state bureaucrats are not cardboard cut-outs. See Bierschenk and Olivier de Sardan (2014); Hull (2012); Chalfin (2010); Hayat (2020); Hoag (2011); and Anders (2010). My intention is not to disparage them righteously by linking their work to imperial projects. In fact, many officials I traveled with were extremely kind and invested in the possibility of improving landscapes and livelihoods through their work. My intention is to describe them well, and to understand how their interventions become sensible to them and others as they work to shape the ways that livestock are grazed.

18. See Behnke, Scoones, and Kerven (1993); Homewood and Rodgers (1984); Sandford (1983). For a discussion of arid lands and their misunderstanding more broadly, see Davis (2016).

19. During my field research the situation at the ministry had been changing dramatically, however. After recruiting a highly qualified rangeland ecologist to manage the ministry, many improvements were being made to draw ecological science into the ministry's policies.

20. In its de-emphasis of overstocking, Savory's program echoed the conclusions of the revisionist work in African rangeland ecology that I described above (sometimes referred to as the "nonequillibrium theory" of rangelands). Otherwise, it bears no similarity.

21. Ashton (1967, 137).

22. Though they are known in vernacular English as "cattle posts," in fact all types of livestock are kept there and the Sesotho term *motebong* does not reference cattle. I keep the vernacular translation here.

23. Notions of overgrazing or undergrazing are often linked in conservation imagination to the concept of "carrying capacity"—the notion that a specific area of land can support a specific number of livestock. This concept is often misapplied in African contexts, where interannual rainfall variability (the "coefficient of variation," or CV) is so high that assigning a set capacity for a pasture is nearly impossible. Such rangelands are known as "nonequilibrium" systems, as opposed to those in more predictable, temperate climates where "equilibrium" systems predominate. Livestock owners in nonequilibrium systems are aware of this, so they see little point in devising an "ideal herd size" and instead work to produce a large herd, even though it may suffer significant losses during years of poor rainfall. It can be difficult to discern the effect of livestock grazing on these non-equilibrium pastures (Homewood and Rodgers [1984]; Behnke, Scoones, and Kerven [1993]; Vetter [2005]). This does not mean that livestock do not impact the range, but rather that their effects can be secondary to climate effects—and that the number of animals that an area of land can support varies dramatically from year to year. The question of whether Lesotho's highland pastures are equilibrium or non-equilibrium is unresolved because of a lack of rangeland ecological science done there. On one hand, the highlands have a subhumid to humid rainfall regime when measured by mean annual precipitation. On the other, rainfall is highly localized and some weather stations show a high enough CV according to the

33 percent limit specified by Ellis (1995) to delineate them as nonequillibrium systems. Additionally, under Lesotho's high stocking levels, efforts to limit grazing in one area will add stress to another. For example, Nüsser (2002) noted that efforts to protect upper subalpine belt areas in Lesotho predictably led to greater stress on lower subalpine areas. Also see Quinlan and Morris (1994).

24. Savory and Parsons (1980); Savory (1988).

25. Dyksterhuis (1949).

26. This figure aggregates the views from YouTube and the Ted Talk website at the time of writing.

27. Savory does not explain, however, whether the time-series photographs, so compelling in their contrast of brown and green vegetation, are simply images of the dry and the rainy season, or whether drought had been a factor.

28. Bartolome (1989); Painter and Belsky (1993). For a similar case in stream restoration, see Lave (2012). Some of his most vociferous critics from the U.S. Jornada Range Experimental Station in New Mexico, where leading rangeland ecology research is conducted. Savory targeted them in the TED talk presentation when one of the slides he used to represent brown, barren land features the Jornada Range sign at the entrance to the station.

29. Briske et al. (2013); Briske, Bestelmeyer, and Brown (2014); see also Briske et al. (2008); McWilliams (2013); Painter and Belsky (1993); Bartolome (1989).

30. Belsky et al. (1999); Painter and Belsky (1993).

31. See Ferguson (1994); Conz (2019); Rantšo (2000); Johnston (1996); Showers (2005).

32. See Ferguson (1994).

33. Common rangelands are a point of pride in Lesotho. A common refrain I heard in conversations with livestock owners, herders, conservation bureaucrats, and many others was, "In Lesotho, there are no fences, there are no private farms" (*Lesotho mona ha ho na terata, ha ho na polase*). They used it as a key distinction between Lesotho and neighboring South Africa.

34. Later, they would propose and test mobile kraals, which could pen animals in overnight. But nobody would use a mobile kraal unless they could sleep near their animals to protect them from livestock thieves. A mobile rondavel would need to accompany the mobile kraal. Without the portable fencing of these mobile kraals, it is highly unlikely that a poorly paid young herder will actively herd the animals into a tight circle all day, for months on end.

35. Eugene Casalis (1861), for example, one of the earliest French missionaries in Basutoland, described this system of pasture resting in 1861.

36. These factors are variable across time, as seeps dry up seasonally, as forage regrows, as herders are replaced by others, and as weather changes. This heterogeneity of time and space is lost on conservation plans that see rangelands as "bins" of annual forage that are either adequate or inadequate to feed livestock.

37. Thank you to David Kneas for pointing this out to me.

38. See Rohde et al. (2006) for an excellent, though brief history of grazing institutions, including a case study on one such grazing association.

39. Artz (1993, 54). See, also, how grazing associations were rolled out in the 1980s as described by Ferguson (1994). For an analogous example to grazing associations, see "syndicates" in Botswana (Peters [1994]). The colonial administration in Basutoland had also

been interested in cooperative societies, as evidenced by colonial reports from 1948 onward that gave in-depth reports on the activities of cooperatives in the territory, described under dedicated "Cooperatives" sections. The reports describe "spontaneous" development and spread of cooperative societies, which "had almost outrun the supervisory capacity of the Co-operative staff" in the administration (Basutoland [1950, 36]). These primarily included wool and mohair cooperatives, through which farmers pooled their clip to fetch good prices, as well as consumer societies, by which groups would pool cash for the bulk purchase of goods with the purpose of resale. In the case of wool and mohair societies, these increased from three registered co-ops with 211 members in 1948 to eight registered with 1,000 members in 1950. The administration clearly supported these societies, and the development industry would later embrace them wholeheartedly. See Aerni-Flessner (2018) on the rise of cooperatives.

40. It was most likely the Maloti-Drakensberg Transfrontier Project. See Büscher (2013) for a detailed analysis of that project.

41. A pseudonym.

42. Gluckman (1940).

43. See Poulter (1979) and Kapa (2013).

44. As Quinlan and Wallis (2003) explain, "dualism" gives the false impression that these are distinct political formations, when in fact chiefs are legally and practically entangled with the state in many ways. See also Leduka (2007) and Kapa (2013) for analyses of how dualism works on the ground. Coplan and Quinlan's (1997) essay on the subject represents the fullest account of dynamics between the state and the nation as it relates to the chieftaincy and identity.

45. According to the 1993 constitution, executive authority is vested in the king but exercised through a parliamentary government that resembles Britain's. The bicameral legislature features a national assembly with 120 members of parliament and a senate, comprising the 22 principal chiefs and 11 senators appointed by the king.

46. See Mamdani's (1996) classic thesis on the strategic support of state governments in urban areas and traditional authorities in rural areas. But see Coquery-Vidrovitch (1976) for an analysis of the long-standing class conflict within African societies governed by a chieftaincy. Also see Ntsebeza (2006) and Oomen (2005) on the enduring power of chiefs in postapartheid South Africa partly owing to their control over land.

47. See Ranger (1983) on the nature of "traditional authorities." Cf. Gulbrandsen (2012).

48. As Moshoeshoe's son, Masopha, described it in 1872, *matsema* was the "bridle that chiefs kept in their people's mouths" (Kimble [1999, 31]).

49. This can be seen in the colonial administration's enactment of the "Laws of Lerotholi" as government policy in 1903. See Rohde et al. (2006).

50. See Edgar (1987).

51. Pim (1935, 48).

52. See Thabane (2002b).

53. Khaketla (1972).

54. See Khaketla (1972). Bardill and Cobbe (1985, 134) suggests that between six hundred and eight hundred civil servants thought to be BCP sympathizers were sacked in the aftermath of the 1970 coup.

55. See Fogelman (2017) for a fantastic account of the situation.

56. See Ferguson (1994).

57. The BCP government that took over in 1993 embraced elements of communism, and it envisioned *matsema* as an important indigenous institution of community work that had been corrupted during the colonial period. Ntsukunyane Mphanya, an intellectual and formerly a high-ranking BCP politician, saw communal work as a quintessentially Sesotho institution. He hoped to promote community work through cooperatives as he has written about in his 1992 book, *Matsema, Mohloli oa Tsoelopele* (Matsema, the Source of Advancement). Mphanya's *A Brief History of the BCP* (2009) explains that *matsema* and cooperatives were at the heart of struggle over power by the BCP, Lekhotla la Bafo, the British, and chiefs. Lekhotla la Bafo accused chiefs of abusing *matsema*; the British saw *matsema* as being at the heart of land degradation problems, namely because they wanted to stop the cultivation of wheat at the behest of the South African government and also at the request of Pim; and the chiefs were abusing the *matsema* system to profit for themselves. The BCP later saw it as critical to reconstitute communal work through cooperatives. In a 2014 interview with Mphanya, I asked him whether *fato-fato* work parties are part of this communalist legacy (see chapter 3), and he rejected the notion outright, explaining that it represented a false version of communal work. This debate reiterates for me yet again that the *res publica* itself is at stake in the work of soil conservation.

58. Government of Lesotho (2014).

59. See Kapa (2013, 131).

60. Criticism of chiefs dates from the Pim Report in 1935 to the Morse Commission in 1960, and the United Nations in 1965, the British Ministry of Overseas Development in 1967, and the World Bank in 1975 (see Leduka 2007, 94). Lesotho's First Five Year National Development Plan (1970–71 to 1974–75) asserted this, illustrating that the position was not exclusively a foreign one. Chiefs have been obviously opposed to any effort to erode their authority. The Chieftainess M.G. Masupha compared their having to consult an elected council in land allocation to be akin to slavery (Leduka [2007, 102]). See Ntsebeza (2005) for an analogous example in South Africa. See Kapa (2013) for an insightful analysis of these challenges and of the marginalization of chiefs. The term "decentralization" dates to a time before the BCP's efforts in the aftermath of military rule. Ferguson (1994) describes the policy during that time as a means of extending BNP control into the hinterland under the moniker of "local participation," the same rationale that would fuel it in later years. In the case described by Ferguson, it had little to do with the role of chiefs and local government councils, the latter of which had not yet been established. With specific reference to the effects of these changes on grazing administration, see Rohde et al. (2006).

61. For example, see Ferguson (1994); Fogelman and Bassett (2017).

62. Pule and Thabane (2004) explain that there is an "inherent vagueness" in who owns land in Lesotho, but that the repeated calls for reform miss the point that poverty rather than land access primarily determines patterns of land use (e.g., whether a farmer can afford agricultural inputs).

63. As Plessis (2018; also see Peters [1994] and Livingston [2019]) points out, in Botswana the movement of cattle deep into commonly held rangelands facilitated social stratification rather than equity. This situation was exacerbated by colonial rule through the imposition of "grazing syndicates" and borehole digging, as well as during the emergence of the liberal democracy when a beef industry emerged. That is, not all "livestock owners" are equal, and neither are they necessarily "rural pastoralists" (see Little [1985]).

64. See Coplan and Quinlan (1997). This grazing fee was still being discussed by government officials during my research.

65. They are known as the 1992 Range Management and Grazing Control (Amendment) Regulations.

66. Principal chiefs, for example, have repeatedly prevented the state government from raising fines or instituting grazing fees. See Turner (2004).

67. Even in failing to pass, they probably had an impact in rangeland management, heightening farmer reluctance to disclose their true herd size in official counts and confounding any measure that might manage grazing by herd size (Ivy and Turner [1996], as cited in ORASECOM [2008, 27]).

68. See Büscher (2013). Tim Quinlan (1995) points out that such programs end up targeting mostly people with small herds, given that they typically attract those livestock owners who are willing to go to a meeting rather than those who own the bulk of livestock.

69. Turner (2004, 177).

70. United Nations Development Programme (2012, 12).

71. These are attempts at making "marginal gains," as described by Guyer (2004). Also see Hoag, Bertoni, and Bubandt (2018) for a distinct example. See Hetherington (2011) on the ways that rural people practice government by engaging creatively with bureaucratic institutions.

72. Turner (2009).

73. See Ballestero (2020) for an analogous ethnographic examination of meetings as sites where water politics take shape.

74. *The Silo-Lisiu* (2014).

75. Here, I'm inspired by Fogelman's (2016) account of land tenure reform timelines in urban Lesotho.

76. For example, Chabal and Daloz (1999). See Ferguson (2006) and Rohde et al. (2006) for critical commentary.

77. Coquery-Vidrovitch (1976, 247); also see Gulbrandsen (2012); King (2019); Coplan and Quinlan (1997).

5. LIVESTOCK PRODUCTION

1. Pim (1935, 5).

2. Thanks for Nikhil Anand for helping me to clarify this point.

3. Ashton (1967); Ferguson (1994); cf. Turkon (2003).

4. Ferguson (1994).

5. For example, see Orlove and Caton (2010).

6. Ferguson (1994).

7. Tsing (2015); also see Tsing et al. (2016).

8. Kimble (1999).

9. My thanks to Pinky Hota for clarifying this point for me.

10. IFAD (2014).

11. Herskovits (1926).

12. E.g., Evans-Pritchard (1940).

13. Mauss (2016).

14. Comaroff and Comaroff (1990); Ferguson (1994); Hutchinson (1996); Turkon (2003).

15. Ferguson (1994); Hutchinson (1996); also see Gudeman (1986); Murray (1981); Piot (1991).

16. Livingston (2019).

17. Ferguson (1994).

18. Comaroff and Comaroff (1990); Hutchinson (1996); see also Piot (1991).

19. Notable exceptions include West (2012), Chalfin (2004), Tsing (2015), and Appel (2019).

20. Dahl and Hjort (1976); Orlove (1977).

21. But see Conz (2017, 2020a) for important exceptions. Though not on commodification, see Govindrajan (2018) for an important account of the intimate kinship between goats and people in India.

22. See Appadurai (1986).

23. Marx (1990, 163).

24. Gifford-Gonzalez and Hanotte (2011).

25. Gifford-Gonzalez and Hanotte (2011).

26. Beinart (2008).

27. Beinart (2008, 9).

28. King (2019); Conz (2017); King and Challis (2017); Mitchell and Challis (2008); Boshoff and Kerley (2013); Dowson (1998).

29. Eldredge (1993, 151); Mothibe and Ntabeni (2002, 55).

30. Kimble (1999, 31–32). Eldredge (1993, 147–50) takes umbrage at the notion that chiefs and commoners were antagonistic toward one another in the precolonial period, accusing Kimble of overemphasizing class relations. But the precolonial order in Basutoland was hardly harmonious, as Motlatsi Thabane (1996, 2002a) incisively shows.

31. Singh (2000).

32. See Phoofolo (2003).

33. See Quinlan (1995); Conz (2020a).

34. Kimble (1999, 135–37). This is in spite of the 1897–99 rinderpest panzootic, which devastated cattle herds in Basutoland and probably led to an increase in small-stock slaughter for meat (Phoofolo 2003).

35. Kimble (1999, 116–17).

36. See Conz (2017).

37. Conz (2020b).

38. Kimble (1999, 116–17).

39. Writing in the 1920s, the general manager of Frasers, a white-owned trading post with stores across Lesotho, reported that, "the rich wool natives do not all live in the mountains, in fact very few of them do so. Many rich wool men are domiciled on the flats . . . and are keeping their flocks and herds in the mountains. . . . When shearing is completed the money is brought to the owners who are living below and finds its way to the different camp stores" (as quoted in Kimble [1999, 220]).

40. This was true for *matsema*, the conscription of commoner labor for work in chief's agricultural fields. Chiefs also generated wealth through the institution of *mafisa*, whereby they would lease out their livestock to commoners. The commoners would tend the livestock and reap a portion of the products (e.g., wool, offspring, etc.), while ultimately building up the chief's herd.

41. Kimble (1999); also see Gutkind and Wallerstein (1976). Cf. Eldredge (1993, 147–51).

42. This mode was not limited to Africa, as Haldon (1993) shows.

43. Swallow and Brokken (1987). Highlands territory was also used by Moshoeshoe to consolidate the rule of his clan's rule over the various tribes that comprise the Basotho. The Tlokoa aristocracy under Sekonyela was one such group. The Tlokoa were expelled to the south by Moshoeshoe in 1853, but later joined forces with Moshoeshoe's successor Letsie I in fighting the British disarmament policy in 1880–81 and were rewarded with a territory in the highlands. Part of this area would later become the District of Mokhotlong, which was relatively unoccupied up until then (Ashton [1967, 4]; see also Eldredge [1993]). Many of the surnames in the Tlokoeng area where I spent most of my time during field research were Setlokoa- or isiXhosa-derived. Some even spoke Xhosa in the home, or at least their parents and grandparents did. Many told me that their grandparents or great grandparents migrated to Mokhotlong from Natal in search of sheep and goat pasture.

44. Beinart (2008); Conz (2017); Driver (1999).

45. Nüsser (2002).

46. "Moshoeshoe has entrusted the chief of Khongoana with a flock of sheep which thrive very much in this region, in spite of the extreme cold which must occur in winter. Here, the pastures are rich and of high quality. In harsh weather, grass and foliage are brought to the animals in their marobeng, which are a type of covered sheep fold. The natives provide this care only for the indigenous breed of sheep and never for those of the colonial breed, which would nevertheless need it as much as the others" (Arbousset 1991 [1840], 78).

47. Ashton (1967, 140).

48. Ashton (1967, 134).

49. Kobisi, Seleteng-Kose, and Moteetee (2019).

50. See Govindrajan (2018) and Haraway (2008) for profound examinations of the intimacy people have with non-human animals.

51. Murray (1981).

52. See Maloka (2004); Murray (1981); and Coplan (1994) for accounts of Basotho experiences of this period.

53. Block and McGrath (2019); Turkon (2003); Kenworthy (2017).

54. *Informative News* (2016).

55. Most of the fiber is processed in South Africa and sold to textile companies in other countries, meaning that value-added manufacturing takes place outside of Lesotho. The iconic wool blankets worn by Basotho, for example, are fabricated mostly in Britain.

56. Tregurtha (n.d.).

57. BKB (2015).

58. Metro (2018).

59. Lesotho has an additional thirty-four privately licensed sheds, many of which also sell to BKB. Prior to 2001, most people sold their clip to the trading posts in Lesotho, the formerly white-owned stores situated across the country who were licensed to purchase clip or other sellers or carry the wool by pack animal to South Africa for sale. In addition, today there are companies that drive through the country with a hand scale and pay out money immediately, as well as shops in the major towns that will purchase the wool and pay out immediately, but they do so for a lower rate than at the woolsheds.

60. This arrangement changed abruptly in 2018, when the Lesotho government abandoned its relationship with BKB for a contract with a Chinese company, a political firestorm that led to tremendous confusion and delays in payment to farmers. The problem is unresolved at the time of writing. Hunter (1987) warned several decades earlier about the potential pitfalls of such a move.

61. Ferguson (1994, 297 n.).

62. Turkon (2003).

63. Herders and livestock owners often said, "If you run into a little problem, you just sell one [and get some cash]." Another man explained, "Sheep take care of all your problems and enable you to eat."

64. Ferguson (1994).

65. Cf. Turkon (2003).

66. As to why he preferred sheep over goats, he said, "Goats die for all sorts of reasons—because of the cold, because of sickness—and the price of wool is high." Additionally, as described below, the market for sheep in butcheries just over the border in South Africa is stronger than for goats. This is because it is occupied by Basotho. In areas of Lesotho that are closer to the eastern border with South Africa, goats are more commonly sold across the border. I was told that Zulu people who live east of Lesotho prefer goat meat.

67. See also Rohde et al. (2006).

68. See Maloka (2004, 9).

69. World Bank (2010, 44).

70. World Bank (2010, 44).

71. These restrictions on the sale of cattle described by Ferguson endure. Rural livestock owners with whom I spoke reported a similar reticence to sell cattle, citing the importance of cattle for bridewealth payments, slaughter at funerals and weddings, or plowing. Small stock can also be used in certain ritual practices. For example, my ethnographic interlocutors noted that sheep might be slaughtered to welcome a newly married woman to her new village. Sheep (and less commonly, goats) might also be slaughtered at funerals or weddings, particularly if a family is not wealthy enough to slaughter a head of cattle. Nevertheless, I saw no general reticence among rural Basotho to sell small stock.

72. Some livestock owners acknowledged to me that it could take time to sell small stock. I certainly saw men bring animals to the kraal at the chief's place for sale who returned home having not sold any. I also met men at the kraal from neighboring valleys where they reported that sales were more difficult and prices not as good. Nevertheless, in general, almost nobody mentioned the difficulty of selling sheep as a problem to be overcome.

73. That the first thirty minutes of a meeting about water and wetlands was dedicated to a discussion of livestock auctions reiterates the challenge of squaring water production with livestock production.

74. Animals sold over the border without paying an export tax were a concern for his office.

75. Auctions failed in the project Ferguson (1994) described thirty years earlier, also.

76. "Fine" is the highest grade, but most farmers in Lesotho prefer medium-fine sheep because fine wool does not grow as well during drought years when sufficient forage is unavailable.

77. Guyer (2004).

78. Livingston (2019).

6. NEGATIVE ECOLOGY

1. On the production of marginality, see Tsing (1993).

2. Dauvergne (1997). Throughout this book, I hope to heed Heather Swanson's (2015) call to consider how "shadow ecologies" in Dauvergne's sense leave their own traces on "core" regions. My focus empirically is on the periphery, yet these highland landscapes matter crucially to Gauteng's viability as a center of population and production. Ferguson's (2006) use of the "shadow" metaphor is closer to what I'm describing.

3. Chakrabarty (2008).

4. Peters (1994). Like rangelands, agricultural land also falls under common land tenure in Lesotho, but use rights (or, "usufruct rights") mean that it's passed generationally within families, drawing croplands much closer to private property. (If a family fails to plant for several years, the chief is free to allocate it to someone else who needs it and who can use it.)

5. Fairhead and Leach (1996); Leach and Mearns (1996); Showers (2005).

6. Peet and Watts (1996).

7. Carruthers (1995); Hughes (2006, 2010); Neumann (1992); Mavhunga (2014); Büscher (2013); West (2006).

8. Some scholars have cautioned against the tendency to presume that local or indigenous forms of land use are necessarily more appropriate than exogenous ones. For example, William Beinart (2000; see also Tilley [2011]) notes the importance of recognizing the ways that African people may have taxed their natural environments, warning against a simple binary of "exploitative colonizer" and "harmless African," the latter of which slips dangerously into "noble savage" stories in which rural people are dehumanized as mere elements of the natural landscape. Sarah Besky (2013) describes this as the "Third World agrarian imaginary" that shapes common perceptions of the rural poor, presenting them as benign stewards of the land at the mercy of failing Third World states.

9. Blaikie (1985). On the scaling problems of environmental thinking, I am indebted also to the work of Tsing (2015); Mitchell (2003); Morton (2013, 2017); Chakrabarty (2021); as well as Sayre's (2017) work on the non-linearity of scale shifts in rangeland ecology.

10. Forman and Alexander (1998).

11. Often the Sesotho word *balisana* is translated as "herdboys," rather than "herders," speaking to both the racial politics of such a translation but also to the typical age.

12. Mbembe (2008).

13. I mean "spacetimes" in two senses: as what Bakhtin (2008) describes as a "chronotope," a frame that organizes the action within a plot and makes it sensible; and in the sense that landscape ecology refers to the structure, function, and change within a landscape (Forman and Godron 1986).

14. Ferguson (1994). See also chapter 5.

15. Herders may be livestock owners themselves, and most livestock owners were once herders. Yet, the social position of herders—particularly herders who work at cattle posts—is very different from a livestock owner, which is why I make this categorical distinction in spite of the overlap.

16. Many Basotho men describe themselves as having been a herder when they were a boy, and they often do so with pride. But there are two types of herders: those who take care of their family's livestock when they return home from school and on the weekends; and those who work full-time at the cattle posts. In rural areas, the second type of herder often "graduates" from the cattle post when he heads to a job in South Africa, or when he acquires enough stock to pay another herder to stay at *motebong* with his herd. The first type is much more common—and in my observation much more likely to talk about herding with pride as an adult.

17. Mudge (2014).

18. See the incredible book by Coplan (1994) on the profound cultural significance of *famo* music.

19. On the complex possibilities of these spaces of freedom, see Tsing (2015).

20. Also see Conz (2020a).

21. This is a term that Gifford-Gonzalez and Hanotte (2011) use to describe the role of goats in the spread of pastoralist peoples across parts of Africa. Also see Tsing (2017).

22. See examples in Weisiger (2011); Melville (1997); Skinner (1976); Beinart (2008); Anderson (2006); Crosby (2004).

23. In 1873–74, when the British colonial officer James Murray Grant traveled through the highlands, he reported "a near-absence of people in the highlands above roughly 1980 masl (King 2019, 56; see Mitchell and Challis [2008]). As Boshoff and Kerley (2013; also see Morake [2010]) show, medium and large ungulates such as eland (*Taurotragus oryx*) and black wildebeest (*Connochaetes gnou*) once inhabited the highlands. These were probably not resident year-round, however, and I doubt they existed in herd sizes that compare to those of livestock today. A thorough study by Grab and Nash (2022) reviewed evidence of medium- to large-sized fauna across Lesotho since the last glacial maximum. They found sixty-one taxa, all but twenty-two of which are now locally extinct. Most were present in the early nineteenth century, but the authors record a punctuated extinction between the period 1845–50, probably owing to hunting campaigns, with other extinctions unfolding afterward probably due to habitat destruction. Also see the fabulous work by Boshoff and Kerley (2013) and Morake (2010).

24. Boshoff and Kerley (2013, 407).

25. Boshoff and Kerley (2013, 29).

26. By 1967, the anthropologist Hugh Ashton (1967, 136) would report that "the growth of the population has so restricted grazing that most Lowlanders have to keep their stock at Highland cattle-posts, and even in the Highlands many people have to keep their animals at cattle-posts rather than at the village." Amy Jacot-Guillarmod (1971, 29), the long-time botanist of Lesotho, would write in 1971 that: "Surveying the country as a whole, it is true to say today that every acre of land in Lesotho is subject to human use in some form or other."

27. Climate interacts with evolutionary history of grazing, and more work needs to be done on this point to account for differences across regions of the world (Díaz et al. [2007]). Yet, the evolutionary history of grazing is a significant factor in determining a plant community's response to grazing with regard to species richness, diversity, life history, and more. See Milchunas, Sala, and Lauenroth (1988); Milchunas and Laurenroth (1993); Díaz et al. (2007); and Leader-Williams (1988).

28. Cingolani, Noy-Meir, and Díaz (2005); Scheffer (2009); Melville (1997).

29. Increased atmospheric CO_2 also disfavors grasses that use the C_4 photosynthetic pathway, which includes some in Lesotho such as *Themeda triandra* and other important forage grasses. See Buitenwerf et al. (2012).

30. As cited in Kimble (1999, 217). There are reasons to be suspicious of colonial accounts. Reports of widespread land degradation during the colonial era may have been fueled by panic and racism that calls their accuracy into question (e.g., Thornton [1931]; Pim [1935]; see Driver [1999]; Showers [2005]). For example, Lesotho is naturally treeless and, at least for the past twenty-three thousand years the highlands have not been dominated by trees (see Scott [1984]; also see May [2000]). Yet, casual observers sometimes presume that the highlands are treeless because of "deforestation," a commonplace narrative that I inherited when I first arrived in Lesotho in 2003. See Showers (2006) for an overview of the history and consequences of that narrative. See Conz (2017) for an expert account of historical perspectives on degradation and soil erosion during the nineteenth century.

31. Sekhesa (1912). Many thanks to Chris Conz for pointing this article out to me.

32. Driver (1999).

33. Showers (2006).

34. The road linking Mokhotlong District to South Africa via Sani Pass on the eastern Drakensberg escarpment is one important example, as explained by Hilliard and Burtt (1987, 14). It had probably been used by people bringing animals from the highlands to Natal during the nineteenth century but between 1914 and 1920 James Lamont, a trader in Mokhotlong, became the first to establish a formal trading post at the base of the pass. By the 1930s, about forty thousand animals a year were using the pass, sometimes two thousand in a single day. Improvements to roads over the years only improved their function as a pathway for disturbance-loving plants, as affirmed by long-term monitoring done by other ecologists. See Kalwij, Robertson, and van Rensburg (2015); Steyn et al. (2017); Carbutt (2012). On the positive effects of paths on plant species diversity, see Root-Bernstein and Svenning (2018).

35. See Fitchett et al. (2017).

36. Shrubs like *Chrysocoma ciliata* are suited to this historical moment, given the tremendous amount of wind-dispersed seeds they produce each year, their ability to grow in even the most compacted and disturbed sites, their ability to endure drought, their capacity to regrow from basal meristems after fire, and their allelopathic properties (Squires and Trollope [1979]; see also Hoag [forthcoming]). That's not to mention their ability to cause fatal illness in lambs that browse them (Van der Vyver et al. [1985]). On the politics of ruderal ecologies, see Stoetzer (2018).

37. Hilliard and Burtt (1987, 14); see also Fitchett et al. (2017).

38. Williams (2005).

CONCLUSION

1. Almost 40 percent of the water Johannesburg draws from the Integrated Vaal River System, the bulk of which is provisioned by Lesotho, is "nonrevenue" water, meaning that it is lost as leaks, stolen, or otherwise not billed for (GreenCape 2017; Gauteng City Region Observatory 2019). On the perils of supply-side municipal water planning elsewhere, see examples from California in Nevarez (1996) and Reisner (1993).

2. See Kaika (2006).

3. Zarfl et al. (2015). The authors of that study show that thirty-seven hundred hydropower dams were planned or under construction in 2014.

4. Khagram (2004); Baviskar (1997).

5. International Commission on Large Dams (2020). As of 2000, this figure was forty-five thousand according to the World Commission on Dams (2000). About 90 percent of those dams were built in the second half of the twentieth century, and about 80 percent of are found in just five countries: China (which has some twenty-two thousand), the United-ed States, India, Japan, and Spain (World Commission on Dams 2000, 8–9). These countries would later go on to be major exporters of dam-building expertise, promoting the construction of new dams across the "developing world."

6. Ansar et al. (2014).

7. For more on the impacts and benefits of dams in Africa and beyond, see Showers (2009), Tsikata (2006); Ansar et al. (2014); Sello (2020). On the meaning of "development" in Lesotho, see Aerni-Flessner (2018).

8. Colson (1971); World Commission on Dams (2000); for Lesotho, see Braun (2010, 2020); Hitchcock and Devitt (2010); Hoover (2001); Horta (1995); Mwangi (2007, 2008); Scudder (2006); Thabane (2000).

9. Cernea (2003); Horowitz (1991).

10. McCully (2001).

11. McCully (2001); Syvitski et al. (2009); Showers (2009).

12. Grill et al. (2019).

13. While the LHWP boasts about the massive amount of water being transferred to South Africa, the LHWP feasibility study for Phase I stated the following: "The proposed transfer of water from the Senqu catchment will not result in any shortfalls in supply from the Senqu/Orange River downstream of the project" (LHDA [1986, iv]). That is, despite the fact the Maliba-Matšo River downstream from the Katse Dam flows at 4 percent of its natural rate (Metsi Consultants [1999]; Arthington et al. [2003]), there are said to be no shortfalls.

14. See McAuslan (1987).

15. Tsing et al. (2020).

16. Kendal, Tehrani, and Odling-Smee (2011); Odling-Smee, Laland, and Feldman (1996); Fuentes (2010).

17. Hutchinson (1957). For a plant, these limit conditions (or, variables) might include maximum and minimum temperature or a similar gradient of soil pH, daily hours of sunlight, tolerance of air pollution, and so on. The ecological space described by the concept is not Euclidean, but these limit conditions can be mapped onto Euclidean geographic space. For example, a given species is said to have a "fundamental" niche, expressing the geographic space where it could potentially occur based on its life requirements, and a "realized" niche, referring to the space in which it actually does occur.

18. See Mathews (2020) for a thorough overview of the concept's use in anthropology and beyond.

19. A kind of "self-devouring growth," as Julie Livingston (2019) describes it. Here, I'm also inspired by the accounts of capitalism's contradictions by Polanyi (1944) and O'Connor (1988), and its ongoing work to overcome them.

20. Martin (1991, 485).

21. Mokuku and Taylor (2015).

22. Carse (2015).

23. Murray's (1981) description of life in the labor reserve was prescient, being echoed a few decades later by those who designated the government's soil conservation efforts, *fato-fato* ("scratching about on the ground like a chicken").

24. Hitchcock et al. (2011, 16).

ACKNOWLEDGMENTS

Endnotes may neaten up the page, but they also submerge some of the names and dates of literature that has been important to me over the course of writing this book. I hope readers will envision this acknowledgments section as extending beyond these paragraphs to include the bibliography that follows. I am so thankful for all the scholars and scholarship out there.

The research for this book began over a decade ago as an inquiry into migration, citizenship, and border administration in Lesotho since the collapse of its labor-export economy. During graduate school, I came to see that these issues were being refracted through Lesotho's "water resources" and the problems and opportunities they called forward. I had lived in Lesotho for two and a half years as a U.S. Peace Corps volunteer, yet I had never thought of Lesotho as a "water exporter" until Anna Tsing asked me some general questions about the country: population, economy, government—the helpful bits of information one might find in an encyclopedia entry. Having mentioned the water scheme, she pushed me to consider looking into it further. I'm so grateful. As I followed water into and through Lesotho, I came to find counterintuitively that an understanding of landscape—of the fluvial and ecological dynamics that make landscapes—was central to water export. That is, in light of concerns about soil erosion and the sedimentation of Lesotho's dam reservoirs, questions about water's flow over the land multiplied and intensified. Does water flow differently over bare ground versus shrub-covered ground, through wetlands or grasslands? When did things get so bad, and why? Was climate responsible for current fluvial problems, or was rural land use at fault? What form of conservation would best maintain an ideal fluvial regime? This is how the project came about.

That's the short version of this book's origin story, anyway. A longer, better one would include my time as a student at the University of Witwatersrand, where I was able to meet and learn from some remarkable scholars, including David Coplan, Zandile Dladla, Kelly Gillespie, Julia Hornberger, Steffie Knoll, Loren Landau, Lewis Manthata, Elliot Moyo, Brenda Njibamum, Phefumula Nyoni, Nedson Pophiwa, Aurelia Segatti, Kathy Shone, Robert Thornton, Chimu Titi, Xolani Tshabalala, Darshan Vigneswaran, Susan Woolf, and Eric Worby. I even had the honor of meeting the late Colin Murray at University of Johannesburg when he presented research he had been doing on the social history of an island in Britain.

The still longer origin story would include my time living in Ha Seshote as a Peace Corps volunteer. There are so many problems with that program, but I feel very fortunate to have gone to Lesotho—such a wonderful and important part of the world. In particular, I'm privileged to have met Sefiri Scepheephe. I admire him more than I think he knows. *Kobo le lemao.* With him, I mourn our mutual friend Khotso Letšikhoana, a giant who used to walk the earth. I admire Kabelo Setala so much, too, achieving all that he has achieved and against all odds. Thank you also to the Sekekete family in Seshote, and to the Matete family in Mokhotlong for their conversation and hospitality. In fact, I'd like to thank the whole of Lesotho and its people for being so welcoming to me over the years I've spent there. Hle, ke lebohile ho menahane.

I'm grateful to the colleagues and friends in Lesotho who helped me in my research and education. Motlatsi Thabane was kind and generous enough to facilitate a research affiliation for me at the National University of Lesotho (NUL). He also disabused me of some naïve lines of thinking over a single cup of coffee one afternoon, for which I'm very appreciative. I thank him and NUL for their hospitality. Moretloa Polaki at NUL's botanic garden taught me so much about Lesotho's flora. I wish I could go botanizing with him again. I would like to thank the Ministry of Forestry and Land Reclamation for facilitating parts of my research, including especially Ratšele Ratšele. I thank the ever-energetic and principled Mabusetsa Lenka Thamae, formerly at the Transformation Resource Centre (TRC) and later at Survivors of Lesotho's Dams (SOLD). I hope that Qalabane Chakela likes what I've written here, and I thank him for helping me to understand the challenges to land conservation. I am still waiting for him to publish his memoirs. Conversations with Bongani Ntloko were extremely helpful. As with just about every research project that has ever been done in Lesotho, Stephen Gill and David Ambrose both offered valuable suggestions for texts and lines of thinking. Many thanks to them both. I'm really happy to have met 'Mamabitsa Makara during my research, whose MSc thesis was amazing and helpful. Lori Pottinger helped usher me into this research, and I'm so indebted to her for her encouragement, suggestions, connections, and her work on the Lesotho Highlands Water Project when she was at International Rivers Network. I learned so much on my research trip to Lesotho with Meredith Root-Bernstein, as well as in our many conversations. Thanks to Charles Fogelman for important conversations about politics, dongas, and more while doing Sunday long runs. There are many others in Lesotho whom I won't name, heeding the convention of providing anonymity to those who have spoken with me for this research. I'm so grateful for their time and insights.

During short stays at the University of Pretoria and the University of KwaZulu-Natal in Pietermaritzburg, I had wonderful conversations with Michelle Greve, Peter le Roux, and Clinton Carbutt. Thanks to them, and thanks also to the Bews Herbarium at UKZN, the SANBI Pretoria National Herbarium, and the NUL Herbarium for allowing me access to their collections.

I'm deeply thankful to my dissertation committee at UC Santa Cruz: Anna Tsing, Andrew Mathews, Danilyn Rutherford, and (externally) James Ferguson. I admire them and their scholarship enormously. Their thinking runs all through these pages (except for any mistakes, which are mine). I need to offer a special thanks to Anna, who gave me so much over the course of the past decade. Talking with Anna is like talking to a visitor from the future, she is always so many steps ahead. Those conversations have been thrilling and so valuable to this book. Thank you.

UC Santa Cruz was an astonishingly great place for the incubation of this research. I learned from Jason Alley, Mark Anderson, David Anthony III, Patricia Alvarez Astacio, Sarah Bakker, Karen Barad, Don Brenneis, Christopher Butler, Heath Cabot, Celina Callahan-Kapoor, Lissa Caldwell, Elizabeth Cameron, Zachary Caple, Nancy Chen, Nellie Chu, Chris Cochran, Salvador Contreras, Luz Córdoba, J. Brent Crosson, the late Ben Crow, Rachel Cypher, Mayanthi Fernando, Elaine Gan, Diane Gifford-Gonzalez, William Girard, Donna Haraway, Susan Harding, Lizzy Hare, Anneke Janzen, Suraiya Jetha, Alix Johnson, Sarah Kelman, Peter Leykam, Daniel Linger, Flora Lu, Andrew Mathews, Stephanie McCallum, Megan Moodie, Olga Nájera-Ramirez, Milad Odabei, Jeffrey Omari, Katy Overstreet, Christian Palmer, Triloki Pandey, Pierre du Plessis, Micha Rahder, Jenny Reardon, Zeb Rifaqat, Lisa Rofel, Kali Rubaii, Kirsten Rudestam, Craig Scheutze, Carolyn Martin Shaw, Megan Shea, Aviva Sinervo, Daniel Solomon, Beth Stephens, Bettina Stoetzer, Heather Swanson, Noah Tamarkin, Nishita Trisal, Kathleen Uzilov, Karen de Vries, Matthew Wolf-Meyer, Adrienne Zihlman, and many others. I'd like to give a special thanks to Zachary Caple, an absolutely brilliant thinker and friend who has influenced me so much.

During a semester at UC Berkeley, I benefited from conversations on rangeland ecology with Felix Ratcliff, James Bartolome, and others.

I'm extremely grateful to my dissertation committee at Aarhus University, Jens-Christian Svenning and Anna Tsing, as well as the internal and external reviewers Anders Barfod, Katherine Homewood, Marcus Nüsser, and Ida Theilade. I must offer a special thank you to Jens-Christian, a remarkable person and thinker who was so patient with me as I fumbled my way through this project. I cherished our conversations, his literature recommendations, and the respect he showed me as a budding ecologist.

At Aarhus University (and elsewhere in Denmark, like Copenhagen, Søby, and Sandbjerg), I learned from Astrid Oberborbeck Andersen, Janelle Marie Baker, Henrik Balslev, Filippo Bertoni, Peder Klith Bøcher, Nathalia Brichet, Nils Bubandt, Rodrigo Cámara-Leret, Marilena Campos, Thiago Cardoso, Xan Chacko, Maria Dahm, Pierre du Plessis, Michael Eilenberg, Natalie Forssman, Peter Funch, Elaine Gan, Frida Hastrup, Kirsten Hastrup, Mathilde Højrup, Samira Kolyaie, Agata Konczal, Morten Nielsen, Jens Mogens Olesen, Spencer Orey, Katy Overstreet, Pil Pedersen, Julia Poerting, Meredith Root-Bernstein, Brody Sandel, Jens-Christian Svenning, Heather Swanson, Line Marie Thorsen, Stine Vestbo, Nina Holm Vohnsen, Gary Whatmough, and basically everyone in the Ecoinformatics and Biodiversity Group. The research program Aarhus University Research on the Anthropocene (AURA) was such a phenomenal intellectual project thanks to Anna Tsing and the co-convenor Nils Bubandt, but also the broader group they assembled. I feel so fortunate to have been a part of it.

My time in Denmark was extremely valuable to this book. A critical reason that I was able to do this research and writing is because of a commitment on the part of the Danish people and their government to fund higher education so that students, postdocs, and faculty can do their work with dignity. The opposite is true in the United States at the moment, with so many precious and brilliant scholars being pushed out of academe because of a broad agreement that scholarship which does not serve industry is superfluous. I feel so fortunate to have benefited from the Danish system that I offer a special thanks to Denmark and the Danish people. I treasured my time there, and I am still sorting through everything I learned and experienced.

I'd like to thank Chitra Venkataramani and Theresa Miller, my co-editors at Engagement blog. I'd also like to thank the authors who have published with us. Their work has taught me so much.

At Smith College and elsewhere in the Connecticut River Valley, I'd like to thank my colleagues (current and former) with whom I've discussed this project, including Jeffrey Ahlman, Felicity Aulino, Lloyd Barba, Alex Barron, Jon Caris, Maya Crandall-Malcolm, Elliot Fratkin, William Girard, Suzanne Gottschang, Jimmy Grogan, Amy Cox Hall, Pinky Hota, Donald Joralemon, Elisa Kim, Elizabeth Klarich, Dana Liebsohn, Patricia Mangan, Zoe McAdoo, Caroline Melly, Matlhabeli Molaoli, Anna Mullany, Sam Ng, Javier Puente, Lee Reale, Claire Seaman, Tracy Tien, Madeline Turner, and Zoë Viñas-Crutcher. Thanks to Tracy Tien and Jon Caris at the Spatial Analysis Lab for the fantastic maps they produced for the book.

Chapter 1 was originally published in the journal *Economic Anthropology*, though it has been revised and portions were split off into the introduction. A revised version of chapter 5 was published in *American Anthropologist*, as well, including an earlier take on figure 14. I thank the journals for permission to reproduce that work here, and I thank the editors and reviewers for their comments and suggestions.

I was fortunate to benefit from the critical feedback on earlier versions of this work of audiences at the University of Berne's Department of Social Anthropology, University of Pennsylvania's Department of Anthropology, Stanford University's Archaeology Research Center, Brown University's Watson Institute, the German Anthropological Association's annual meeting, the Five Colleges African Studies Council, and a PhD course jointly offered by University of Cape Town and Aarhus University. I'd particularly like to thank my hosts at those institutions, Laura Affolter, Nikhil Anand, Ben Baker, Sarah Besky, Lesley Green, Thomas Kirsch, Linda Pickbourn, and Pierre du Plessis. I benefited from conversations and feedback on this work from Jeffrey Ahlman, Jessie Barnes, Melissa Beresford, Zachary Caple, Ashley Carse, Dean Chahim, Nellie Chu, Kim Dionne, Jacob Doherty, Amelia Fiske, William Girard, Lesley Green, Maron Greenleaf, Miia Halme-Tuomisaari, Maira Hayat, Corinne Hoag, Pinky Hota, Matthew Hull, Rachel King, Thomas Kirsch, David Kneas, Caroline Melly, Katwiwa Mule, Pierre du Plessis, Sayd Randle, Meredith Root-Bernstein, Caterina Scaramelli, Sefiri Seepheephe, Kefiloe Sello, Heather Swanson, Anna Weichselbraun, Greg White, Eric Worby, Cassandra Workman, Amber Wutich, and Jerry Zee. I'm so grateful to those who read the entire manuscript, including the profoundly generous (de-anonymized) reviewers Nikhil Anand, Laura Ogden, and Rebecca Lave, as well as Andrea Ballestero, Scott MacLochlainn, and Chris Conz. They made the book so much better.

Field research was made possible by the Department of Anthropology at UC Santa Cruz, the Center for Tropical Research in Ecology, Agriculture, and Development at UC Santa Cruz, and the Science and Justice Research Center at UC Santa Cruz; the Danmarks Grundsforskningsfond as part of the Aarhus University Research on the Anthropocene project; the Wenner-Gren Dissertation Research Grant; the Social Sciences Research Council International Dissertation Fellowship Program; the Thomas Jefferson Fund at the French Embassy of the United States; and Smith College. Writing of this book manuscript was made possible by a sabbatical from Smith College, as well as fellowships from Smith College's Jean Picker Program; the American Council of Learned Societies; the Wenner-Gren Hunt Postdoctoral Fellowship; and the National Endowment for the Humanities. I am so grateful to them all.

At UC Press, I thank Kate Marshall and Enrique Ochoa-Kaup for their guidance and assistance, as well as the copy editor, Andrew Frisardi. Thanks to the Critical Environments Series editors, Rebecca Lave and Julie Guthman, too.

I hope the text lives up to the potential granted to it by all these people and institutions. Mistakes are all mine.

Finally, my family, immediate and extended. Endless thanks to my parents, Peter and Eugenia. Endless, endless thanks for their love and support. Thanks to

Bret, Melissa, and Atticus. To Greg and Lovie Fralick, the late Nadine and Stanley Fralick, Maureen Fralick and Doug Keenum. And, to Corinne, Corinne, Corinne! Corinne has done so much to make this book possible, materially and intellectually: restructuring her career and social life through all the relocations; helping me through scholarly log-jams; doing serious double-duty on childcare; and all manner of other important things from Phomolong to Point Reyes, from McNeill's to Melville, from Lake Merritt to Mokhotlong, and from Skejbygårdsvej to Roe Avenue. Thank you. I love you. And, of course, thank you to Eamon and to Eske, two cosmically beautiful and captivating young kids with so much depth and intelligence, so full of future and light and breath, on their way and already there. I love you guys to pieces.

WORKS CITED

Adams, WilliamM. 1993. *Wasting the Rain: Rivers, People, and Planning in Africa.* Minneapolis: University of Minnesota Press.

Aerni-Flessner, John. 2018. *Dreams for Lesotho: Independence, Foreign Assistance, and Development.* Notre Dame, IN: University of Notre Dame Press.

———. N.d. "Water, Land, Sovereignty: The Pre-History of the Lesotho Highlands Water Project, c1930s–1976." Unpublished paper.

African News Agency. 2015. "Botswana Set to Draw Water from Lesotho Highlands Project." *Engineering News,* November 25, www.engineeringnews.co.za/article/botswana-set -to-draw-water-from-lesotho-highlands-project-2015-11-25/rep_id:4136 (accessed May 24, 2022).

Alatout, Samer. 2009. "Bringing Abundance into Environmental Politics: Constructing a Zionist Network of Water Abundance, Immigration, and Colonization." *Social Studies of Science* 39 (3): 363–94.

Althusser, Louis. 1971. "Ideology and Ideological State Apparatuses (Notes toward an Investigation)." In *Lenin and Philosophy and Other Essays,* edited by Ben Brewster, 127–86. New York: Monthly Review Press.

American Rivers, Friends of the Earth, and Trout Unlimited. 1999. *Dam Removal Success Stories: Restoring Rivers through Selective Removal of Dams That Don't Make Sense.* Washington, DC: American Rivers.

Anand, Nikhil. 2017. *Hydraulic City: Water and the Infrastructures of Citizenship in Mumbai.* Durham, NC: Duke University Press.

Anand, Nikhil, Akhil Gupta, and Hannah Appel, eds. 2018. *The Promise of Infrastructure.* Durham, NC: Duke University Press.

Anders, Gerhard. 2010. *In the Shadow of Good Governance: An Ethnography of Civil Service Reform in Africa.* Leiden, Netherlands: Brill.

Andersen, Astrid Oberborbeck. 2016. "Infrastructures of Progress and Dispossession: Collective Responses to Shrinking Water Access among Farmers in Arequipa, Peru." *Focaal—Journal of Global and Historical Anthropology* 74: 28–41.

———. 2019. "Assembling Commons and Commodities: The Peruvian Water Law between Ideology and Materialisation." *Water Alternatives* 12 (2): 470–87.

Anderson, David. 2002. *Eroding the Commons: The Politics of Ecology in Baringo, Kenya, 1890s–1963.* London: James Currey.

Anderson, Virginia DeJohn. 2006. *Creatures of Empire: How Domestic Animals Transformed Early America.* Oxford: Oxford University Press.

Ansar, Atif, et al. 2014. "Should We Build More Large Dams? The Actual Costs of Hydropower Megaproject Development." SSRN Scholarly Paper ID 2406852. Rochester, NY: Social Science Research Network, https://papers.ssrn.com/abstract=2406852 (accessed April 12, 2022).

Appel, Hannah. 2019. *The Licit Life of Capitalism: U.S. Oil in Equatorial Guinea.* Durham, NC: Duke University Press.

Apter, Andrew H. 2005. *The Pan-African Nation: Oil and the Spectacle of Culture in Nigeria.* Chicago: University of Chicago Press.

Arbousset, Thomas. 1991 [1840]. *Missionary Excursions.* Translated by David Ambrose and Alfred Brutsch. Morija, Lesotho: Morija Museum and Archives.

Arendt, Hannah. 2006. *Eichmann in Jerusalem: A Report on the Banality of Evil.* Edited by Amos Elon. New York: Penguin.

Arthington, Angela H., et al. 2003. "Environmental Flow Requirements of Fish in Lesotho Rivers Using the DRIFT Methodology." *River Research and Applications* 19 (5–6): 641–66.

Arthur, L.J., C.M. Wagner, and B. Hein. 1997. "Lesotho Highlands Water Project—Design of the 'Muela Hydropower Station." In *Proceedings of the Institution of Civil Engineers-Civil Engineering* 120: 43–53.

Artz, N.E. 1993. "Local Participation, Equity, and Popular Support in Lesotho's Range Management Area Programme." *African Journal of Range and Forage Science* 10 (1): 54–62.

Ashmore, Peter. 2015. "Towards a Sociogeomorphology of Rivers." *Emerging Geomorphic Approaches to Guide River Management Practices.* Special issue of *Geomorphology* 251 (December): 149–56.

Ashpole, Marie. 2004. "Ninham Shand—He Walked Tall!" *Civil Engineering: Magazine of the South African Institution of Civil Engineering* 12 (6): 5–7.

Ashton, Hugh. 1967. *The Basuto: A Social Study of Traditional and Modern Lesotho.* 2nd ed. Oxford: Oxford University Press.

Bachelard, Gaston. 1983. *Water and Dreams: An Essay on the Imagination of Matter.* Dallas: Dallas Institute of Humanities and Culture.

Bainbridge, William, Bore Motsamai, and Christopher Weaver, eds. 1991. "Report of the Drakensberg/Maluti Conservation Programme." Pietermaritzburg, South Africa: Natal Parks Board.

Bakhtin, Mikhail M. 2008. *The Dialogic Imagination: Four Essays.* Edited by Michael Holquist. Translated by Caryl Emerson and Michael Holquist. Austin: University of Texas Press.

Bakker, Karen. 2003. *An Uncooperative Commodity: Privatizing Water in England and Wales.* Oxford: Oxford University Press.

Ballestero, Andrea. 2019a. "The Anthropology of Water." *Annual Review of Anthropology* 48 (1): 405–21.

———. 2019b. *A Future History of Water*. Durham, NC: Duke University Press.

Bardill, John, and James Cobbe. 1985. *Lesotho: Dilemmas of Dependence in Southern Africa*. Boulder, CO: Westview.

Barnes, Jessica. 2014. *Cultivating the Nile: The Everyday Politics of Water in Egypt*. Durham, NC: Duke University Press.

Bartolome, James. 1989. "Review of *Holistic Resource Management* by Allan Savory." *Journal of Soil and Water Conservation* 44 (6): 591–92.

Basutoland. 1900–1901. "Annual Report for 1900–01." Basutoland Colonial Report. Maseru, Lesotho.

———. 1933. "Annual Report on the Social and Economic Progress of the People of Basutoland, 1933." Basutoland Colonial Report. Maseru, Lesotho.

———. 1948. "Annual Report of the Department of Agriculture for the Year Ending 30 September 1948." Basutoland Colonial Report. Maseru, Lesotho.

———. 1950. "Annual Report of the Department of Agriculture for the Year Ending 30 September 1950." Basutoland Colonial Report. Maseru, Lesotho.

Baviskar, Amita. 1997. *In the Belly of the River: Tribal Conflicts over Development in the Narmada Valley*. Oxford: Oxford University Press.

———. 2004. "Between Micro-Politics and Administrative Imperatives: Decentralisation and the Watershed Mission in Madhya Pradesh, India." *European Journal of Development Research* 16 (1): 26–40.

Bega, Sheree. 2021. "Southern Africa's 'Water Tower' Slipping towards Ecosystem Collapse." *Mail and Guardian*, June 26, 2021.

Behnke, Roy H., Ian Scoones, and Carol Kerven, eds. 1993. *Range Ecology at Disequilibrium: New Models of Natural Variability and Pastoral Adaptation in African Savannas*. London: Overseas Development Institute.

Beinart, William. 1984. "Soil Erosion, Conservationism and Ideas about Development: A Southern African Exploration, 1900–1960." *Journal of Southern African Studies* 11 (1): 52–83.

———. 1989. "Introduction: The Politics of Colonial Conservation." *Journal of Southern African Studies* 15 (2): 143–62.

———. 2000. "African History and Environmental History." *African Affairs* 99 (305): 269–302.

———. 2008. *The Rise of Conservation in South Africa: Settlers, Livestock, and the Environment, 1770–1950*. Oxford: Oxford University Press.

Beinart, William, Karen Brown, and Daniel Gilfoyle. 2009. "Experts and Expertise in Colonial Africa Reconsidered: Science and the Interpenetration of Knowledge." *African Affairs* 108 (432): 413–33.

Bell, F.G., and D.R. Haskins. 1997. "A Geotechnical Overview of Katse Dam and Transfer Tunnel, Lesotho, with a Note on Basalt Durability." *Engineering Geology* 46 (2): 175–98.

Belsky, A.J., A. Matzke, and S. Uselman. 1999. "Survey of Livestock Influences on Stream and Riparian Ecosystems in the Western United States." *Journal of Soil and Water Conservation* 54 (1): 419–31.

Beresford, David, and Mike Pitso. 1986. "Leaders Held as Lesotho 'Blockade' Takes Effect/Opposition Politicians Accused of Conspiracy with South Africa." *The Guardian*, January 15.

Besky, Sarah. 2013. *The Darjeeling Distinction: Labor and Justice on Fair-Trade Tea Planta-tions in India*. Berkeley: University of California Press.

Bhabha, Homi. 1990. "DissemiNation: Time, Narrative, and the Margins of the Modern Nation." In *Nation and Narration*, edited by Homi Bhabha, 291–322. London: Routledge.

Bierschenk, Thomas, and Jean-Pierre Olivier de Sardan. 2014. *States at Work: Dynamics of African Bureaucracies*. Leiden: Brill.

BKB. 2015. "Lesotho 2014/2015." Fibretrack Report. Compiled by Phillip Fourie, August 6, 2015. Pietermaritzburg, South Africa: BKB.

Blaikie, Piers. 1985. *The Political Economy of Soil Erosion in Developing Countries*. London: Longman.

Block, Ellen, and Will McGrath. 2019. *Infected Kin: Orphan Care and AIDS in Lesotho*. Medical Anthropology: Health, Inequality, and Social Justice. New Brunswick, NJ: Rutgers University Press.

Blue, Brendon, and Gary Brierley. 2016. "'But What Do You Measure?' Prospects for a Constructive Critical Physical Geography." *Area* 48 (2): 190–97.

Bond, Patrick. 2002. *Unsustainable South Africa: Environment, Development, and Social Protest*. London: Merlin.

Bond, Patrick, and Molefi Mafereka ka Ndlovu. 2010. "When Mega Projects Crowd Out Development: Coega and Lesotho Dams." In *Development Dilemmas in Post-Apartheid South Africa*, edited by Bill Freund and Harald Witt. Pietermaritzburg, South Africa: University of KwaZulu-Natal Press.

Boshoff, William, and Graham I.H. Kerley. 2013. *Historical Incidence of Larger Mammals in the Free State Province (South Africa) and Lesotho*. Port Elizabeth, South Africa: Centre for African Conservation Ecology, Nelson Mandela Metropolitan University.

Bowker, Geoffrey C., and Susan Leigh Star. 1999. *Sorting Things Out: Classification and Its Consequences*. Cambridge, MA: MIT Press.

Braun, Yvonne A. 2010. "Gender, Large-Scale Development, and Food Insecurity in Lesotho: An Analysis of the Impact of the Lesotho Highlands Water Project." *Gender and Development* 18 (3): 453–64.

———. 2020. "Environmental Change, Risk, and Vulnerability: Poverty, Food Insecurity, and HIV/AIDS amid Infrastructural Development and Climate Change in Southern Africa." *Cambridge Journal of Regions, Economy, and Society* 13 (2): 267–91.

Briske, David D., Brandon T. Bestelmeyer, and Joel R. Brown. 2014. "Savory's Unsubstantiated Claims Should Not Be Confused with Multipaddock Grazing." *Rangelands* 36 (1): 39–42.

Briske, David D., et al. 2008. "Rotational Grazing on Rangelands: Reconciliation of Perception and Experimental Evidence." *Rangeland Ecology and Management* 61 (1): 3–17.

Briske, David D., et al. 2013. "The Savory Method Can Not Green Deserts or Reverse Climate Change: A Response to the Allan Savory TED Video." *Rangelands* 35 (5): 72–74.

Buitenwerf, Robert, et al. 2012. "Increased Tree Densities in South African Savannas: >50 Years of Data Suggests CO_2 as a Driver." *Global Change Biology* 18 (2): 675–84.

Burgess, Tom. 2016. "Water: At What Cost? The State of the World's Water 2016." Briefing. New York: WaterAid, https://washmatters.wateraid.org/publications/water-at-what -cost-the-state-of-the-of-the-worlds-water-2016 (accessed May 11, 2022).

Büscher, Bram. 2013. *Transforming the Frontier: Peace Parks and the Politics of Neoliberal Conservation in Southern Africa*. Durham, NC: Duke University Press.

Caple, Zachary. 2017. "Holocene in Fragments: A Critical Landscape Ecology of Phosphorus in Florida." PhD diss., University of California, Santa Cruz.

Carbutt, Clinton. 2012. "The Emerging Invasive Alien Plants of the Drakensberg Alpine Centre, Southern Africa." *Bothalia* 42 (2): 71–85.

Carlson, K.A. 1913. "Forestry in Relation to Irrigation in South Africa." *Agricultural Journal of the Union of South Africa* 5: 219–34.

Caromba, Laurence. 2017. "Redrawing the Map of Southern Africa? A Critical Analysis of the Arguments for the Unification of South Africa and Lesotho." *Politikon* 44 (1): 93–109.

Carruthers, Jane. 1995. *The Kruger National Park: A Social and Political History*. Pietermaritzburg, South Africa: University of Natal Press.

Carse, Ashley. 2015. *Beyond the Big Ditch: Politics, Ecology, and Infrastructure at the Panama Canal*. Cambridge, MA: MIT Press.

Casalis, Eugene. 1965 [1861]. *The Basuto, or Twenty-Three Years in South Africa*. Cape Town, South Africa: C. Struik.

Castells, Manuel. 2002. "The Space of Flows." In *The Castells Reader on Cities and Social Theory*, edited by Ida Susser, 314–65. Oxford: Blackwell.

Cattelino, Jessica. 2008. *High Stakes: Florida Seminole Gaming and Sovereignty*. Durham, NC: Duke University Press.

Cernea, Michael M. 2003. "For a New Economics of Resettlement: A Sociological Critique of the Compensation Principle." *International Social Science Journal* 55 (175): 37–45.

Chabal, Patrick, and Jean-Pascal Daloz. 1999. *Africa Works: Disorder as Political Instrument*. London: James Currey.

Chakela, Qalabane K. 1981. *Soil Erosion and Reservoir Sedimentation in Lesotho*. Uppsala: Scandinavian Institute of African Studies.

———, ed. 1999. *State of the Environment in Lesotho—1997*. Maseru: National Environment Secretariat, Ministry of Environment, Gender, and Youth Affairs.

Chakela, Qalabane K., and Michael Stocking. 1988. "An Improved Methodology for Erosion Hazard Mapping, Part II: Application to Lesotho." *Geografiska Annaler*, ser. A, *Physical Geography* 70 (3): 181–89.

Chakela, Q[alabane K.], J. Molapo, and T.G. Putsoane. 1989. "Erosion Hazard Mapping of the SADCC Region, Part III: Lesotho." 25. Soil and Water Conservation and Land Utilization Sector. Maseru: Southern African Development Coordination Conference.

Chakrabarty, Dipesh. 2008. *Provincializing Europe: Postcolonial Thought and Historical Difference*. Princeton, NJ: Princeton University Press.

———. 2021. *The Climate of History in a Planetary Age*. Chicago: University of Chicago Press.

Chalfin, Brenda. 2004. *Shea Butter Republic: State Power, Global Markets, and the Making of an Indigenous Commodity*. New York: Routledge.

———. 2010. *Neoliberal Frontiers: An Ethnography of Sovereignty in West Africa*. Chicago: University of Chicago Press.

Chatanga, Peter, and Erwin JJ Sieben. 2019. "Ecology of Palustrine Wetlands in Lesotho: Vegetation Classification, Description, and Environmental Factors." *Koedoe* 61 (1): 16.

Chatanga, Peter, and Lerato Seleteng-Kose. 2021. "Montane Palustrine Wetlands of Lesotho: Vegetation, Ecosystem Services, Current Status, Threats, and Conservation." *Wetlands* 41 (6): 67.

Choy, Timothy K., et al. 2009. "A New Form of Collaboration in Cultural Anthropology: Matsutake Worlds." *American Ethnologist* 36 (2): 380–403.

Chu, Julie Y. 2014. "When Infrastructures Attack: The Workings of Disrepair in China." *American Ethnologist* 41 (2): 351–67.

Cingolani, Ana M., Imanuel Noy-Meir, and Sandra Díaz. 2005. "Grazing Effects on Rangeland Diversity: A Synthesis of Contemporary Models." *Ecological Applications* 15 (2): 757–73.

Cobbe, James H. 1980. "Integration among Unequals: The Southern African Customs Union and Development." *World Development* 8 (4): 329–36.

Colson, Elizabeth. 1971. *The Social Consequences of Resettlement: The Impact of the Kariba Resettlement upon the Gwembe Tonga*. Manchester, England: Manchester University Press.

Comaroff, John L., and Jean Comaroff. 1990. "Goodly Beasts, Beastly Goods: Cattle and Commodities in a South African Context." *American Ethnologist* 17 (2): 195–216.

Constable, Nicole. 2009. "The Commodification of Intimacy: Marriage, Sex, and Reproductive Labor." *Annual Review of Anthropology* 38: 49–64.

Convention on Biological Diversity. 1995. "Biological Diversity in Lesotho: First Country Report to the COP." Maseru, Lesotho: Convention on Biological Diversity.

Conz, Christopher. 2017. "'Wisdom Does Not Live in One House': Compiling Environmental Knowledge in Lesotho, Southern Africa, c.1880–1965." PhD diss., Boston University.

———. 2019. "Origins and Pathways of Agricultural Demonstration in Lesotho, Southern Africa, 1924–1960s." *Agricultural History* 93 (2): 233–63.

———. 2020a. "Sheep, Scab Mites, and Society: The Process and Politics of Veterinary Knowledge in Lesotho, Southern Africa, c. 1900–1933." *Environment and History* 26 (3): 383–412.

———. 2020b. "(Un)Cultivating the Disease of Maize: Pellagra, Policy, and Nutrition Practice in Lesotho, c. 1933–1963." *Journal of Southern African Studies* 46 (3): 509–26.

Coplan, David. 1994. *In the Time of Cannibals: The Word Music of South Africa's Basotho Migrants*. Chicago: University of Chicago Press.

———. 2000. "Unconquered Territory: Narrating the Caledon Valley." *Journal of African Cultural Studies* 13 (2): 185–206.

———. 2001. "A River Runs through It: The Meaning of the Lesotho-Free State Border." *African Affairs* 100 (398): 81–116.

Coplan, David B., and Tim Quinlan. 1997. "A Chief by the People: Nation versus State in Lesotho." *Africa: Journal of the International African Institute* 67 (1): 27–60.

Coquery-Vidrovitch, Catherine. 1976. "The Political Economy of the African Peasantry and Modes of Production." In *The Political Economy of Contemporary Africa*, edited by P. Gutkind and Immanuel Wallerstein, 90–111. London: Sage.

Coronil, Fernando. 1997. *The Magical State: Nature, Money, and Modernity in Venezuela*. Chicago: University of Chicago Press.

Creamer, Terence. 2016. "Bid Deadlines Loom for Two Key Water-Transfer Components of Lesotho Highlands Project." *Engineering News*, December 16, 2016.

Crosby, Alfred W. 2004. *Ecological Imperialism: The Biological Expansion of Europe, 900–1900*. 2nd ed. Cambridge: Cambridge University Press.

Crush, Jonathan, et al. 2010. *Migration, Remittances, and "Development" in Lesotho*. Migration Policy Series 52. Cape Town, South Africa: Institute for Democracy in South Africa (IDASA).

———. 2017. *Harnessing Migration for Inclusive Growth and Development in Southern Africa*. Special Report. Waterloo, ON: Southern African Migration Programme.

———. 2021. *Stocktaking on Labour Migration in Southern Africa*. Report for the Southern African Migration Management (SAMM) Project. Pretoria, South Africa: International Labour Organization.

Dahl, Gudrun, and Anders Hjort. 1976. *Having Herds: Pastoral Herd Growth and Household Economy*. Department of Social Anthropology, University of Stockholm.

Dauvergne, Peter. 1997. *Shadows in the Forest: Japan and the Politics of Timber in Southeast Asia*. Cambridge, MA: MIT Press.

Davenport, Rodney. 1969. "African Townsmen? South African Natives (Urban Areas) Legislation through the Years." *African Affairs* 68 (271): 95–109.

Davis, Diana K. 2016. *The Arid Lands: History, Power, Knowledge*. Illustrated ed. Cambridge, MA: MIT Press.

Davis, Matt, Søren Faurby, and Jens-Christian Svenning. 2018. "Mammal Diversity Will Take Millions of Years to Recover from the Current Biodiversity Crisis." *Proceedings of the National Academy of Sciences* 115 (44): 11262–67.

Díaz, Sandra, et al. 2007. "Plant Trait Responses to Grazing—a Global Synthesis." *Global Change Biology* 13 (2): 313–41.

Dodson, Belinda. 2005. "A Soil Conservation Safari: Hugh Bennett's 1944 Visit to South Africa." *Environment and History* 11 (1): 35–53.

Dore, Mohammed H.I. 2005. "Exporting Fresh Water: Is There an Economic Rationale?" *Water Policy* 7 (3): 313–27.

Dowson, Thomas A. 1998. "Rain in Bushman Belief, Politics, and History: The Rock-Art of Rain-Making in the South-Eastern Mountains, Southern Africa." In *The Archaeology of Rock-Art*, edited by Christopher Chippindale and Paul S.C. Taçon, 73–88. Cambridge: Cambridge University Press.

Driver, Thackwray. 1999. "Anti-Erosion Policies in the Mountain Areas of Lesotho: The South African Connection." *Environment and History* 5 (1): 1–25.

Dubow, Saul. 1992. "Afrikaner Nationalism, Apartheid and the Conceptualization of 'Race.'" *Journal of African History* 33 (2): 209.

Dyksterhuis, E.J. 1949. "Condition and Management of Range Land Based on Quantitative Ecology." *Journal of Range Management* 2 (3): 104–15.

Edgar, Robert. 1987. *Prophets with Honour: A Documentary History of Lekhotla La Bafo*. Johannesburg, South Africa: Ravan.

Eldredge, Elizabeth A. 1993. *A South African Kingdom: The Pursuit of Security in Nineteenth-Century Lesotho*. Cambridge: Cambridge University Press.

Ellenberger, D. Fred. 1912. *History of the Basotho, Ancient and Modern*. London: Caxton.

Ellis, Jim. 1995. "Climate Variability and Complex Ecosystem Dynamics: Implications for Pastoral Development." In *Living with Uncertainty: New Directions in Pastoral Development in Africa*, edited by Ian Scoones, 37–46. London: International Institute for Environment and Development.

Erasmus, Zmitri. 2008. "Race." In *New South African Keywords*, edited by Nick Shepherd and Steven Robins, 169–81. Athens: Ohio University Press.

Etherington, Norman. 2001. *The Great Treks: The Transformation of Southern Africa, 1815–1854*. New York: Pearson.

Evans, Ivan Thomas. 1997. *Bureaucracy and Race: Native Administration in South Africa*. Perspectives on Southern Africa 53. Berkeley: University of California Press.

Evans-Pritchard, E.E. 1940. *The Nuer: A Description of the Modes of Livelihood and Political Institutions of a Nilotic People*. Oxford: Oxford University Press.

Fairhead, James, and Melissa Leach. 1996. *Misreading the African Landscape Society and Ecology in a Forest-Savanna Mosaic*. Cambridge: Cambridge University Press.

Ferguson, James. 1994. *The Anti-Politics Machine: "Development," Depoliticization, and Bureaucratic Power in Lesotho*. Minneapolis: University of Minnesota Press.

———. 1999. *Expectations of Modernity: Myths and Meanings of Urban Life on the Zambian Copperbelt*. Berkeley: University of California Press.

———. 2006. *Global Shadows: Africa in the Neoliberal World Order*. Durham, NC: Duke University Press.

———. 2015. *Give a Man a Fish: Reflections on the New Politics of Distribution*. Durham, NC: Duke University Press.

Fitchett, Jennifer M., et al. 2017. "Chrysocoma Ciliata L. (Asteraceae) in the Lesotho Highlands: An Anthropogenically Introduced Invasive or a Niche Coloniser?" *Biological Invasions* (June): 1–18.

Fogelman, Charles. 2016. "Measuring Gender, Development, and Land: Data-Driven Analysis and Land Reform in Lesotho." *World Development Perspectives* 1: 36–42.

———. 2017. "The Bureaucratisation of Politicians in Lesotho." Op-ed. *Daily Maverick*, February 28, www.dailymaverick.co.za/article/2017-03-01-op-ed-the-bureaucratisation-of-politicians-in-lesotho (accessed May 22, 2022).

Fogelman, Charles, and Thomas J. Bassett. 2017. "Mapping for Investability: Remaking Land and Maps in Lesotho." *Geoforum* 82 (June): 252–58.

Folch, Christine. 2019. *Hydropolitics: The Itaipu Dam, Sovereignty, and the Engineering of Modern South America*. Princeton, NJ: Princeton University Press.

Forman, Richard T.T., and Lauren E. Alexander. 1998. "Roads and Their Major Ecological Effects." *Annual Review of Ecology and Systematics* 29 (January): 207–31.

Forman, Richard T.T., and Michael Godron. 1986. *Landscape Ecology*. New York: Wiley.

Forman, Richard T.T., et al. 2002. *Road Ecology: Science and Solutions*. 2nd ed. Washington, DC: Island.

Fratkin, Elliot. 1997. "Pastoralism: Governance and Development Issues." *Annual Review of Anthropology* 26: 235–61.

Fuentes, Agustín. 2010. "Naturalcultural Encounters in Bali: Monkeys, Temples, Tourists, and Ethnoprimatology." *Cultural Anthropology* 25 (4): 600–624.

Furlong, Kathryn. 2006. "Hidden Theories, Troubled Waters: International Relations, the 'Territorial Trap,' and the Southern African Development Community's Transboundary Waters." *Political Geography* 25 (4): 438–58.

Gauteng City Region Observatory. 2019. "Water Security Perspective for the Gauteng City-Region." Johannesburg, South Africa: Gauteng City Region Observatory, https://cdn.gcro.ac.za/media/documents/GCR_Water_Security_Perspective_for_web_2019.pdf#page=42 (accessed April 12, 2022).

Gay, John. 1984. "Basotho Attitudes to Erosion and Conservation." In *Lesotho: Environment and Management*, 61–68. Lesotho Miscellaneous Documents no. 1. Roma: National University of Lesotho.

Geisler, Charles. 2015. "New Terra Nullius Narratives and the Gentrification of Africa's 'Empty Lands.'" *Journal of World-Systems Research* 18 (1): 15–29.

Germond, Paul. 1967. *Chronicles of Basutoland*. Morija, Lesotho: Morija Sesuto Book Depot.

Gibson-Graham, J.K. 2006. *The End of Capitalism (As We Knew It): A Feminist Critique of Political Economy*. Minneapolis: University of Minnesota Press.

Gifford-Gonzalez, Diane, and Olivier Hanotte. 2011. "Domesticating Animals in Africa: Implications of Genetic and Archaeological Findings." *Journal of World Prehistory* 24 (1): 1–23.

Gleick, Peter H., et al. 2018. *The World's Water Volume 9: The Report on Freshwater Resources*. CreateSpace.

Gluckman, Max. 1940. "Analysis of a Social Situation in Modern Zululand." *Bantu Studies* 14 (1): 1–30.

Goodspeed, Peter. 1988. "Tiny Lesotho Aims to Escape Pretoria's Grip." *Toronto Star*, sec. H.

GOPA. N.d. Protection of the Orange-Senqu Water Sources—SPONGE—Project. See this related report at the project website: https://gopasa.co.za/gopaGroupGermanyProjects /Lesotho%20(Orange-Senqu%20Water%20Protection).pdf (accessed June 12, 2022).

Government of Lesotho. 1970a. "Tikoloho ea Sehlabathebe e Leboha 'Muso ka Motebo." *Molia: Pampiri E Hlophisitsoeng le ho Phatlalatsoa ke ba Lekala la Phatlalatso ea Litaba* 2 (103), July 3. Maseru, Lesotho: Government of Lesotho.

———. 1970b. "R.C.S. E Tla Thusa Lesotho ka Lijo tse Tla Ja R1,344,785." *Molia: Pampiri E Hlophisitsoeng le ho Phatlalatsoa ke ba Lekala la Phatlalatso ea Litaba*. 2 (119), August 14. Maseru, Lesotho: Government of Lesotho.

———. 2014. National Decentralisation Policy. Ministry of Local Government, Chieftainship and Parliamentary Affairs, www.undp.org/content/dam/lesotho/docs/Other/Final _Decentralization_Policy_(PDF).pdf (accessed July 23, 2021).

———. N.d.a. "About Lesotho." At www.gov.ls/about/default.php (accessed March 7, 2013).

———. N.d.b. "Tourism." At www.gov.ls/about/tourism.php (accessed March 7, 2013).

Govindrajan, Radhika. 2018. *Animal Intimacies: Interspecies Relatedness in India's Central Himalayas*. Chicago: University of Chicago Press.

Grab, Stefan W., and Christine L. Deschamps. 2004. "Geomorphological and Geoecological Controls and Processes Following Gully Development in Alpine Mires, Lesotho." *Arctic, Antarctic, and Alpine Research* 36 (1): 49–58.

Grab, Stefan W., and David J. Nash. 2022. "'But What Silence! No More Gazelles . . . : Occurrence and Extinction of Fauna in Lesotho, Southern Africa, since the Late Pleistocene." *Quaternary International* 611–12 (February): 91–105.

Gramsci, Antonio. 1971. *Selections from the Prison Notebooks*. Translated by Quintin Hoare and Geoffrey Nowel Smith. New York: International.

Green, Lesley. 2020. *Rock | Water | Life: Ecology and Humanities for a Decolonial South Africa*. Durham, NC: Duke University Press Books.

GreenCape. 2017. "Water: Market Intelligence Report 2017." Cape Town, South Africa: GreenCape.

Grill, G., et al. 2019. "Mapping the World's Free-Flowing Rivers." *Nature* 569: 215–21.

Grove, Richard H. 1989. "Scottish Missionaries, Evangelical Discourses, and the Origins of Conservation Thinking in Southern Africa, 1820–1900." *Journal of Southern African Studies* 15 (2): 163–87.

———. 1996. *Green Imperialism: Colonial Expansion, Tropical Island Edens, and the Origins of Environmentalism, 1600–1860*. Cambridge: Cambridge University Press.

Gudeman, Stephen. 1986. *Economics as Culture: Models and Metaphors of Livelihood.* London: Routledge.

Gulbrandsen, Ørnulf. 2012. *The State and the Social: State Formation in Botswana and Its Pre-Colonial and Colonial Genealogies.* New York: Berghahn.

Gupta, Akhil. 2012. *Red Tape: Bureaucracy, Structural Violence, and Poverty in India.* Durham, NC: Duke University Press.

Gutkind, Peter C.W., and Immanuel Wallerstein, eds. 1976. *The Political Economy of Contemporary Africa.* London: Sage.

Guyer, Jane I. 2004. *Marginal Gains: Monetary Transactions in Atlantic Africa.* Chicago: University of Chicago Press.

Haldon, John F. 1993. *The State and the Tributary Mode of Production.* London: Verso.

Hamilton, Carolyn, ed. 1995. *The Mfecane Aftermath: Reconstructive Debates in Southern African History.* Johannesburg: Wits University Press.

Haraway, Donna. 1989. *Primate Visions: Gender, Race, and Nature in the World of Modern Science.* New York: Routledge.

———. 2008. *When Species Meet.* Minneapolis: University of Minnesota Press.

Hastrup, Kirsten, and Cecilie Rubow, eds. 2014. *Living with Environmental Change: Waterworlds.* New York: Routledge.

Hastrup, Kirsten, and Frida Hastrup, eds. 2017. *Waterworlds: Anthropology in Fluid Environments.* New York: Berghahn.

Hayat, Maira. 2020. "The Bureaucrat's Wage: (De)Valuations of Work in an Irrigation Bureaucracy." *Anthropology of Work Review* 41 (2): 86–96.

Hecht, Gabrielle. 2012. *Being Nuclear: Africans and the Global Uranium Trade.* Cambridge, MA: MIT Press.

———. 2018. "Interscalar Vehicles for an African Anthropocene: On Waste, Temporality, and Violence." *Cultural Anthropology* 33 (1): 109–41.

Helmreich, Stefan. 2007. "An Anthropologist Underwater: Immersive Soundscapes, Submarine Cyborgs, and Transductive Ethnography." *American Ethnologist* 34 (4): 621–41.

———. 2011. "Nature/Culture/Seawater." *American Anthropologist* 113 (1): 132–44.

———. 2014. "Waves: An Anthropology of Scientific Things (The 2014 Lewis Henry Morgan Lecture)." *HAU: Journal of Ethnographic Theory* 4 (3): 265–84.

Herskovits, Melville J. 1926. "The Cattle Complex in East Africa." *American Anthropologist* 28 (1): 230–72.

Hetherington, Kregg. 2011. *Guerrilla Auditors: The Politics of Transparency in Neoliberal Paraguay.* Durham, NC: Duke University Press.

Hilliard, Olive Mary, and Brian Laurence Burtt. 1987. "The Botany of the Southern Natal Drakensberg." *Annals of Kirstenbosch Botanic Gardens* 15. Royal Botanical Gardens, Kew, http://kbd.kew.org/kbd/detailedresult.do?id=270849 (accessed April 12, 2022).

Hirst, Stanley. 1995. "Soil Erosion and Sediment Yield Studies in Catchments of the Lesotho Highlands Water Project." Position paper. Maseru: Lesotho Highlands Development Authority.

Hitchcock, Robert. 2015. "The Lesotho Highlands Water Project: Dams, Development, and the World Bank." *Sociology and Anthropology* 3 (10): 526–38.

Hitchcock, Robert, and Paul Devitt. 2010. "Who Drives Resettlement? The Case of Lesotho's Mohale Dam." *African Study Monographs* 31 (2): 57–106.

Hitchcock, Robert, et al. 2011. "Panel of Environmental Experts: Report No. 58." Maseru: Lesotho Highlands Water Project. At https://dokumen.tips/documents/lesotho-high lands-water-project-lhwp-report-58-revopdf-lesotho-highlands.html?page=1 (accessed May 23, 2022).

Hoag, Colin. 2011. "Assembling Partial Perspectives: Thoughts on the Anthropology of Bureaucracy." *PoLAR: Political and Legal Anthropology Review* 34 (1): 81–94.

———. 2014a. "Dereliction at the South African Department of Home Affairs: Time for the Anthropology of Bureaucracy." *Critique of Anthropology* 34 (4): 410–28.

———. 2014b. "Water in Lesotho: Contradiction, Disjuncture, Death." *Engagement* (blog), December 1, https://aesengagement.wordpress.com/2014/12/01/water-in-lesotho-con tradiction-disjuncture-death (accessed April 12, 2022).

———. Forthcoming. "Interpreting Dwarf Shrub Patterns in the Lesotho Highlands." In: *Rubber Boots Methods for the Anthropocene: Doing Fieldwork in Multispecies Worlds*, edited by Nils Bubandt, Astrid O. Andersen, Rachel Cypher. Minneapolis: University of Minnesota Press.

Hoag, Colin, and Jens-Christian Svenning. 2017. "African Environmental Change from the Pleistocene to the Anthropocene." *Annual Review of Environment and Resources* 42 (1): 27–54.

———. N.d. "Livestock Grazing Intensity and Soil Resources Determine Shrub Densities in Lesotho's High-Altitude Rangelands." Unpublished ms.

Hoag, Colin, Filippo Bertoni, and Nils Bubandt. 2018. "Wasteland Ecologies: Undomestication and Multispecies Gains on an Anthropocene Dumping Ground." *Journal of Ethnobiology* 38 (1): 88–104.

Holechek, Jerry, Rex D. Pieper, and Carlton H. Herbel. 2011. *Range Management: Principles and Practices*. 6th ed. Boston: Prentice Hall.

Holleman, Hannah. 2018. *Dust Bowls of Empire: Imperialism, Environmental Politics, and the Injustice of "Green" Capitalism*. New Haven, CT: Yale University Press.

Homewood, K.M., and W.-A. Rodgers. 1984. "Pastoralism and Conservation." *Human Ecology* 12 (4): 431–41.

Hoover, Ryan. 2001. *Pipe Dreams: The World Bank's Failed Efforts to Restore Lives and Livelihoods of Dam-Affected People in Lesotho*. Berkeley, CA: International Rivers Network.

Horowitz, Michael M. 1991. "Victims Upstream and Down." *Journal of Refugee Studies* 4 (2): 164–81.

Horta, Korinna. 1995. "The Mountain Kingdom's White Oil: The Lesotho Highlands Water Project." *Ecologist* 25 (6): 227–31.

Hosken, Graeme, Shaun Smillie, and Neo Goba. 2016. "Water the New Gold." *Times LIVE*, January 25.

Hughes, David McDermott. 2006. *From Enslavement to Environmentalism: Politics on a Southern African Frontier*. Seattle: University of Washington Press.

———. 2010. *Whiteness in Zimbabwe: Race, Landscape, and the Problem of Belonging*. New York: Palgrave Macmillan.

Hull, Matthew S. 2012. *Government of Paper: The Materiality of Bureaucracy in Urban Pakistan*. Berkeley: University of California Press.

Hunter, John P. 1987. "The Economics of Wool and Mohair Production and Marketing in Lesotho." ISAS Research Report 16. Roma, Lesotho: Institute for Southern African Studies.

Hutchinson, G. Evelyn. 1957. "Concluding Remarks." *Cold Spring Harbor Symposia on Quantitative Biology* 22 (January): 415–27.

Hutchinson, Sharon. 1996. *Nuer Dilemmas: Coping with Money, War, and the State.* Berkeley: University of California Press.

IFAD (International Fund for Agricultural Development). 2014. "The Kingdom of Lesotho. Wool and Mohair Promotion Project." Report No. 3549-LS. IFAD: Maseru, Lesotho.

Illich, Ivan. 1985. *H2O and the Waters of Forgetfulness: Reflections on the Historicity of "Stuff."* Dallas: Dallas Institute of Humanities and Culture.

Informative News. 2016. "Wool and Mohair Farmers Face Poverty." January 19. Maseru, Lesotho. Informative, www.informativenews.co.ls/index.php?option=com_content&view=article&id=409:wool-and-mohair-farmers-face-poverty-as-the-country-experiences-first-hand-effects-of-climate-change&catid=10:news&Itemid=107 (accessed April 12, 2022).

International Commission on Large Dams. 2020. "World Register of Dams: General Synthesis." See https://www.icold-cigb.org/GB/world_register/general_synthesis.asp (accessed May 23, 2022).

Isaacman, Allen F., and Barbara S. Isaacman. 2013. *Dams, Displacement, and the Delusion of Development: Cahora Bassa and Its Legacies in Mozambique, 1965–2007.* Athens: Ohio University Press.

Jacks, Graham Vernon, and Robert Orr Whyte. 1939. *The Rape of the Earth: A World Survey of Soil Erosion.* London: Faber and Faber.

Jacot-Guillarmod, Amy. 1962. "The Bogs and Sponges of the Basutoland Mountains." *South African Journal of Science* 56 (6): 179–82.

———. 1971. *Flora of Lesotho.* Lehre, Germany: Cramer.

Jehanno, P., et al., SOGREAH Consulting Engineers, and France GRENOBLE. 1987. "Calculation of Sediment Deposition in the Katse Reservoir, Lesotho." *Hydrology in Mountainous Regions II—Artificial Reservoirs, Water and Slopes*, edited by Richard O. Sinninger and Michel Monbaron, 51–58. Proceedings of Two International Symposia, Lausanne, Switzerland, August 1990. IAHS Publication no. 194. Oxfordshire, UK: International Association of Hydrological Sciences.

Johnston, Deborah. 1996. "The State and Development: An Analysis of Agricultural Policy in Lesotho, 1970–1993." *Journal of Southern African Studies* 22 (1): 119–37.

Kabi, Pascalinah. 2017. "Water Project under Threat from Sludge." *Lesotho Times*, April 7, http://lestimes.com/water-project-under-threat-from-sludge (accessed April 12, 2022).

Kaika, Maria. 2006. "Dams as Symbols of Modernization: The Urbanization of Nature Between Geographical Imagination and Materiality." *Annals of the Association of American Geographers* 96 (2): 276–301.

Kalwij, Jesse M., Mark P. Robertson, and Berndt J. van Rensburg. 2015. "Annual Monitoring Reveals Rapid Upward Movement of Exotic Plants in a Montane Ecosystem." *Biological Invasions* 17 (12): 3517–29.

Kamara, Joseph K., Kingsley Agho, and Andre M.N. Renzaho. 2019. "Understanding Disaster Resilience in Communities Affected by Recurrent Drought in Lesotho and Swaziland—A Qualitative Study." *PLOS ONE* 14, no. 3 (March 1): e0212994.

Kapa, Motlamelle Anthony. 2013. "Chiefs, Democracy, and Popular Participation: The Case of Lesotho." *African Studies* 72 (1): 121–37.

Keck, Frederic, and Andrew Lakoff. 2013. "Figures of Warning." *Limn*, June 15, 2013.

Kendal, Jeremy, Jamshid J. Tehrani, and John Odling-Smee. 2011. "Human Niche Construction in Interdisciplinary Focus." *Philosophical Transactions of the Royal Society B: Biological Sciences* 366: 785–92.

Kenworthy, Nora. 2017. *Mistreated: The Political Consequences of the Fight against AIDS in Lesotho*. Nashville, TN: Vanderbilt University Press.

Khaba, Liphapang, and James Andrew Griffiths. 2017. "Calculation of Reservoir Capacity Loss Due to Sediment Deposition in the 'Muela Reservoir, Northern Lesotho." *International Soil and Water Conservation Research* 5 (2): 130–40.

Khagram, Sanjeev. 2004. *Dams and Development: Transnational Struggles for Water and Power*. Ithaca, NY: Cornell University Press.

Khaketla, B. Makalo. 1972. *Lesotho, 1970: An African Coup under the Microscope*. Berkeley: University of California Press.

Kiage, Lawrence M. 2013. "Perspectives on the Assumed Causes of Land Degradation in the Rangelands of Sub-Saharan Africa." *Progress in Physical Geography* 37 (5): 664–84.

Kimble, Judith M. 1999. *Migrant Labour and Colonial Rule in Basutoland, 1890–1930*. 1. Grahamstown, South Africa: Institute of Social and Economic Research, Rhodes University.

King, Rachel. 2019. *Outlaws, Anxiety, and Disorder in Southern Africa: Material Histories of the Maloti-Drakensberg*. New York: Palgrave Macmillan.

King, Rachel, and Sam Challis. 2017. "The 'Interior World' of the Nineteenth-Century Maloti-Drakensberg Mountains." *Journal of African History* 58 (2): 213–37.

Kings, Sipho. 2015. "Water Restrictions Begin in Gauteng." *M&G Online*, October 28, https://mg.co.za/article/2015-10-28-rand-water-begins-water-restrictions (accessed May 24, 2022).

Kings, Sipho, et al. 2015. "South Africa's Great Thirst Has Begun." *M&G Online*, January 23, https://mg.co.za/article/2015-01-22-south-africas-great-thirst-has-begun (accessed May 24, 2022).

Kirsch, Stuart. 2014. *Mining Capitalism: The Relationship between Corporations and Their Critics*. Oakland: University of California Press.

Knight, Jasper, and Stefan Grab. 2015. "The Drakensberg Escarpment: Mountain Processes at the Edge." In *Landscapes and Landforms of South Africa*, edited by Stefan Grab and Jasper Knight, 47–55. World Geomorphological Landscapes. Cham, Germany: Springer.

———. 2021. "Stratigraphy of Late Quaternary Mountain Slope Landforms and Deposits in Southern Africa and Their Significance for the Dynamics of Mountain Sediment Systems." *South African Journal of Geology* 124 (4): 863–78.

Kobisi, Khotso, Lerato Seleteng-Kose, and Annah Moteetee. 2019. "Invasive Alien Plants Occurring in Lesotho: Their Ethnobotany, Potential Risks, Distribution and Origin." *Bothalia* 49 (1): a2543.

Kohn, Eduardo. 2013. *How Forests Think: Toward an Anthropology beyond the Human*. Berkeley: University of California Press.

Kopytoff, Igor. 1986. "The Cultural Biography of Things: Commoditization as Process." In *The Social Life of Things: Commodities in Cultural Perspective*, edited by Arjun Appadurai, 64–91. Cambridge: Cambridge University Press.

Kynoch, Gary, and Theresa Ulicki. 2000. "'It Is Like the Time of Lifaqane': The Impact of Stock Theft and Violence in Southern Lesotho." *Journal of Contemporary African Studies* 18 (2): 179–206.

Lakoff, Andrew. 2016. "The Indicator Species: Tracking Ecosystem Collapse in Arid California." *Public Culture* 28 (2[79]): 237–59.

Latour, Bruno. 2004. "Why Has Critique Run Out of Steam? From Matters of Fact to Matters of Concern." *Critical Inquiry* 30: 225–48.

Lave, Rebecca. 2012. *Fields and Streams: Stream Restoration, Neoliberalism, and the Future of Environmental Science*. Athens: University of Georgia Press.

Lave, Rebecca, Christine Biermann, and Stuart N. Lane, eds. 2018. *The Palgrave Handbook of Critical Physical Geography*. Cham, Switzerland: Palgrave Macmillan.

Lawton, John H. 1999. "Are There General Laws in Ecology?" *Oikos* 84 (2): 177–92.

Leach, Melissa, and Robin Mearns, eds. 1996. *The Lie of the Land: Challenging Received Wisdom on the African Environment*. Portsmouth, NH: Heinemann.

Leader-Williams, N. 1988. *Reindeer on South Georgia*. Cambridge: Cambridge University Press.

Lederman, Rena. 2006. "The Perils of Working at Home: IRB 'Mission Creep' as Context and Content for an Ethnography of Disciplinary Knowledges." *American Ethnologist* 33 (4): 482–91.

Leduka, Resetselemang C. 2007. "Recycled Fable or Immutable Truth? Reflections on the 1973 Land-Tenure Reform Project in Lesotho and Lessons for the Future." *Africa Today* 53 (3): 91–111.

Lelimo, Martin Moloantoa. 1998. *The Question of Lesotho's Conquered Territory: It's Time for an Answer*. Morija, Lesotho: Morija Museum and Archives.

Lesotho Bureau of Statistics. 2013a. "2012 Biodiversity, Land Use and Cover 2010/11." Statistical Report no. 16 of 2013. Maseru: Lesotho Bureau of Statistics.

———. 2013b. "2012 Solid Waste, Water and Sanitation." Statistical Report no. 19. Maseru: Lesotho Bureau of Statistics.

———. 2016. "2016 Census—Summary of Key Findings." Maseru: Lesotho Bureau of Statistics.

Lesotho Highlands Development Authority (LHDA). 1981. *Feasibility Study*. Maseru: Government of Lesotho.

———. 1986. *Treaty of the Lesotho Highlands Water Project*. Maseru: Government of Lesotho.

———. 2014. "Press Release—Unveiling Ceremony at Tlokoeng Launches Phase II of the Lesotho Highlands Water Project." Maseru: Lesotho Highlands Development Authority.

———. 2019. "Annual Report 2018/2019." Maseru: Lesotho Highlands Development Authority. See www.lhda.org.ls/lhdaweb/Uploads/documents/Annual_Reports/Annual_Report_2018_19.pdf (accessed May 24, 2022).

———. 2021. "Water Sales." Maseru: Lesotho Highlands Development Authority. See www.lhda.org.ls/lhdaweb/Uploads/documents/royalties/WaterRoyalties.pdf (accessed May 24, 2022).

———. N.d.a. "Environmental Management Plan." Lesotho Highlands Development Authority Archives. Maseru: Lesotho Highlands Development Authority.

———. N.d.b. "Lesotho Highlands Water Project." Brochure, Public Relations Branch. Maseru: Lesotho Highlands Development Authority.

Lewis, F., et al. 2015. "Mapping Climate Change Vulnerability and Potential Economic Impacts in Lesotho: A Case Study of the Katse Dam Catchment." Pietermaritzburg, South Africa: Institute of Natural Resources NPC.

Li, Fabiana. 2009. "Documenting Accountability: Environmental Impact Assessment in a Peruvian Mining Project." *PoLAR: Political and Legal Anthropology Review* 32 (2): 218–36.

Li, Tania Murray. 2007. *The Will to Improve: Governmentality, Development, and the Practice of Politics.* Durham, NC: Duke University Press.

Linquist, Stefan, et al. 2016. "Yes! There Are Resilient Generalizations (or 'Laws') in Ecology." *Quarterly Review of Biology* 91 (2): 119–31.

Linton, Jamie. 2010. *What Is Water? The History of a Modern Abstraction.* Vancouver: University of British Columbia Press.

Little, Peter D. 1985. "Absentee Herd Owners and Part-Time Pastoralists: The Political Economy of Resource Use in Northern Kenya." *Human Ecology* 13 (2): 131–51.

Livingston, Julie. 2019. *Self-Devouring Growth: A Planetary Parable as Told from Southern Africa.* Durham, NC: Duke University Press.

LMS. 2017. "Lesotho's National Climate Change Policy." Maseru, Lesotho: Ministry of Energy and Meteorology.

Lundahl, Mats, and Lennart Petersson. 1991. *The Dependent Economy: Lesotho and the Southern African Customs Union.* Boulder, CO: Westview.

Lundahl, Mats, Colin McCarthy, and Lennart Petersson. 2003. *In the Shadow of South Africa: Lesotho's Economic Future.* Burlington, VT: Ashgate.

Lynteris, Christos. 2014. "Introduction: The Time of Epidemics." *Cambridge Journal of Anthropology* 32 (1): 24–31.

Lyons, Kristina Marie. 2020. *Vital Decomposition: Soil Practitioners and Life Politics.* Durham, NC: Duke University Press.

Magubane, Bernard Makhosezwe. 1979. *The Political Economy of Race and Class in South Africa.* New York, NY: Monthly Review Press.

Makara, 'Mambitsa. 2013. "Assessment of Spatial and Temporal Soil Loss in and out Lesotho Using RUSLE Model and GIS." MSc thesis, Harare, University of Zimbabwe.

Malhi, Yadvinder. 2017. "The Concept of the Anthropocene." *Annual Review of Environment and Resources* 42: 77–104.

Maliehe, Sean M. 2021. *Commerce as Politics: The Two Centuries of Struggle for Basotho Economic Independence.* New York: Berghahn Books.

Maloka, Eddy. 2004. *Basotho and the Mines: A Social History of Labour Migrancy in Lesotho and South Africa, c. 1890–1940.* Dakar, Senegal: CODESRIA.

Maloti-Drakensberg Transfrontier Project. 2007. *Spatial Assessment of Biodiversity Priorities in the Lesotho Highlands: Executive Summary.* Maseru: Lesotho Department of Environment.

———. N.d. "Conservation & Development Strategy (2008–2028) for the Maloti-Drakensberg Transfrontier Conservation Area." Maloti-Drakensberg Transfrontier Project. Maseru, Lesotho.

Mamdani, Mahmood. 1996. *Citizen and Subject: Contemporary Africa and the Legacy of Late Colonialism.* Princeton, NJ: Princeton University Press.

Marneweck, Gary, and P. Grundling. 1999. *Wetlands of the Upper Catchment Areas of Bokong, Maliba-Matšo and Matsoku Rivers in the Leribe, Mokhotlong and Butha-Buthe*

Districs of Lesotho. Report for Lesotho Highlands Development Authority. Maseru: Lesotho Highlands Development Authority.

Martin, Emily. 1991. "The Egg and the Sperm: How Science Has Constructed a Romance Based on Stereotypical Male-Female Roles." *Signs: Journal of Women in Culture and Society* 16 (3): 485–501.

Marx, Karl. 1990. *Capital: Volume I*. Translated by Ben Fowkes. New York: Penguin.

Mathews, Andrew S. 2011. *Instituting Nature: Authority, Expertise, and Power in Mexican Forests*. Cambridge, MA: MIT Press.

———. 2018. "Landscapes and Throughscapes in Italian Forest Worlds: Thinking Dramatically about the Anthropocene." *Cultural Anthropology* 33 (3): 386–414.

———. 2020. "Anthropology and the Anthropocene: Criticisms, Experiments, and Collaborations." *Annual Review of Anthropology* 49 (1): 67–82.

Mauss, Marcel. 2016. *The Gift*. Translated by Jane I. Guyer. Expanded ed. Chicago: HAU Books.

Mavhunga, Clapperton Chakanetsa. 2014. *Transient Workspaces: Technologies of Everyday Innovation in Zimbabwe*. Cambridge, MA: MIT Press.

May, E.D. 2000. *The Indigenous Forests of Lesotho: Their Former Occurrence*. Morija, Lesotho: Morija Printing Works.

Mbembe, Achille. 2001. *On the Postcolony*. Translated by Janet Roitman. Berkeley: University of California Press.

———. 2008. "The Aesthetics of Superfluity." In *Johannesburg: The Elusive Metropolis*, 37–67. Durham, NC: Duke University Press.

———. 2017. *Critique of Black Reason*. Translated by Laurent Dubois. Durham, NC: Duke University Press.

McAuslan, Patrick. 1987. "Lesotho Highlands Water Project and Water Law." *Lesotho Law Journal* 3 (2): 41–65.

McCracken, John. 1982. "Experts and Expertise in Colonial Malawi." *African Affairs* 81 (322): 101–16.

McCully, Patrick. 2001. *Silenced Rivers: The Ecology and Politics of Large Dams*. London: Zed.

McWilliams, James E. 2013. "All Sizzle and No Steak." *Slate*, April 22, www.slate.com/articles/life/food/2013/04/allan_savory_s_ted_talk_is_wrong_and_the_benefits_of_holistic_grazing_have.html (accessed May 24, 2022).

Médard, Jean-Pierre. 1982. "The Underdeveloped State in Tropical Africa: Political Clientelism or Neo-Patrimonialism." In *Private Patronage and Public Power: Political Clientelism in the Modern State*, edited by C. Clapham, 162–92. London: Frances Pinter.

Mehta, Lyla. 2001. "The Manufacture of Popular Perceptions of Scarcity: Dams and Water-Related Narratives in Gujarat, India." *World Development* 29 (12): 2025–41.

Mehta, Lyla, William Derman, and Emmanuel Manzungu, eds. 2017. *Flows and Practices: The Politics of Integrated Water Resources Management in Eastern and Southern Africa*. Harare, Zimbabwe: Weaver.

Meissner, Richard, and Anthony R. Turton. 2003. "The Hydrosocial Contract Theory and the Lesotho Highlands Water Project." *Water Policy* 5 (2): 115–26.

Melly, Caroline. 2017. *Bottleneck: Moving, Building, and Belonging in an African City*. Chicago: University of Chicago Press.

Melville, Elinor G.K. 1997. *A Plague of Sheep: Environmental Consequences of the Conquest of Mexico*. Cambridge: Cambridge University Press.

Mensah, Samuel N.-A., and Vannie Naidoo. 2011. "Migration Shocks: Integrating Lesotho's Retrenched Migrant Miners." *International Migration Review* 45 (4): 1017–42.

Messeri, Lisa. 2016. *Placing Outer Space: An Earthly Ethnography of Other Worlds*. Durham, NC: Duke University Press.

Metro. 2018. "Wool and Mohair Farmers Call for Assistance." *Metro News*, October 5, sec. Business, www.maserumetro.com/news/business/wool-and-mohair-farmers-call-for-assistance (accessed May 24, 2022).

Metsi Consultants. 1999. "The Establishment and Monitoring of Instream Flow Requirements for River Courses Downstream of LHWP Dams." LHDA Contract 648. Maseru: Lesotho Highlands Development Authority.

Milchunas, D.G., O.E. Sala, and W.K. Lauenroth. 1988. "A Generalized Model of the Effects of Grazing by Large Herbivores on Grassland Community Structure." *American Naturalist* 132 (1): 87–106.

Milchunas, D.G., and W.K. Lauenroth. 1993. "Quantitative Effects of Grazing on Vegetation and Soils Over a Global Range of Environments." *Ecological Monographs* 63 (4): 328–66.

Mitchell, Don. 2003. "Dead Labor and the Political Economy of Landscape—California Living, California Dying." In *Handbook of Cultural Geography*, 233–248. London: Sage.

Mitchell, Peter, and Sam Challis. 2008. "A 'First' Glimpse into the Maloti Mountains: The Diary of James Murray Grant's Expedition of 1873–74." *Southern African Humanities* 20 (2): 399–461.

Mitchell, Timothy. 2002. *Rule of Experts: Egypt, Techno-Politics, Modernity*. Berkeley: University of California Press.

———. 2011. *Carbon Democracy: Political Power in the Age of Oil*. New York: Verso.

Miyazaki, Hirokazu. 2004. *The Method of Hope: Anthropology, Philosophy, and Fijian Knowledge*. Palo Alto, CA: Stanford University Press.

Mohapatra, Sanket, Dilip Ratha, and Ani Silwal. 2011. "Migration and Development Brief 17." New York: World Bank.

Mokhethi, Sechaba, and Pascalinah Kabi. 2021. "Lesotho's 'White Gold': Water, Water Everywhere . . . but Not a Drop to Drink for Local Communities." *Daily Maverick*, April 11, www.dailymaverick.co.za/article/2021-04-11-lesothos-white-gold-water-water-everywhere-but-not-a-drop-to-drink-for-local-communities (accessed May 24, 2022).

Mokotjomela, Thabiso, Ute Schwaibold, and Neville Pillay. 2009. "Does the Ice Rat Otomys Sloggetti Robertsi Contribute to Habitat Change in Lesotho?" *Acta Oecologica* 35 (3): 437–43.

Mokuku, Chaba. 2004. *Lesotho: Second State of the Environment Report, 2002*. Maseru: National Environment Secretariat, Ministry of Tourism, Environment, and Culture, Government of Lesotho.

Mokuku, Tšepo, and Jim Taylor. 2015. "Tlokoeng Valley Community's Conceptions of Wetlands: Prospects for More Sustainable Water Resources Management." *Journal of Education for Sustainable Development* 9 (2): 196–212.

Molapo, Reentsent. 2018. "LHWP Dam Levels: Is There a Threat to Water Transfer and Electricity Generation?" Avani Lesotho, March 3, www.lhda.org.ls/lhdaweb/Uploads/Documents/Newsroom/News/LHWP_DAM_LEVELS_IS%20THERE_A_THREAT

_TO_WATER_TRANSFER_AND_ELECTRICITY_GENERATION_BY_DM_DOD .pdf (accessed May 24, 2022).

Monyane, Chelete. 2005. "Lesotho's Transition to Democratic Rule: An Era of 'Fragile' Democracy." MA thesis, University of Kwa-Zulu Natal, Pietermaritzburg.

Moodie, T. Dunbar. 1975. *The Rise of Afrikanerdom: Power, Apartheid, and the Afrikaner Civil Religion*. Berkeley: University of California Press.

Moore, Amelia. 2019. *Destination Anthropocene: Science and Tourism in the Bahamas*. Oakland: University of California Press.

Morake, Puleng. 2010. "Documenting Historical Faunal Change in Lesotho and the Adjoining Eastern Free State of Southern Africa." Masters thesis, University of the Witwatersrand, Johannesburg.

Morita, Atsuro. 2017. "Multispecies Infrastructure: Infrastructural Inversion and Involutionary Entanglements in the Chao Phraya Delta, Thailand." *Ethnos* 82 (4): 738–57.

Morton, Timothy. 2013. *Hyperobjects: Philosophy and Ecology after the End of the World*. Minneapolis: University of Minnesota Press.

———. 2017. *Dark Ecology: For a Logic of Future Coexistence*. New York: Columbia University Press.

Moshoeshoe II, King. 1988. "Punish Pretoria, but Not Lesotho." *New York Times*, July 5, sec. A.

Mosse, David. 2003. *The Rule of Water. Statecraft, Ecology, and Collective Action in South India*. Oxford: Oxford University Press.

———. 2005. *Cultivating Development: An Ethnography of Aid Policy and Practice*. New York: Pluto.

———. 2013. "The Anthropology of International Development." *Annual Review of Anthropology* 42 (1): 227–46.

Mothibe, Tefetso, and Maria Ntabeni. 2002. "The Role of the Missionaries, Boers, and British in Social and Territorial Changes, 1833–1868." In *Essays on Aspects of the Political Economy of Lesotho, 1500–2000*, edited by Neville W. Pule and Motlatsi Thabane, 35–57. Roma: Department of History, National University of Lesotho.

Mott MacDonald. 2013. *Strategic Performance Assessment of the Lesotho Wetlands Restoration and Conservation Project—Millennium Challenge Account Lesotho*. Contract No. WS-F-045–12. Washington, DC: Millennium Challenge Corporation.

Mphanya, Ntsukunyane. 1992. *Matsema, Mohloli oa Tsoelopele*. Morija, Lesotho: Morija Sesuto.

———. 2009. *A Brief History of the BCP*. Morija, Lesotho: Morija Sesuto.

Mrázek, Rudolf. 2002. *Engineers of Happy Land: Technology and Nationalism in a Colony*. Princeton Studies in Culture/Power/History. Princeton, NJ: Princeton University Press.

Mudge, Andrew. 2014. *The Forgotten Kingdom*. Cape Town, South Africa: Binary Film Works.

Mukwada, Geoffrey. 2022. "Current Crisis and Future Woes: The Case of Climate Change in the Drakensberg Mountains Region of Southern Africa and Its Socio-Economic Impacts in the Region." In *Mountain Landscapes in Transition: Effects of Land Use and Climate Change*, edited by Udo Schickhoff, R.B. Singh, and Suraj Mal, 449–67. Sustainable Development Goals Series. Cham, Germany: Springer.

Muller, Mike. 2018. "Cape Town's Drought: Don't Blame Climate Change." *Nature* 559: 174–76.

———. 2020. "Urgent Covid-19 Decisions Divert the Focus from Growing Water Supply Crisis." *Business Day Live*, July 20, www.businesslive.co.za/bd/opinion/2020-07-20-urgent -covid-19-decisions-divert-the-focus-from-growing-water-supply-crisis (accessed May 24, 2022).

Murray, Colin. 1981. *Families Divided: The Impact of Migrant Labour in Lesotho*. Cambridge: Cambridge University Press.

Mwangi, Oscar. 2007. "Hydropolitics, Ecocide, and Human Security in Lesotho: A Case Study of the Lesotho Highlands Water Project." *Journal of Southern African Studies* 33 (1): 3–17.

———. 2008. "Environmental Change and Human Security in Lesotho: The Role of the Lesotho Highlands Water Project in Environmental Degradation." *African Security Review* 17 (3): 58–70.

Nash, David J., and Stefan W. Grab. 2010. "'A Sky of Brass and Burning Winds': Documentary Evidence of Rainfall Variability in the Kingdom of Lesotho, Southern Africa, 1824–1900." *Climatic Change* 101 (3–4): 617–53.

Nastar, Maryam. 2014. "The Quest to Become a World City: Implications for Access to Water." *Cities* 41: 1–9.

Neimanis, Astrida. 2017. *Bodies of Water: Posthuman Feminist Phenomenology*. New York: Bloomsbury Academic.

Nel, Werner, and Paul Sumner. 2008. "Rainfall and Temperature Attributes on the Lesotho–Drakensberg Escarpment Edge, Southern Africa." *Geografiska Annaler*, ser. A, *Physical Geography* 90 (1): 97–108.

Neumann, Roderick P. 1992. "Political Ecology of Wildlife Conservation in the Mt. Meru Area of Northeast Tanzania." *Land Degradation and Development* 3 (2): 85–98.

Nevarez, Leonard. 1996. "Just Wait Until There's a Drought: Mediating Environmental Crises for Urban Growth." *Antipode* 28 (3): 246–72.

Niang, Isabelle, et al. 2014. "Africa." In *Climate Change 2014—Impacts, Adaptation and Vulnerability: Regional Aspects*, edited by Christopher B. Field and Vicente R. Barros, 1199–1266. Part B, *Regional Aspects*. Contribution of Working Group II to the Fifth Assessment Report of the Intergovernmental Panel on Climate Change. Cambridge: Cambridge University Press.

Nobe, K.C., and David William Seckler. 1979. "An Economic and Policy Analysis of Soil-Water Problem and Conservation Programs in the Kingdom of Lesotho." LASA Research Report 3. Maseru: Ministry of Agriculture, Lesotho.

Ntaote, Billy. 2010. "Mixed Reaction to Independence Day." *Lesotho Times*, October 4.

Ntsebeza, Lungisile. 2005. *Democracy Compromised: Chiefs and the Politics of the Land in South Africa*. Leiden: Brill.

Nüsser, Marcus. 2002. "Pastoral Utilization and Land Cover Change: A Case Study from the Sanqebethu Valley, Eastern Lesotho." *Erdkunde* 56 (2): 207–21.

Nüsser, Marcus, and Stefan W. Grab. 2002. "Land Degradation and Soil Erosion in the Eastern Highlands of Lesotho, Southern Africa." *Die Erde* 133: 291–311.

Obadare, Ebenezer. 2016. *Humor, Silence, and Civil Society in Nigeria*. Rochester, NY: University of Rochester Press.

O'Connor, James. 1988. "Capitalism, Nature, Socialism: A Theoretical Introduction." *Capitalism Nature Socialism* 1 (1): 11–38.

Odling-Smee, F. John, Kevin N. Laland, and Marcus W. Feldman. 1996. "Niche Construction." *American Naturalist* 147 (4): 641–48.

Ogden, Laura A. 2011. *Swamplife: People, Gators, and Mangroves Entangled in the Everglades*. Minneapolis: University of Minnesota Press.

Oomen, Barbara. 2005. *Chiefs in South Africa: Law, Power and Culture in the Post-Apartheid Era*. Oxford: James Currey.

ORASECOM (Orange-Senqu River Commission). 2008. "Protection of the Orange-Senqu Water Sources 'Sponges Project' Lesotho." Inventory Report 001/2008. Maseru, Lesotho: Orange-Senqu River Commission.

ORASECOM and Lesotho Department of Water Affairs. 2018. "Protecting the Source of Lesotho's 'White Gold.'" Final report. Maseru: Orange-Senqu River Commission.

Organization for Economic Co-Operation and Development (OECD). 2021. "Details of Public Revenues: Lesotho." OECD.Stat. https://stats.oecd.org/Index.aspx?DataSetCode =REVLSO (accessed May 24, 2022).

Orlove, Ben. 1977. *Alpacas, Sheep, and Men: The Wool Export Economy and Regional Society of Southern Peru*. New York: Academic Press.

Orlove, Ben, and Steven C. Caton. 2010. "Water Sustainability: Anthropological Approaches and Prospects." *Annual Review of Anthropology* 39 (1): 401–15.

Otto, Ton, and Nils Bubandt. 2010. *Experiments in Holism: Theory and Practice in Contemporary Anthropology*. New York: Wiley.

Painter, Elizabeth L., and A. Joy Belsky. 1993. "Application of Herbivore Optimization Theory to Rangelands of the Western United States." *Ecological Applications* 3 (1): 2–9.

Peet, Richard, and Michael Watts, eds. 1996. *Liberation Ecologies: Environment, Development, Social Movements*. London: Routledge.

Peters, Pauline E. 1994. *Dividing the Commons: Politics, Policy, and Culture in Botswana*. Charlottesville: University Press of Virginia.

Petrović, Tanja. 2018. "Political Parody and the Politics of Ambivalence." *Annual Review of Anthropology* 47 (1): 201–216.

Petryna, Adriana. 2018. "Wildfires at the Edges of Science: Horizoning Work Amid Runaway Change." *Cultural Anthropology* 33 (4): 570–95.

Phoofolo, Pule. 2003. "Face to Face with Famine: The BaSotho and the Rinderpest, 1897–1899." *Journal of Southern African Studies* 29 (2): 503–27.

Pim, Alan W. 1935. "Financial and Economic Position of Basutoland: Report of the Commission Appointed by the Secretary of State for Dominion Affairs." London: HMSO. Cmd. 4907.

Piot, Charles D. 1991. "Of Persons and Things: Some Reflections on African Spheres of Exchange." *Man*, n.s., 26 (3): 405–24.

Plessis, Pierre L. du. 2018. "Gathering the Kalahari: Tracking Landscapes in Motion." *ProQuest Dissertations and Theses*. Ph.D. Dissertation, Santa Cruz, California: University of California, Santa Cruz.

———. 2022. "Tracking Meat of the Sand: Noticing Multispecies Landscapes in the Kalahari." *Environmental Humanities* 14 (1): 49–70.

Polanyi, Karl. 1944. *The Great Transformation: The Political and Economic Origins of Our Time*. Boston: Beacon.

Posel, Deborah. 2001. "Race as Common Sense: Racial Classification in Twentieth-Century South Africa." *African Studies Review* 44 (2): 87–113.

Poulter, Sebastian. 1979. *Legal Dualism in Lesotho*. Morija, Lesotho: Morija Sesuto Book Depot.

Preez, P.J. du, and L.R. Brown. 2011. "Impact of Domestic Animals on Ecosystem Integrity of Lesotho High Altitude Peatlands." In *Ecological Biodiversity*, edited by Oscar Grillo and Gianfranco Venora, 249–70. Rijeka, Croatia: InTech.

Pule, Neville W. 1999. "Power Struggles in the Basutoland Congress Party, 1991-1997." *Lesotho Social Science Review* 5 (1): 1–30.

Pule, Neville W., and Motlatsi Thabane. 2004. "Lesotho's Land Tenure Regimes: Experiences of Rural Communities and the Calls for Land Reform." *Journal of Modern African Studies* 42 (2): 283–303.

Quinlan, Tim. 1995. "Grassland Degradation and Livestock Rearing in Lesotho." *Journal of Southern African Studies* 21 (2): 491–507.

Quinlan, Tim, and Craig D. Morris. 1994. "Implications of Changes to the Transhumance System for Conservation of the Mountain Catchments in Eastern Lesotho." *African Journal of Range & Forage Science* 11 (3): 76–81.

Quinlan, Tim, and Malcolm Wallis. 2003. "Local Governance in Lesotho: The Central Role of Chiefs." In *Grassroots Governance? Chiefs in Africa and the Afro-Caribbean*, edited by Donald Iain Ray and P.S. Reddy, 145–72. Calgary, Alberta: University of Calgary Press. See http://dspace.ucalgary.ca/bitstream/1880/48646/5/UofCPress_Grassroots Governance_2003.pdf (accessed May 24, 2022).

Raffles, Hugh. 2002. *In Amazonia: A Natural History*. Princeton, NJ: Princeton University Press.

Ranger, Terrence. 1983. "The Invention of Tradition in Colonial Africa." In *The Invention of Tradition*, edited by Eric Hobsbawm and Terrence Ranger. Cambridge: Cambridge University Press.

Rantšo, Tšepiso A. 2000. "Asparagus Production and Sustainable Rural Livelihoods in Lesotho." *Review of Southern African Studies* 4 (2): 15–34.

Reisner, Marc. 1993. *Cadillac Desert: The American West and Its Disappearing Water*. New York: Penguin.

Robinson, Cedric J. 2000. *Black Marxism the Making of the Black Radical Tradition*. Chapel Hill: University of North Carolina Press.

Rocheleau, Dianne, Philip E. Steinberg, and Patricia A. Benjamin. 1995. "Environment, Development, Crisis, and Crusade: Ukambani, Kenya, 1890-1990." *World Development* 23 (6): 1037–51.

Rodriguez, Sylvia. 2006. *Acequia: Water Sharing, Sanctity, and Place*. Santa Fe, NM: School for Advanced Research.

Rogers, Douglas. 2015. *The Depths of Russia: Oil, Power, and Culture after Socialism*. Ithaca, NY: Cornell University Press.

Rohde, Richard F., et al. 2006. "Dynamics of Grazing Policy and Practice: Environmental and Social Impacts in Three Communal Areas of Southern Africa." *Environmental Science and Policy* 9 (3): 302–16.

Root-Bernstein, Meredith, and Jens-Christian Svenning. 2018. "Human Paths Have Positive Impacts on Plant Richness and Diversity: A Meta-Analysis." *Ecology and Evolution* 8 (22): 11111–21.

Rosenberg, Scott. 2004. *Historical Dictionary of Lesotho*. New ed. African Historical Dictionaries, no. 90. Lanham, MD: Scarecrow Press.

Ruiters, Greg, and David A. McDonald, eds. 2004. *The Age of Commodity: Water Privatization in Southern Africa*. London: Routledge.

Rutherford, Danilyn. 2012. *Laughing at Leviathan: Sovereignty and Audience in West Papua*. Chicago: University of Chicago Press.

———. 2018. *Living in the Stone Age: Reflections on the Origins of a Colonial Fantasy*. Chicago: University of Chicago Press.

Rutherford, Michael C., Ladislav Mucina, and Leslie Powrie. 2006. "Biomes and Bioregions of South Africa." In *The Vegetation of South Africa, Lesotho, and Swaziland*, edited by Ladislav Mucina and Michael C. Rutherford, 31–50. Strelitzia 19. Pretoria: South African National Biodiversity Institute.

Sahlins, Marshall D. 1976. *The Use and Abuse of Biology: An Anthropological Critique of Sociobiology*. Ann Arbor: University of Michigan Press.

Sanders, Peter. 2010. *"Throwing Down White Man": Cape Rule and Misrule in Colonial Lesotho, 1871–1884*. Morija, Lesotho: Morija Museum and Archives.

Sandford, Stephen. 1983. *Management of Pastoral Development in the Third World*. New York: Wiley.

Satsuka, Shiho. 2015. *Nature in Translation: Japanese Tourism Encounters the Canadian Rockies*. Durham, NC: Duke University Press.

Savory, Allan. 1988. *Holistic Resource Management*. Covelo, CA: Island.

———. 1991. "Holistic Resource Management: A Conceptual Framework for Ecologically Sound Economic Modelling." *Ecological Economics* 3 (3): 181–91.

Savory, Allan, and Stanley D. Parsons. 1980. "The Savory Grazing Method." *Rangelands* 2 (6): 234–37.

Sayre, Nathan F. 2017. *The Politics of Scale: A History of Rangeland Science*. Chicago: University of Chicago Press.

Scheffer, Marten. 2009. *Critical Transitions in Nature and Society*. Princeton, NJ: Princeton University Press.

Schmidt, Jeremy J. 2017. *Water: Abundance, Scarcity, and Security in the Age of Humanity*. New York: New York University Press.

Schmitz, Gerard, and Firouz Rooyani. 1987. *Lesotho Geology, Geomorphology, Soils*. Roma: National University of Lesotho.

Schnitzler, Antina von. 2016. *Democracy's Infrastructure: Techno-Politics and Protest after Apartheid*. Princeton, NJ: Princeton University Press.

Scott, James C. 1998. *Seeing Like a State: How Certain Schemes to Improve the Human Condition Have Failed*. New Haven, CT: Yale University Press.

Scott, Louis. 1984. "Palynological Evidence for Quaternary Paleoenvironments in Southern Africa." In *Southern African Prehistory and Paleoenvironments*, edited by Richard G. Klein, 65–80. Rotterdam: Balkemn.

Scudder, Thayer. 2006. *The Future of Large Dams: Dealing with Social, Environmental, Institutional, and Political Costs*. London: Earthscan.

Sekhesa, Nathan. 1912. "Makhulo a Felile." *Leselinyana la Lesotho*, October 3, 419.

Sello, Kefiloe. 2020. "Rivers That Become Dams: An Ethnography of Water Commodification in Lesotho." PhD diss., University of Cape Town.

Sene, K.J., et al. 1998. "Rainfall and Flow Variations in the Lesotho Highlands." *International Journal of Climatology* 18 (3): 329–45.

Sharp, Lesley A. 2000. "The Commodification of the Body and Its Parts." *Annual Review of Anthropology* 29 (1): 287–328.

Showers, Kate Barger. 2002. "Water Scarcity and Urban Africa: An Overview of Urban-Rural Water Linkages." *World Development* 30 (4): 621–48.

———. 2005. *Imperial Gullies: Soil Erosion and Conservation in Lesotho.* Columbus: Ohio University Press.

———. 2006. "From Forestry to Soil Conservation: British Tree Management in Lesotho's Grassland Ecosystem." *Conservation and Society* 4 (1): 1–35.

———. 2009. "Congo River's Grand Inga Hydroelectricity Scheme: Linking Environmental History, Policy and Impact." *Water History* 1 (1): 31–58.

Singh, M. 2000. "Basutoland: A Historical Journey into the Environment." *Environment and History* 6 (1): 31–70.

Sivapalan, M., et al. 2014. "Socio-Hydrology: Use-Inspired Water Sustainability Science for the Anthropocene." *Earth's Future* 2 (4): 2013EF000164.

Skinner, T.E. 1976. "A Comparison between the Effects of Continuous Grazing by Angora Goats and Merino Sheep on Veld in the Central Lower Karoo." *Proceedings of the Annual Congresses of the Grassland Society of Southern Africa* 11 (1): 131–34.

Smith, A.D. 2010. "Bankrupt Lesotho Pleads to be Swallowed Up by South Africa: Popular Pressure for Unity Comes as Pretoria Closes Border to Workers." *Guardian Weekly*, June 11, p. 12.

Smith, H.J., et al. 2000. "Soil Loss Modelling in the Lesotho Highlands Water Project Catchment Areas." *South African Geographical Journal* 82 (2): 64–69.

Squires, V.R., and W.S.W. Trollope. 1979. "Allelopathy in the Karoo Shrub, Chrysocoma Tenuifolia." *South African Journal of Science* 75: 88–89.

Statistics South Africa. 2020. "General Household Survey." P0318. Pretoria, South Africa: Statistics South Africa. See www.statssa.gov.za/publications/P0318/P03182018.pdf (accessed May 24, 2022).

Steyn, Christien, et al. 2017. "Alien Plant Species That Invade High Elevations Are Generalists: Support for the Directional Ecological Filtering Hypothesis." *Journal of Vegetation Science* 28 (2): 337–46.

Stocking, Michael. 1995. "Soil Erosion in Developing Countries: Where Geomorphology Fears to Tread!" *Catena* 25 (1): 253–67.

Stocking, Michael, Qalabane Chakela, and Henry Elwell. 1988. "An Improved Methodology for Erosion Hazard Mapping Part I: The Technique." *Geografiska Annaler*, ser. A, *Physical Geography* 70 (3): 169–80.

Stoetzer, Bettina. 2018. "Ruderal Ecologies: Rethinking Nature, Migration, and the Urban Landscape in Berlin." *Cultural Anthropology* 33 (2): 295–323.

Stoler, Ann Laura. 2009. *Along the Archival Grain: Epistemic Anxieties and Colonial Common Sense.* Princeton, NJ: Princeton University Press.

———, ed. 2013. *Imperial Debris: On Ruins and Ruination.* Durham, NC: Duke University Press.

Strang, Veronica. 2004. *The Meaning of Water.* Oxford: Berg.

Swallow, Brent M., and Ray P. Brokken. 1987. "Cattle Marketing Policy in Lesotho." Network Paper no. 14. ALPAN—African Livestock Policy Analysis Network. Addis Ababa, Ethiopia: International Livestock Centre for Africa.

Swanson, Heather Anne. 2015. "Shadow Ecologies of Conservation: Co-Production of Salmon Landscapes in Hokkaido, Japan, and Southern Chile." *Geoforum* 61 (May): 101–10.

———. 2017. "Methods for Multispecies Anthropology: Analysis of Salmon Otoliths and Scales." *Social Analysis* 61 (2): 81–99.

Swanson, Maynard W. 1968. "Urban Origins of Separate Development." *Race* 10 (1): 31–40.

Syvitski, James P.M., et al. 2009. "Sinking Deltas Due to Human Activities." *Nature Geoscience* 2 (10): 681–86.

Taussig, Michael. 1997. *The Magic of the State.* New York: Routledge.

Tempelhoff, Johann W.N. 2003. *The Substance of Ubiquity: Rand Water, 1903–2003.* Vanderbijlpark, South Africa: Kleio.

Tennyson, Larry. 2012. "Review and Assessment of Integrated Watershed Management Project." Maseru: Ministry of Forestry and Land Reclamation, Government of Lesotho.

Thabane, Motlatsi. 1996. "A Mutual-Benefit Utopia Where Exploitation Was Unknown? Elizabeth Eldredge's Liberal Interpretation of Social Relations in Nineteenth-Century Lesotho." *South African Historical Journal* 34 (1): 240–48.

———. 2000. "Shifts from Old to New Social and Ecological Environments in the Lesotho Highlands Water Scheme: Relocating Residents of the Mohale Dam Area." *Journal of Southern African Studies* 26 (4): 633–54.

———. 2002a. "The Nature of Social Relations in the Nineteenth Century." In *Essays on Aspects of the Political Economy of Lesotho, 1500–2000,* edited by Neville W. Pule and Motlatsi Thabane, 59–77. Roma: Department of History, National University of Lesotho.

———. 2002b. "Aspects of Colonial Society and Economy, 1868–1966." In *Essays on Aspects of the Political Economy of Lesotho, 1500–2000,* edited by Neville W. Pule and Motlatsi Thabane, 103–30. Roma: Department of History, National University of Lesotho.

———. 2006. "Developing Lesotho's Water Resources: The Lesotho Highlands Water Scheme." In *A History of Water,* vol. 2, *The Political Economy of Water,* edited by Richard Coopey and Terje Tvedt, 368–89. London: Tauris.

Thamae, Mabusetsa Lenka, and Lori Pottinger. 2006. *On the Wrong Side of Development: Lessons Learned from the Lesotho Highlands Water Project.* Maseru, Lesotho: Transformation Resource Centre.

Thornton, Russell. 1931. "Report on Pastoral and Agricultural Conditions in Basutoland." Unpublished, in file Lesotho National Archives 212.

Tilley, Helen. 2011. *Africa as a Living Laboratory: Empire, Development, and the Problem of Scientific Knowledge, 1870–1950.* Chicago: University of Chicago Press.

Tlali, Caswell. 2012. "Masupha Sole Back as Water Adviser." *The M&G Online,* November 2, 2012, https://mg.co.za/article/2012-11-02-00-masupha-sole-back-as-water-adviser (accessed on May 10, 2022).

Tregurtha, Norma. N.d. "Enhancing the Structure and Performance of Value Chains: A Case Study of the Lesotho Wool and Mohair Sector." See www.value-chains.org/dyn/bds/docs/452/Tregurtha.pdf (accessed on May 24, 2022).

Trimble, Stanley W, and Pierre Crosson. 2000. "U.S. Soil Erosion Rates: Myth and Reality." *Science* 289: 248–50.

Tsikata, Dzodzi A. 2006. *Living in the Shadow of the Large Dams: Long Term Responses of Downstream and Lakeside Communities of Ghana's Volta River Project.* Leiden: Brill.

Tsing, Anna Lowenhaupt. 1993. *In the Realm of the Diamond Queen: Marginality in an Out-of-the-Way Place.* Princeton, NJ: Princeton University Press.

———. 2000. "The Global Situation." *Cultural Anthropology* 15 (3): 327–60.

———. 2005. *Friction: An Ethnography of Global Connection*. Princeton, NJ: Princeton University Press.

———. 2009. "Supply Chains and the Human Condition." *Rethinking Marxism* 21 (2): 148–76.

———. 2015. *The Mushroom at the End of the World: On the Possibility of Life in Capitalist Ruins*. Princeton, NJ: Princeton University Press.

———. 2017. "The Buck, the Bull, and the Dream of the Stag: Some Unexpected Weeds of the Anthropocene." *Suomen Antropologi: Journal of the Finnish Anthropological Society* 42 (1): 3–21.

Tsing, Anna Lowenhaupt, et al. 2016. *Arts of Living on a Damaged Planet: Stories from the Anthropocene*. Minneapolis: University of Minnesota Press.

Tsing, Anna Lowenhaupt, Andrew S. Mathews, and Nils Bubandt. 2019. "Patchy Anthropocene: Landscape Structure, Multispecies History, and the Retooling of Anthropology; An Introduction to Supplement 20." *Current Anthropology* 60 (S20): S186–97.

Tsing, Anna Lowenhaupt, et al. 2020. "Feral Atlas: The More-Than-Human Anthropocene." Palo Alto, CA: Stanford University Press. See http://feralatlas.org (accessed May 24, 2022).

Turkon, David. 2003. "Modernity, Tradition, and the Demystification of Cattle in Lesotho." *African Studies* 62 (2): 147–69.

Turner, Stephen D. 2004. "A Land without Fences: Range Management in Lesotho." In *Rights, Resources, and Rural Development Community-Based Natural Resource Management in Southern Africa*, edited by Christo Fabricius and Eddie Kock, 174–81. Sterling, VA: Earthscan.

———. 2009. "Promoting Food Security in Lesotho: Issues and Options." Report. Maseru. Lesotho: Priority Support Program.

Turpie, Jane, et al. 2021. "Accounting for Land Cover Changes and Degradation in the Katse and Mohale Dam Catchments of the Lesotho Highlands." *African Journal of Range and Forage Science* 38 (1): 53–66.

United Nations Development Programme (UNDP). 2012. "Capacity Building and Knowledge Management for Sustainable Land Management in Lesotho." PIMS 3044. Maseru, Lesotho: UNDP.

Van der Vyver, Fh, et al. 1985. "Valsiekte (Falling Disease): A Nervous Disorder in Lambs Suspected of Being Caused by the Plant Chrysocoma-Tenuifolia." *Journal of the South African Veterinary Association-Tydskrif Van Die Suid-Afrikaanse Veterinere Vereniging* 56 (2): 65–68.

van Zinderen Bakker, E.M., and M.J.A. Werger. 1974. "Environment, Vegetation, and Phytogeography of the High-Altitude Bogs of Lesotho." *Plant Ecology* 29 (1): 37–49.

Vayda, Andrew, and Bradley Walters. 1999. "Against Political Ecology." *Human Ecology* 27 (1): 167–79.

Vetter, Susi. 2005. "Rangelands at Equilibrium and Non-Equilibrium: Recent Developments in the Debate." *Journal of Arid Environments* 62 (2): 321–41.

Walker, Peter A. 2005. "Political Ecology: Where Is the Ecology?" *Progress in Human Geography* 29 (1): 73–82.

Wallerstein, Immanuel. 2004. *World-Systems Analysis: An Introduction*. Durham, NC: Duke University Press.

Waters, Colin N., et al. 2016. "The Anthropocene Is Functionally and Stratigraphically Distinct from the Holocene." *Science* 351 (6269): aad2622.

Weber, Max. 1978. *Economy and Society*. Translated by Guenther Roth and Claus Wittich. Berkeley: University of California Press.

Weisiger, Marsha L. 2011. *Dreaming of Sheep in Navajo Country*. Seattle: University of Washington Press.

West, Paige. 2006. *Conservation Is Our Government Now: The Politics of Ecology in Papua New Guinea*. Durham, NC: Duke University Press.

———. 2012. *From Modern Production to Imagined Primitive: The Social World of Coffee from Papua New Guinea*. Durham, NC: Duke University Press.

Whatmore, Sarah J. 2009. "Mapping Knowledge Controversies: Science, Democracy, and the Redistribution of Expertise." *Progress in Human Geography* 33 (5): 587–98.

White, Richard. 1983. *The Roots of Dependency: Subsistance, Environment, and Social Change among the Choctaws, Pawnees, and Navajos*. Lincoln: University of Nebraska Press.

Whitington, Jerome. 2019. *Anthropogenic Rivers: The Production of Uncertainty in Lao Hydropower*. Ithaca, NY: Cornell University Press.

Wilcock, Deirdre, Gary Brierley, and Richard Howitt. 2013. "Ethnogeomorphology." *Progress in Physical Geography: Earth and Environment* 37 (5): 573–600.

Williams, Raymond. 2005. *Culture and Materialism: Selected Essays*. New York: Verso.

Wolpe, Harold. 1972. "Capitalism and Cheap Labour-Power in South Africa: From Segregation to Apartheid." *Economy and Society* 1 (4): 425–56.

Workman, Cassandra. 2013. "A Critical Ethnography of Globalization in Lesotho, Africa: Syndemic Water Insecurity and the Micro-Politics of Participation." PhD diss., University of South Florida, Tampa.

World Bank. 1991. "Lesotho Highlands Water Project, Phase 1A: Staff Appraisal Report, 1991." Report no. 8853. Washington, DC: World Bank.

———. 1995. *Lesotho Poverty Assessment*. Report no. 13171-LSO. Washington, DC: World Bank.

———. 2010. "Project Performance Assessment Report (Document #54359). Lesotho Highlands Water Project, Phase 1B, Community Development Support Project." Washington, DC: World Bank.

———. 2016. *Lesotho*. Data Bank. See http://data.worldbank.org/country/Lesotho (accessed May 24, 2022). Washington, DC: World Bank.

———. 2019. "Lesotho Poverty Assessment: Progress and Challenges in Reducing Poverty." Report no. 144347-LSO. Washington, DC: World Bank.

World Commission on Dams. 2000. *Dams and Development, a New Framework for Decision-Making: The Report of the World Commission on Dams*. London and Sterling, VA: Earthscan.

Wynter, Sylvia. 2003. "Unsettling the Coloniality of Being/Power/Truth/Freedom: Towards the Human, after Man, Its Overrepresentation—An Argument." *CR: The New Centennial Review* 3 (3): 257–337.

Xinhua General Overseas News Service. 1986. "Lesotho's Leader Visits South Africa." Xinhua General Overseas News Service, March 26. Gaborone, Botswana.

Yusoff, Kathryn. 2018. *A Billion Black Anthropocenes or None*. Minneapolis: University of Minnesota Press.

Zarfl, Christiane, et al. 2015. "A Global Boom in Hydropower Dam Construction." *Aquatic Sciences* 77 (1): 161–70.

Zee, Jerry C. 2017. "Holding Patterns: Sand and Political Time at China's Desert Shores." *Cultural Anthropology* 32 (2): 215–41.

Zunckel, Kevan. 2003. "Managing and Conserving Southern African Grasslands with High Endemism: The Maloti-Drakensberg Transfrontier Conservation and Development Program." *Mountain Research and Development* 23 (2): 113–18.

A-B-C rotational grazing system: as vertical transhumance, 87, 137; history of, 87, 137; in relation to Sponges Project, 87–88; seasonal livestock movements according to, 12, 87–88; structure of, 87. *See also* rotational grazing

abundance. *See* forage, shrubs, water, water abundance

active herding: as element in Sponges Project grazing reform, 13, 84–88, 99, 120–21, 134, 139, 164n34. *See also* Khubelu Sponges Project

active storage, of reservoirs: as impacted by reservoir sedimentation, 46, 50–51; definition of, 46; in relation to dead storage, 46, 50–51. *See also* dead storage, live storage, storage

Aerni-Flessner, Johnathan, 74, 148n26, 155nn56,58, 160nn19,20, 161n28, 165n39, 174n7

Africa: cattle in, 102–113, 118–21, 135–38, 152n9, 161n41; colonization of, 3, 8, 33, 48–49, 105–8, 152n90; dams in, 148n23, 174n7; depiction as empty in colonial narratives, 3, 48–49, 152n90; independence of countries in, 3, 5, 74, 102, 160n20; land degradation narratives in, 48–50, 75, 83–84, 86, 112–13, 118–21, 123–24, 135–38, 145, 171n8; perceptions of farming and farmers in, 48–50, 75, 83–84, 102–8, 112–13, 118–19, 123, 135–36, 145, 171n8; rangeland ecology in, 21, 83–84, 86, 123–24, 135–38, 145, 163nn20,23; scholarly traditions

about, 21, 23, 83–84, 124; the state in, 66, 99, 107, 165n46; treatment of African people during apartheid, 2, 8, 33, 48–49, 161n41. *See also specific countries and cities*

African National Congress (ANC), 73, 148n27

African studies, 21, 23

Afrikaans, 12, 101, 115–116, 126. *See also* Afrikaners

Afrikaners: Afrikaner farmer complaints about grazing in Lesotho, 9–10, 32, 48–50; ancestry of, 5–6, 32, 48; as farmers in Orange Free State, 9–10, 32, 48–50, 106; as political constituency of National Party, 5–6, 9–10, 32, 48–50; fleeing British rule in the Cape, 32, 48, 106; "Great Trek," 32, 48; relationship with British, 5–6, 9–10, 32, 48–50; settler colonialism of, 5–6, 9–10, 26, 32–33, 48–49, 106, 125. *See also* Afrikaans

aid: from international organizations, 6, 25, 28, 34, 72–75, 77, 84, 96–97; importance to Lesotho's economy, 6, 28, 34, 72–75, 77. *See also* conservation, development

Anthropocene, 2, 15, 20–21, 123, 142–43, 147n1, 152n89

apartheid: Bantustans as element in, 7–8, 10, 30, 102, 114; beginning of, 2, 5–8, 149n42; contradictions of, 8, 10, 30; end of, 2, 8–9, 30, 102, 114; fight against, 2, 6, 8, 36, 73; impacts on Lesotho, 1–3, 5–10, 25, 30, 36, 64, 73, 102, 108, 114, 122, 145; international sanctions against, 6, 8, 36, 73; landscape effects of, 25, 122, 145; legacy of, 2–3, 5–6, 8, 10, 25, 30, 64, 73, 102, 108, 114, 145; logic of, 1–3, 8, 10, 102, 108; structure of, 2–3, 6, 8, 10, 102, 108, 149n42

aphorisms, 13, 38–40, 43, 59, 84–85, 121, 134, 144, 146, 156n75. *See also* proverbs

auctions: of livestock, 89, 113, 170nn73,75; of wool, 110. *See also* livestock

Australia, 33

Ballenden, Peter, 5, 9–10

Bantustans, 7–8, 8*map*, 30, 33, 102, 108, 114, 119. *See also* apartheid

bare soil: as index of land degradation, 124. *See also* degradation

basalt: in contrast to sandstone of lowlands, 47, 50–51; in geology of highlands, 31, 47, 50–51, 127. *See also* sandstone

Basotho National Party (BNP), 75, 94–95, 95*table*, 161nn34,36,38, 165n54, 166nn57,60. *See also* National movement

Basutoland: agriculture in, 9–10, 32, 49, 100, 105–8, 165nn35,39, 168n34; anxiety about highland landscapes in, 9–10, 49, 54–55, 94, 100; class relations in, 93–94, 103, 106–7, 168nn30,40; colonization of, 5, 32, 93–95, 100, 105–6, 153nn28,29, 165n39; formation of, 32; independence of, 94–95; relationship to Britain, 5–6, 9–10, 32, 49, 93–95, 100, 105–6, 153nn28,29; relationship to South Africa, 5–6, 9–10, 32, 49, 105–6, 153n28; soil conservation in, 9–10, 49, 54–55, 94, 100. *See also* Lesotho

Basutoland Congress Party (BCP), 75, 94–95, 161nn34,36, 165n54, 166nn57,60. *See also* Congress movement

Basutoland Progressive Association (BPA), 93–94. *See also* Lekhotla la Bafo

Bechuanaland, 49, 153n28. *See also* Botswana

bedload, 14, 53. *See also* sedimentation, soil erosion

bewys, 101

bitter Karoo bush, 54–55. See also *Chrysocoma ciliata*, shrubs

BKB, 110, 169n59, 170n60

Blaikie, Piers, 23, 125, 145

Bophuthatswana, 8*map*, 33. *See also* Bantustans

borders: Drakensberg mountains as forming, 31–32, 114; movement of livestock across, 25, 102–3, 110–15, 130, 170nn66,74, 173n34; settler colonial impact on Lesotho's, 8*map*, 32, 106, 125, 148n26; South Africa's power to close

Lesotho's borders, 36, 125, 148n27; use in regulating flow of labor from Bantustans and Lesotho, 2–3, 8, 10, 33, 125; use in regulating flow of Lesotho's water, 2–3, 10, 15, 28–29

Botswana, 19–20, 37, 49, 118–19, 153n28, 155n61, 164n39, 166n63

bovine mystique, 104–5, 108, 111–13, 118. *See also* commodities, livestock, ovicaprine mystique

bridewealth, 69, 104, 108, 170n71. See also *lobola*

Britain: British aid to Lesotho, 73, 77; British Commonwealth, 5–6; British colonialism in Lesotho, 5–7, 9–10, 32–33, 48–49, 73–75, 92–94, 100, 106, 113, 115, 137–38, 153nn28,29, 166n57, 169n43, 172n23; British colonialism in South Africa, 5–6, 9–10, 32, 48–49, 153nn28,29; British indirect rule, 75, 81, 93–94, 96, 144, 153n30, 166n57; British soil conservation efforts, 9–10, 48–50, 96, 100, 113, 137–38, 160n8, 166n57; Lesotho independence from, 6, 8–9, 35, 73–74, 77, 94, 160n20, 166n57; textile industry in, 105, 169n55

British indirect rule. *See* Britain, indirect rule

bureaucracy: bureaucratic administration of apartheid, 149n42; bureaucratic ecology, 20, 80–81, 99, 118, 149n45; bureaucratic reforms, 11–14, 24, 60–62, 80–99, 134–35, 144–145; critique of, 81–83, 162nn10,14, 163n17. *See also* conservation bureaucrats, meetings

bureaucrats. *See* bureaucracy, conservation bureaucrats

burning of rangelands, 23, 25, 54, 121, 128, 133–36, 139, 173n36. *See also* fire

Butha-Buthe: district of, x*map*, 6; town of, 114, 149n43, 161n36

by-products: 14–16, 139, 145. *See also* production, Williams, Raymond

cabinet ministers, 93. *See also* Lesotho government

Caledon River, 7*map*, 68, 158n45

canal: Panama Canal, 66; use in water production, 120

Cape Colony, 32, 153nn28,29

Cape Town, 2, 7*map*, 8*map*

Cape Province, 7*map*, 8*map*, 48

capitalism: alienation under, 29, 43; contradictions of, 149n41, 150n56, 174n19; effects on environment, 143, 149n41, 150n56, 174n19; nature of, 162n9; racial capitalism; 1, 143, 145. *See also* commodities

Carse, Ashley, 66

catchment: as object of concern, 23–24, 43, 47–48, 52–53, 57, 66, 100; as unit of scale, 30, 66; definition of, 153n16; management of, 24, 53, 68, 77, 118; of Lesotho Highlands Water Project, 10–11, 14–16, 47–48, 51–53, 57, 67–68, 70–72, 98, 100, 120. *See also* Integrated Catchment Management, upstream

cattle posts: as spaces of freedom, 131–32, 135, 139; descriptions of, 12, 13*fig*, 58, 84, 87–88, 106–8, 112, 123, 125–134, 127*fig*, 137, 150n46, 163n22, 172n16; history of, 87, 106–7, 172n26; life at, 12–13, 84–85, 87–88, 111, 115, 121, 129–132; *Motebong ha ho lisoe* (one is not herded at the cattle posts), 13, 84–85, 121, 134. *See also* herders, herding

Chakela, Qalabane, 51

channelization: of global flows, 16; of water, 17, 52, 64, 66–67, 75, 121, 126, 138. *See also* soil erosion

chieftaincy: history of, 25, 92–97, 99, 103, 165n46, 168nn30,40; perceptions of, 17, 20, 57, 81, 93–95, 166nn57,60, 168n30; responsibilities of, 12, 75, 81, 88, 91–94, 171n4; structure of, 9, 91, 93, 165nn44,45. *See also* headman, indirect rule, legal dualism, principal chiefs, ward chiefs

Chrysocoma ciliata (sehala-hala), 12, 54–56, 55*fig*, 56*fig*, 60, 126–27, 137–38, 159nn52,53, 173n36. *See also* shrubs

civil service, 15, 35, 39, 57, 65, 91, 94, 97, 165n54

civilization, 3

clean-break commodities, 105, 118. *See also* commodities

climate: as influence on environmental patterns, 16, 22, 25, 59, 81, 83–84, 120, 136, 139, 145, 163n23, 172n27; of Lesotho, 30, 40–41, 83–84, 136, 139, 145. *See also* climate change

climate change, 2, 16, 30, 40–41, 86, 120. *See also* Anthropocene, climate

colonialism: impact on land and land management, 24, 49–50, 54–55, 65, 73–75, 81, 83–84, 92–97, 106, 136–39, 156n57, 159n52; indirect rule, 75, 81, 93–94, 144, 153n30; in Lesotho, 5–10, 23–24, 26, 31–33, 49–50, 65, 73–75, 77, 81, 92–97, 105–8, 113, 125, 136–38, 156n57, 164n39; in South Africa, 5–10, 26, 31–33, 48–49, 105–6; legacies of, 3, 54–55, 74–75, 77, 83, 92–97, 99, 137–38, 144, 159n52. *See also* settler colonialism

commodities: clean-break commodities, 105, 118; exchange of, 3, 29, 103–105, 118; labor as, 16, 41, 148n19; livestock as, 12, 25, 100, 102–105, 108, 111–12, 118, 120–21, 135–36; production of, 1, 5, 10–11, 15–16, 23–25, 29–30, 36–37, 41–44, 67, 77, 100, 102–5, 118, 120–22, 148n19; recalcitrant commodities, 118, 152n9; water as, 1, 5, 10–11, 15–16, 23–24, 29–30, 36–37, 41–44, 67, 77, 100, 102, 121–22, 145

common land tenure, 13, 85, 87, 90, 95–96, 99, 123, 159n52, 164n33, 166n63, 171n4

compensation: for *fato-fato* workers, 63, 66, 70, 72, 74–75; for herding work, 13, 111, 115, 130; for people impacted by dams, 34, 72, 78, 142, 162n43. *See also* resettlement

Congress movement, 94–95, 95*table*. *See also* Basutoland Congress Party (BCP)

conquered territories, 8*map*, 32, 148n26

conservation: conservation-development industry, 57, 83, 92, 104; conservation organizations and initiatives, 11, 18–19, 21, 37, 59–61, 63–78, 84–85, 87–92, 96–99, 113, 120–21. *See also* soil conservation, conservation bureaucrats

conservation bureaucrats: beliefs regarding the importance of management to rangeland health by, 11–15, 17, 20, 39–40, 54–62, 69–73, 80–99, 120–21, 149n45; ideas about ecology by, 10–14, 17–22, 24, 39–40, 54–61, 69–71, 80–81, 84–87, 118, 120–21, 124–25, 134, 139, 144–45, 159n52; interactions with herders and livestock owners by, 14–15, 21–22, 69–73, 85, 88–92; perceptions of chiefs by, 17, 80–84, 91–92, 95–98; perceptions of herders and livestock owners by, 11, 20, 69–72, 84–85, 104–5, 113, 118, 120–21, 134, 139, 145; perceptions of wetlands by, 11, 17–19, 24, 54, 84–85; use of metaphor by, 18–19, 39–40

Coplan, David, 165n44, 169n52, 172n18

Coquery-Vidrovitch, Catherine, 99

corral (*kraal*), 11–12, 57, 84, 89–90, 107, 115, 125, 131, 134, 164n34, 170n72

core: core-periphery relations, 4, 6, 11, 64, 145, 171n2. *See also* marginality

councils: history of, 92–96, 166n60; local councilors, 19, 39, 59–60, 90–98, 113, 136, 166n60; local councils, 81, 91–98; relationships with chiefs, 91–98, 95*table*, 166n60; responsibilities of, 91, 93, 95–98. *See also* chieftaincy, legal dualism

coup d'etat, 6, 36, 73, 94–95, 148n27, 165n54

critique: limits of, 21

cropland: inundation of, 34, 154n46; ownership of, 171n4; plowing of, 108, 112, 123, 170n71

currency, 35

dams: as part of global industry, 141–42, 174n5; as part of the Lesotho Highlands Water Project, 1, 3–4, 6, 7map, 9–10, 22, 26–30, 34–38, 46–53, 56, 59, 66–72, 78, 82, 118, 120, 141–42, 154n46, 155n61, 157n5, 158n45, 174n13; as "temples of modernity," 3; impacts of, 34, 38, 61, 72, 78, 141–42, 154n46, 157n20, 162n43, 174nn5,13; sedimentation problems associated with, 4–5, 10–11, 14–17, 23–24, 43–54, 59, 61, 65, 67–71, 118, 120, 125, 141–44, 157n18, 158nn45,48, 160n17; financing of, 6, 155n49

"day zero," 2

dead storage, 46, 50. See also live storage, storage

decentralization, 95–97, 166n60

degradation: definitions of, 20, 124; of land, 4, 9, 57, 61, 70–73, 80, 97, 104, 106, 112, 118, 121, 123–26, 135–39, 144–45; of wetlands, 17–19, 46, 57, 59, 85, 121, 126, 126fig, 128, 133, 139, 151n68

demand: of labor, 8; of water, 3, 6, 10, 141; of wool, 105

demonstration, 59–60

desiccation, 54–55, 107

deportation, 8

development: anthropology of, 66, 103–5 124; concept of, 88, 124, 155n56, 160n20; "developmentalism," 74; development industry, 14, 19, 57, 82–83, 92, 96, 102–5, 144; development initiatives, 14, 34, 65, 74–75, 82, 88–92, 95–96, 103–5, 112–13, 135; development refugees, 142; economic development, 2, 28, 75, 96, 141, 155n56; ntlafatso, 88, 91–92, 94–97, 95table; village development committees, 95. See also ntlafatso

diamond mining, 6, 32, 34. See also mining

Disaster Risk Reduction Policy, 39

Disaster Management Authority, 39

disorientation: regarding historiography of the landscape, 15–16, 20, 56, 124, 135; regarding the nature of water, 135; while walking through cattle post areas, 129

displacement. See resettlement

dissolution: of Bantustans, 8, 30, 114; of development-conservation initiatives, 82; of Lesotho into South Africa, 8–9, 30, 35

districts: administrative districts of Lesotho, xmap, 169n43; livestock production in Mokhotlong District, 109, 113, 173n34; rivalries between districts of Lesotho, 58

diversion furrows, 39–40, 68–69, 71–72, 77. See also soil conservation

diversion tunnel, 5, 45, 48, 51. See also Lesotho Highlands Water Project

downstream impacts of dams, 61, 142, 157n20, 174n13

Drakensberg Mountains: as refuge, 31–32, 106; as site of anxiety, 20, 106, 151n75; climate of, 31, 37; geography of, 31, 37, 153n18; historical ecology of, 157n13, 173n34

dreams: entrepreneurial dreamworlds, 103, 108, 118–19, 130

dredging, 5, 43, 48, 68. See also reservoirs

drivers: of landscape change, 138; of regional economic integration, 28

Driver, Thackwray, 10

drought: as characteristic of Lesotho, 30, 38, 44, 61, 121; as driver of landscape change, 17, 44, 121, 137–38; dam reservoirs as indices of, 37; drought-resistance of shrubs, 54, 59, 121, 138, 173n36; historical incidence of, 2–3, 30, 32–33, 37–38, 41, 69, 101, 106–7, 122, 156n78; stemming from El Niño Southern Oscillation, 37. See also climate change, floods, rainfall

Dust Bowl, 48

dwarf shrubs. See shrubs

earthquakes. See reservoir-induced seismicity

ecology: Allan Savory's Holistic Resource Management, 11–14, 81, 84–88, 90–93, 97–99, 134, 163n20, 164nn27,28; cultural ecology, 21; political ecology, 124; rangeland ecology, 13, 22, 81, 83–88, 97–99, 137, 163nn19,23, 164n28. See also bureaucratic ecology; negative ecology, Savory, Allan

El Niño Southern Oscillation (ENSO), 37, 156n78

elections, 75, 94–96

electricity: electrification, 34; hydroelectricity, 6, 28, 34–35, 45–46, 155n52

elites, 3, 24–25, 36, 66–67, 75, 78, 93–94, 97, 143–45

empire: and imperialism, 16, 83–84, 119, 135–36, 143; imperial debris, 14, 83–84; green imperialism, 16, 72

encroachment. See shrubs

engineers: engineering forage, 25, 121, 133–135, 139; engineering storage, 5, 10, 25, 66–67, 139, 144; hydro-engineering, 1, 6, 27, 52, 66–67, 141–43; social engineering, 25, 41, 104; water engineers, 4–6, 10, 15–18, 20, 24, 37, 44–52, 62, 77, 120, 124–25, 145, 158n48, 162n10

entrepreneurship, 103, 108, 110, 114, 117–19

environmental change, 20, 22, 138. See also degradation

ephemeral streams, 12, 17

equilibrium: rangeland ecology theory of, 163nn20,23

erosion. *See* soil erosion
eSwatini, 49, 153n28
ethnoscience, 21, 48, 157n6
Euryops decumbens, 128. *See also* shrubs
evolutionary history of rangelands, 137,
139, 172n27

Fanakalo, 14
farming: crop agriculture, 16, 123–24, 133;
farmers in South Africa, 5, 9, 29, 32, 48–50,
106, 155n49, 164n33; fodder cropping, 25,
116–17, 121, 123–24, 133; land ownership,
164n33; of livestock, 14, 16, 19, 54, 85, 87, 98,
103–114, 116–19, 124, 130, 164n39, 170nn60,76.
See also livestock
fato-fato, 24–25, 63–67, 70, 72, 75–78.
See also Integrated Catchment Management,
Integrated Water Resource Management, soil
conservation
feasibility study: for LHWP, 36, 49–52,
55, 174n13
fees: for attending school, 102; for gun license,
32; for impounded livestock, 81, 89–92,
97, 99, 123, 136; for use of rangelands, 96,
167nn64,66
fences: absence of, 13, 84–85, 87, 134, 164n33;
use in rangeland reforms, 13, 87. *See also*
common land tenure
Ferguson, James, 74, 95, 102–5, 111–13,
166n60, 170n71
Festuca caprina, 55, 134. *See also* grasses
fines: for impounded livestock, for impounded
livestock, 81, 89–92, 97, 99, 123, 136
fire: effects on landscape, 25, 54, 134–35, 173n36;
use in pasture management 23, 25, 121, 128,
133–36, 139. *Also see* burning
flooding, 2, 9–10, 17, 39, 46, 48–50, 52, 61. *See also*
drought, rainfall
flows: as concept in social theory, 15–16; natural
river flow regime, 17–18, 46–47, 142, 174n13;
of people across borders, 2–3, 10, 16, 33, 125;
of water to South Africa, 3, 15–16, 23, 28–29,
37, 45–46, 51, 67, 142, 145–46; of water over
land, 1, 4–5, 9–12, 14–17, 20, 22–24, 39, 42–48,
54, 59–72, 80, 88, 100, 120–21, 135, 143–144.
See also fluvial, overflowing Katse Dam,
water abundance
fluvial: definition of, 15; fluvial economy, 14–16,
85; fluvial imagination, 5, 9, 17, 24, 45, 48, 58,
61–62, 76, 100, 120–21, 135, 143, 150n51; fluvial
landscape, 10, 15, 17, 61, 71; fluvial pedagogy,
19, 24, 44–45, 53–61, 67; fluvial theory, 1, 10,
16, 22, 48–50, 135, 143, 162n43; fluvial water,

14, 22, 42–44, 48, 53, 61, 67, 69, 135, 144.
See also flows, volumetric water
fodder, 25, 116–17, 121, 123–24, 133. *See also*
forage, grasses
Food Self-Sufficiency Programme, 74.
See also *fato-fato*
foothills: geography of, 6, 37, 87, 94, 153n17
forage: abundance or scarcity of, 17, 25, 41, 60,
81, 83, 87–88, 123–24, 134, 164n36, 170n76,
173n29; engineering forage, 25, 121, 133–135,
139; livestock preferences for, 15, 20, 25,
54, 127, 134, 139, 145, 159n52; palatable and
unpalatable forage, 11, 15, 25, 54, 60, 68,
85–86, 121, 133–34, 139. *See also* fodder, grasses
Frasers trading post, 168n39
Free State Province (South Africa), x*map*, 29, 37,
48, 106, 148n28, 154n40
frontline states: Lesotho's status as, 6.
See also apartheid
future: climate future, 3, 6, 10, 61; dams as bridge
between past and, 3. *See also* "temples of
modernity"

gabions, 24, 39–40, 40*fig*, 63, 68, 70–72, 71*fig*, 77,
144. *See also* soil conservation
geopolitics, 1, 6, 20, 42, 66, 151n73
globalization, 16
gold: gold mining, 1–2, 6, 9, 32–33, 141; gold rush,
. 2, 32; water as "white gold," 18, 28. See also
mining
governance: as *puso*, 88, 91–95, 95*table*, 97, 99;
conservation as, 17, 77. *See also* chieftaincy,
ntlafatso
Grant, James Murray, 172n23
grasses: annual grasses, 11, 86, 127, 133; burning
to encourage, 23, 25, 54, 121, 128, 133–36, 139,
173n36; fodder production, 25, 116–17, 121,
123–24, 133; forage grasses, 11, 55, 60, 68,
85–86, 133–34, 159n52, 173n29; in relation
to shrubs, 11, 54–55, 59, 81, 86, 128, 134, 139,
159nn52,58, 173n36; perennial grasses, 11, 86,
134. *See also* shrubs, plants, fodder, forage
Gray rhebok (*Pelea capreolus*), 137
grazing: grazing density and grazing intensity,
122–23; grazing patterns of herders, 12–13,
87–88; history Lesotho's A-B-C rotational
grazing system, 87–88, 137; *maboella*
(*leboella*, sing; rested pasture), 79, 87, 93;
overgrazing, 48–49, 54, 59, 62, 84–85, 88, 98,
120–21, 125, 137, 159n53, 163n23; overresting
and undergrazing, 84–85, 88, 98, 120–21,
163n23; rotational grazing, 81–89, 97, 134.
See also grazing associations

grazing associations, 14–15, 19, 24, 56–58, 82–91, 95–98. *See also* user associations
Great Britain. *See* Britain
"green imperialism," 16, 72. *See also* Grove, Richard
Grove, Richard, 16
gullies. *See* soil erosion
Gun War, 32, 153n28

headman, 93. *See also* chieftaincy
Helichrysum trilineatum, 12, 126, 129. *See also* shrubs
heritage sites, 36
herders: as cultural symbol, 27, 121, 130–31, 135, 172n16; as sources of anxiety, 20, 84–85, 87, 92, 96, 99, 120–21, 130–35, 139, 145; challenges facing, 13, 87–88, 108, 111, 114–15, 118, 122, 125, 129–30; descriptions of, 13, 18, 84–85, 108, 111, 120–21, 124, 128–34, 171n15, 172n16; perspectives of, 88, 111, 114, 116, 121, 124, 128–36, 170n63. *See also* herding
herding: active and passive, 13, 84–88, 99, 120–21, 134, 139, 164n34; freedom and, 131–32, 135, 139; lifestyle of, 12–13, 84–85, 87–88, 111, 115, 121, 129–132; techniques, 18, 25, 85–87, 92, 120–21, 128–34, 139. *See also* cattle posts, grazing, herders
Herskovits, Melville, 104
highlands: as sources of anxiety, 9–10, 49, 54–55, 94, 100; climate of, 29–31, 41, 58, 131; geology of, 31, 47, 50–51, 127; relationship between lowlands and highlands, 31, 57–58, 65, 76, 110, 131, 145; settlement of, 103, 105–7, 118, 136–38. *See also* lowlands
Hirst, Stanley, 52
historiography. *See* landscape
Holistic Resource Management, 11–14, 81, 84–88, 90–93, 97–99, 134, 163n20, 164nn27,28. *See also* Savory, Allan
Holocene, 2. *See also* Anthropocene
humanitarian assistance. *See* aid
"hut tax," 6–7, 32
Hutchinson, G. Evelyn, 143
hydroelectricity: in relation to the Lesotho Highlands Water Project, 6, 28, 34–35, 45–46, 155n52; 'Muela hydroelectric station, 6, 27–29, 34, 45–48, 53, 67–72, 157n5, 158n48; pump-storage scheme, 35; rural electrification, 34
hydrology: as opposed to terrestrial or fluvial, 5; hydrologic cycle, 58; hydrologic science, 29; hydrologic statistics, 6, 37; reservoir-induced seismicity, 38. *See also* fluvial

hypervolume, 143. *See also* niche construction

ice rats, 59, 125–26
identity: as factor in ecological process, 4, 139; national identity, 2, 10, 28, 92, 135, 165n44
ignorance: of sedimentation problems in the Lesotho Highlands Water Project, 11, 53, 61–62, 158n43; perceived ignorance of rural people, 11
imperial debris, 14, 83–84. *See also* empire
imperialism. *See* empire, "green imperialism"
in-stream flow requirements (IFR), 142. *See also* rivers
incorporation (of Lesotho into South Africa), 8–9, 30, 35
independence: of Afrikaners from British rule, 5, 32; of Bantustans, 8, 30, 33; of former colonies, 3, 6, 73; of herders, 131–32, 139; of Lesotho, 6–9, 33, 35–36, 73–74, 77, 94, 155n56, 160n20; of South Africa, 2, 30, 102, 114, 148n21; post-independence politics in Lesotho, 94–97, 99, 154n39, 155n56, 160n20. *See also* colonialism
India, 3, 168n21, 174n5
indirect rule, 75, 81, 93–94, 144, 153n30. *See also* colonialism
inequality, 2, 15, 154n39
infrastructure: natural infrastructure, 66, 143; of dams, 27, 66, 77–78, 142–43; of distribution and production, 4, 41, 64, 66, 99; storage infrastructure, 3, 6, 10, 18, 24, 29, 35, 64, 66, 143–44; urban water infrastructure, 3, 34–35, 53–54, 141, 173n1
Integrated Catchment Management (ICM), 53, 77, 159n49. *See also* Integrated Watershed Management Project
Integrated Water Resource Management (IWRM), 159n49. *See also* Integrated Catchment Management
Integrated Watershed Management Project, 65
interdisciplinarity, 22, 123
Inulanthera thodei, 12, 127. *See also* shrubs

jackals, 131. *See also* herders, herding
Johannesburg: geography of, 7*map*; history of, 1, 6; relationship between Lesotho and, 1–4, 6, 29, 122, 142; water demand in, 1–2, 4, 6, 10, 37, 50, 147n4, 173n1
jokes: about Lesuhla's *lekalapense*, 116; about South Africa's reliance on Lesotho's water, 3; *fato-fato* as, 65–66, 75, 78; landscape theory within, 11–12, 14, 58, 70, 133
Jonathan, Leabua, 6, 36, 73–75, 77, 94–95, 161n36

Katse Dam and Reservoir: as components of
    LHWP, 5–6, 28, 34, 45–46, 48, 174n13; as icon
    of water abundance or drought, 27–28, 37, 46,
    47*fig*; impacts from, 34, 38, 154n46; soil
    erosion and sedimentation concerns at,
    46–48, 51–52, 142, 158nn45,48
Khubelu River Valley, 12, 56
Khubelu Sponges Project, 11, 18–19, 84–85,
    87–92, 96–99, 113, 120–21
Kimberly, South Africa, 32
King, Rachel, 30
kraal (corral), 11–12, 57, 84, 89–90, 107, 115, 125,
    131, 134, 164n34, 170n72

labor: commodification of, 16, 41, 148n19; labor
    migration, 4, 15, 23–25, 32–35, 104, 145,
    149n42, 161n41; labor reserves, 2, 4, 6–9,
    8*map*, 10, 14–16, 26, 30, 33, 35, 41–42, 103,
    108, 114, 117–18, 122, 136, 139, 142–45, 175n23;
    performative labor, 66. See also *fato-fato*,
    matsema, work parties
land: agricultural, 123, 171n4; expropriation of,
    7–8, 33; grazing land, 13, 34, 85, 87, 90, 95–96,
    123; tenure of, 13, 85, 87, 95–96, 99, 155n55,
    162n12, 167n75, 171n4. See also degradation
landscape: changes in, 17–20, 135–38;
    historiography of, 11–12, 16–23, 58, 61, 71–73,
    124–25, 135–38, 143; history of, 11–12, 17, 22,
    25–26, 56–58, 135–38; patterns in, 12, 14,
    17–18, 20, 24, 58, 61, 120–28, 138–39; theory
    of, 10–12, 16–23, 45, 54–61, 71–73, 87–88,
    124–25, 135–38, 143. See also patterns
laziness: as attribute of herders, 72, 84–85, 121,
    131, 139
leaky water infrastructure, 2–3, 34–35,
    141, 173n1
legal dualism, 88, 91–94, 165n44. See also indirect
    rule, chieftaincy, councils
lekalapense, 115–117, 117*fig*. See also livestock, wool
Lekhotla la Bafo (Commoners League), 93,
    166n57. See also Basutoland Progressive
    Association (BPA)
Leribe District, x*map*, 57–58
Lesotho Fund for Community Development
    (LFCD), 75
Lesotho government: civil service of, 15, 35,
    39, 57, 65, 91, 94, 97, 165n54; resistance to
    incorporation into South Africa, 35; structure
    of, 88, 91–94, 165n44. See also legal dualism
Lesotho Highlands Development Authority
    (LHDA), 27, 36–37, 45–48, 51–52, 67–73, 78,
    148n18, 152n2, 162n43
Lesotho Highlands Revenue Fund (LHRF), 75

Lesotho Highlands Water Commission
    (LHWC), 36, 51, 68, 70, 152n2, 154n42
Lesotho Highlands Water Project (LHWP):
    feasibility studies for, 36, 49–52, 55–56,
    155n61, 174n13; history of, 1–2, 4–7, 9–10,
    34–37, 44, 48–54; Phase 1, 28, 34–35, 51–52,
    55–56, 154n42, 161n39, 174n13; Phase 2, 3, 35,
    148n17, 154n42, 158nn30,45; sedimentation
    problems associated with Lesotho's dams,
    4–5, 10–11, 14–17, 23–24, 43–54, 59, 61,
    65, 67–71, 118, 120, 125, 141–44, 157n18,
    158nn45,48, 160n17; structure of, 7*map*,
    28–29, 45–46, 48; treaty for, 1, 3, 6, 34, 36, 51,
    142, 152n2, 154n40, 155n49. See also Lesotho
    Highlands Development Authority, Lesotho
    Highlands Water Commission, Lesotho
    Fund for Community Development, Lesotho
    Highlands Revenue Fund
Lesotho Meteorological Society, 41.
    See also rainfall
Lesotho National Wool and Mohair Growers
    Association (LNWMGA), 108–9, 115. See also
    livestock, mohair, wool
Lesotho Peoples Charter Movement, 35.
    See also sovereignty, dissolution
Lesotho Woodlots Project, 161n36
Letsie III, King of Lesotho, 98
lifaqane (*Mfecane*), 32, 153n20
lightning: as threat to herders, 131.
    See also herders
lipitso. See *pitso*
live storage (of reservoirs): as impacted by
    reservoir sedimentation, 46, 50–51; definition
    of, 46; in relation to dead storage, 46, 50–51.
    See also active storage, dead storage, storage
livelihoods, 4, 16, 23, 40, 98, 107, 118, 122, 131, 135,
    142, 145, 163n17
livestock: auctions of, 89, 113, 170nn73,73; cattle,
    25, 33, 68, 90, 92, 102–13, 118, 130, 135–36,
    150n46, 170n71; commodification of, 12,
    25, 100, 102–105, 108, 111–12, 118, 120–21,
    135–36; for meat production, 25, 103, 105,
    108, 110, 115–117, 133; for wool and mohair
    production, 4, 23, 25–26, 47–48, 98, 100, 103,
    105–110, 115–18, 121, 124, 126, 130–33, 136–39,
    157n15, 164n39, 168n39, 169n59, 170nn66,76;
    impoundment of, 88–98, 123, 136; numbers
    of, 49, 103, 105–109, 109*fig*, 112–13, 118,
    135–37; small stock (sheep and goats), 25,
    92, 102–14, 117–19, 130, 135–37, 170n71; use of
    salt and molasses in livestock production,
    25, 121, 133–34, 139. See also commodities,
    lekalapense, mohair, wool, meat

lobola, 69, 104, 108, 170n71. *See also* bridewealth
local councils: history of, 81, 92–96, 166n60; local councilors, 19, 39, 59–60, 90–98, 113, 136, 166n60; relationships with chiefs, 91–98, 95*table*, 166n60; responsibilities of, 91, 93, 95–98. *See also* legal dualism, chieftaincy
log books, 82
lowlands: climate of, 37–38, 41; control over pastures in, 25, 106–7; geography of, 31, 37, 153nn17,18, 172n26; geology of, 31, 47, 50–51; lowlands water scheme, 38; relationship between highlands and lowlands, 31, 57–58, 65, 76, 110, 131, 145. *See also* highlands, foothills

maele. See proverbs
malitšoekere. See Helichrysum trilineatum
Maloka, Eddy, 169n52
Maloti Chain, 31
Maloti-Drakensberg Transfrontier Project, 37, 97, 165n40
management: in relation to rangeland condition, 11–13, 15, 17–20, 23–25, 40, 49–50, 56–62, 67–72, 77, 80–81, 83–101, 120–21, 125, 128, 139, 143–45; of contradictions in storage reserves, 10; of reservoir levels, 14, 24, 45–46, 50; of urban water, 2–3, 34–35, 141, 173n1. *See also* grazing; reservoirs
Mapholaneng, 115, 130
Mapholaneng River, 12
marginality: of herders within Lesotho society, 118, 121–22, 125, 131–32, 139; of highlands within Lesotho, 118, 121; of Lesotho within South Africa, 26, 66, 103, 118, 121–22, 125, 130, 139; ploughing marginal lands, 16, 123. *See also* core, periphery
Martin, Emily, 143
Marx, Karl, 33, 105
Maseru, 28, 34, 36, 65, 73
masculinity, 115, 118, 129
materiality: of landscape patterns, 20–21; of water, 18, 24, 42, 44, 135, 150n48
Matsoku Weir and Reservoir, 5–6, 34, 48
Mauss, Marcel, 29, 104
Mbembe, Achille, 130
McAuslan, Patrick, 36
McCully, Patrick, 44
meat, 4, 11, 69, 114, 116, 119, 168n34, 170n66. *See also* livestock, mohair, wool
medicines: for livestock, 15, 25, 117, 135. See also *nyopo-nyopo*

meetings, 3, 15, 19, 21, 39–40, 56–57, 78, 82, 89–92, 89*fig*, 92, 97–98, 113, 167n68, 170n73. *See also* bureaucracy, *pitso*
members: of grazing associations, 82, 89–91; of parliament, 93, 165n45
metaphors: for sheep, 111; for water, 18, 28; in landscape theory, 14, 18–19, 58–59, 122, 150n66. *See also* theory
Metolong Water Scheme, 38
metsele-tsele. See stonelines
Mfecane (lifaqane), 32, 153n20
migration (of labor), 4, 15, 23–25, 32–35, 104, 145, 149n42, 161n41. *See also* mining
mining: labor migration for, 4, 9, 25, 33–34, 100, 103, 108, 112, 130, 145; mechanization of mines, 9, 33; mineworkers, 2, 6, 9–10, 14, 32–33, 75–76, 104, 111–14, 117, 119, 129–30, 153n30, 154nn38,39; of diamonds, 6, 32, 34; of gold, 1–2, 6, 9, 32–33, 141; sheep as mines, 111. *See also* migration
ministers: cabinet ministers of Lesotho, 35, 93, 96; prime minister of Lesotho, 3, 6, 35–36, 49, 73, 76, 93; prime minister of South Africa, 3, 6, 49
ministries of government, 18–19, 21, 40, 56–57, 59–61, 63–65, 70, 72, 75, 77, 84, 88–92, 97–98, 101, 113, 136, 149n45, 163n19
mires, 12. *See also* wetlands
missionaries, 32, 93–94, 107, 153n22, 157n13, 164n35
mohair, 4, 25–26, 98, 103, 106–110, 109*fig*, 117, 124, 130, 133, 137, 164n39. *See also* livestock, meat, wool
Mohale Dam and Reservoir, 6, 28, 34, 37, 45, 48, 52–53, 156n69, 158n45, 161n39
Mokhoabo-Motšo Valley, 12
Mokhotlong: district of, x*map*, 17–18, 38, 41, 56, 58, 63, 78, 109–10, 113–14, 124, 130–31, 137, 158n45, 169n43; town of, 3, 31, 39, 78, 85, 111, 173n34
molasses (*nyopo-nyopo*), 25, 121, 133–34, 139
Molia, 74. *See also* Jonathan, Leabua
Mont-Aux-Sources, 48
Moshoeshoe I, King of Lesotho, 27, 32, 87, 106–7, 169n43
Moshoeshoe II, King of Lesotho, 36
motebong. See cattle posts
motsele-tsele. See stonelines
Motšerimeli, 60, 125
mountains. *See* highlands
mountain reedbok (*Redunca fulvorufula*), 137

Mphanya, Ntsukunyane, 166n57
'Muela Dam and Reservoir, 4–6, 27–29, 34, 43, 45–48, 51–53, 59, 67–73, 157n5, 158n48
multispecies anthropology, 22
multispecies politics, 15, 126, 145, 150n50
Murray, Colin, 9, 33, 149n42, 160n6, 169n52, 175n23

Namibia, 12, 19–20, 37
national identity, 2, 10, 28, 92, 135, 165n44
National movement, 75, 94–95, 95*table*, 161nn34,36,38, 165n54, 166nn57,60. *See also* Basotho National Party (BNP)
National Party (South Africa), 5. *See also* apartheid
national water, 15, 29–30, 38, 41–44, 53, 61, 67, 131, 143–44
Natives Land Act of 1913 (South Africa), 33. *See also* land
natural history, 21–22, 25
n-dimensional hypervolume, 143, 174n17
negative ecology, 122–3, 138–39
Nehru, Jawarharlal, 3
niche construction, 143, 174n17
Nkandla Estate (of Jacob Zuma), 78
non-place-based factors (in land degradation), 23, 125, 130, 145. *See also* Blaikie, Piers, degradation
ntlafatso, 88, 91–92, 94–97, 95*table*; *ntlafatso ea mobu*, 65. *See also* development
nutrients: for livestock, 133–34, 139; soil nutrients, 12, 22, 86, 126, 133, 142. See also *nyopo-nyopo*
nyopo-nyopo, 121, 133–34, 139. *See also* medicines

oil: petroleum, 5; as payment for soil conservation work, 74
operations (water engineering): sedimentation as problem of, 24, 45–46
Orange Free State, 5, 8*map*, 9, 32, 48, 108, 153n28. *See also* Free State Province
Orange/Senqu River, 6, 12, 37, 48–50, 174n13
overflowing Katse Dam, 27–28, 46–47, 47*fig*
overgrazing. *See* grazing
overresting. *See* grazing
ovicaprids, 103, 105, 111–15, 118–19. *See also* bovine mystique, livestock, ovicaprine mystique
ovicaprine mystique, 103, 105, 108, 111, 117–19. *See also* bovine mystique, commodities, livestock

Oxbow Scheme, 6. *See also* Lesotho Highlands Water Project (LHWP)

palatable forage, 11, 60, 68, 85–86, 133–34
Panama Canal, 66
parliament, of Lesotho, 9, 93, 165n45. *See also* Lesotho government
passbooks, 8
pass laws, 8, 33
patterns: interpretation of landscape patterns, 12, 14, 17–18, 20, 24, 58, 61, 120–28, 138–39; of rainfall, 37, 61; of transhumance, 87, 137
payment: for herding work, 13, 111, 115, 130; to *fato-fato* workers, 63, 66, 70, 72, 74–75; to people impacted by dams, 34, 72, 78, 142, 162n43. *See also* compensation
peasantariat, 66, 145
pedagogy: fluvial pedagogy, 19, 24, 44–45, 53–61, 67; for natural resource stewardship, 30, 151n72, 159n50
Pentzia cooperi (*selingoana*), 12. *See also* shrubs
perennial grasses, 11, 86, 134. *See also* grasses
perennial streams, 12
periphery: core-periphery relations of Lesotho in Southern Africa, 7, 11, 25, 64, 125; imperial peripheries, 16, 33; peripheral position of herders in Lesotho, 121, 125, 130, 135. *See also* marginality
permits: for bringing animals into South Africa, 113; for grazing, 57, 80, 89–91; for work and residence, 8, 33, 114
petroleum, 5. *See also* commodities
Phuthaditjhaba, 114–15
Pim, Alan: British colonial agent, 49–50, 94, 100, 166n57; "Pim Report," 49, 87, 94, 100, 157n15, 166nn57,60
pitso, 3, 57, 89. *See also* meetings
plants: as index of soil erosion, 54–62, 85; as object of concern to water engineers and conservation bureaucrats, 11, 20, 49, 53–62, 121; evolutionary history of rangeland plant community, 137, 139, 172n27; fodder cropping, 25, 116–17, 121, 123–24, 133; palatable and unpalatable forage, 11, 15, 25, 54, 60, 68, 85–86, 121, 133–34, 139; plant community assembly, 12, 21, 122; plant community response to grazing, 121, 137; plant species diversity, 81, 83, 124, 135, 137, 172n27, 173n34; tree-planting initiatives, 49, 53, 63, 73, 85, 161n36; wetland plant community, 59, 125–128. *See also* grasses, shrubs

Polanyi, Karl, 148n19, 150n56, 174n19
Polihali Dam and Reservoir, 3, 6, 35, 46, 53, 56–57, 78, 109, 148n17, 158nn30,45
postapartheid South Africa: economics of, 29; position of chieftaincy within, 165n46
precipitation. *See* rainfall
Pretoria, x*map*, 6, 7*map*, 8*map*, 10, 36, 50
prime ministers: of Lesotho, 3, 6, 35–36, 49, 73, 76, 93; of South Africa, 3, 6, 49
principal chiefs, 35, 57, 89, 93, 165n45, 167n66. *See also* chieftaincy
production: by-products, 14–16, 139, 145; of commodities, 1, 5, 10–11, 15–16, 23–25, 29–30, 36–37, 41–44, 67, 77, 100, 102–5, 118, 120–22, 148n19; of livestock, 12, 25, 100, 102–105, 108, 111–12, 118, 120–21, 135–36; of petroleum, 5; of water, 1, 5, 10–11, 15–16, 23–24, 29–30, 36–37, 41–44, 67, 77, 100, 102, 121–22, 145. *See also* commodities
projects: as means of doing conservation and development, 14, 18–19, 49, 57, 63–65, 70–78, 82–92, 95–99, 103–4, 110–13, 121, 123–24, 142, 144, 160n6, 161n36, 162n4; commodification as project, 5; Khubelu Sponges Project, 11, 18–19, 84–85, 87–92, 96–99, 113, 120–21; "projectification," 82. *See also* conservation, development
protectorate status (under British Crown), 32, 153n28. *See also* Britain, colonialism
proverbs, 13, 38–40, 43, 59, 84–85, 121, 134, 144, 146, 156n75. *See also* aphorisms
provincializing universal categories, 43, 122–23
pump-storage scheme, 35. *See also* hydroelectricity, storage
puso, 88, 91–97, 95*table*, 99. *See also* chieftaincy, governance

Qacha's Nek District, x*map*, 31, 37, 137
Qwa-Qwa, 8*map*, 102, 110–11, 113–17, 119, 130. *See also* Bantustans, Phuthaditjhaba

race: apartheid, 1–10, 25, 30, 36, 64, 73, 102, 108, 114, 122, 145, 149n42; horse race, 114; racial capitalism, 1, 143, 145; water production as racial project, 1–10, 145–46. *See also* apartheid
rainfall: climate change, 2, 16, 30, 40–41, 86, 120; drought, 2–3, 17, 30, 32–33, 37–38, 41, 44, 61, 69, 101, 106–7, 121–22, 137–38, 156n78; drought-resistance of shrubs, 54, 59, 121, 138, 173n36; flood, 2, 9–10, 17, 39, 46, 48–50, 52, 61; impact on land condition, 16, 22, 25, 59, 81, 83–84, 120, 136, 139, 145, 163n23, 172n27; in

relation to El Niño Southern Oscillation, 37; patterns of, 37, 61; rain shadow, 37; Sesotho terms for types of, 41, 58, 156n76. *See also* drought, floods, water
Rand Water, 155n49
rangeland: definition of, 81; rangeland ecology, 13, 22, 81, 83–88, 97–99, 137, 163nn19,23, 164n28. *See also* grazing, livestock, rotational grazing
recalcitrant commodities, 118, 152n9. *See also* commodities
reform: of rangeland management, 11–14, 24, 60–62, 80–99, 134–35, 144–145; of the chieftaincy, 93–99. *See also* bureaucracy, chieftaincy
reservoir-induced seismicity, 38
reservoirs: amount of water in, 6, 37, 45, 50, 53, 142, 155n49, 156n69; as components of the Lesotho Highlands Water Project, 5–6, 7*map*, 27–29, 34, 45–46; as icon of water abundance or scarcity, 27–28, 37, 46, 47*fig*; building popular concern for, 11–12, 24, 27–28, 48, 54–62, 69–73, 144; dredging of, 5, 43, 48, 67–68; Lesotho as storage reservoir, 1–2, 9–10, 15, 24, 26, 30–35, 62, 65–66, 77–78, 103, 108, 118–19, 122–23, 136, 142–46; management of, 14, 18, 24, 28–29, 45–48, 66, 84–85; sedimentation of, 4–5, 10–12, 14–17, 23–24, 43–54, 59, 61, 65, 67–71, 118, 120, 125, 141–46, 157n18, 158nn45,48, 160n17. *See also* dams, reservoir-induced seismicity, sedimentation
resettlement: for people impacted by dams, 34, 72, 78, 142, 162n43
retirement, 4, 25, 103, 108, 114, 118, 145. *See also* livestock, mining
revenues: foreign revenue, 34, 109, 161n39; "nonrevenue" water, 173n1; non-tax revenue, 154n40; water revenue, 3, 34, 38–39, 62, 75, 77, 154n40, 161n39. *See also* Lesotho Highlands Revenue Fund, water royalties
rinderpest epizootic, 33, 106, 168n34
rivers: as body of flowing sediments, 44; as icon of national water, 28; ecological function of, 46–47, 142; effects of dams on, 16, 46–47, 61, 142, 157n20, 174n13; flooding in, 9–10, 17, 39, 46, 48–50, 52, 61; geography of, 6, 7*map*, 12, 29, 37, 48, 67–68; healthy river activism, 38, 141–42; sediment monitoring in, 36, 50, 52–53. *See also* upstream
roads: as evidence of development, 28, 38–39; effects on plant community, 54, 137–38, 173n34; effects on runoff and erosion, 40, 121, 126, 137–38; road construction and

maintenance, 39–40, 51, 74, 121, 137–38; visibility of *fato-fato* projects from the roadside, 61, 76

rodents, 19, 59, 125–26. *See also* ice rats

rotational grazing: A-B-C rotational grazing system, 12, 87–88, 137; Allan Savory's rotational grazing plan, 11–14, 81, 84–88, 90–93, 97–99, 134, 163n20, 164nn27,28; transhumance, 87, 137. *See also* Khubelu Sponges Project, Savory, Allan

royalties. *See* water royalties

rural: perceptions of rural people, 11, 14, 45, 49–50, 54, 57–58, 61–62, 67, 72, 83, 104–5, 113, 120–21, 124, 143–44, 171n8; rural livelihoods, 4, 16, 23, 40, 98, 107, 118, 122, 131, 135, 142, 145, 163n17. *See also* conservation, marginality

Rural Water Supply (RWS), 38

salt, 24, 121, 133–34. *See also* livestock, *nyopo-nyopo*

sandstone, 31, 47, 50–51, 138. *See also* basalt

Sandton, 122

Savory, Allan: biography of, 86; controversy surrounding, 86; Holistic Resource Management, 11–14, 81, 84–88, 90–93, 97–99, 134, 163n20, 164nn27,28. *See also* Khubelu Sponges Project, rotational grazing

scarcity: forage scarcity, 17, 25, 41, 60, 81, 83, 87–88, 123–24, 134, 164n36, 170n76, 173n29; water scarcity, 3–4, 37–38, 41, 156n64. *See also* abundance

Schnitzler, Antina von, 30, 53–54

Seate River, 12

seboku. See *Themeda triandra*

sediment: movement and accumulation of, 39–40, 45–54, 61, 63–64, 67–68, 71, 120, 128, 142–143, 146, 157n20, 158n45, 160n17; sedimentation problems associated with Lesotho's dams, 4–5, 10–11, 14–17, 23–24, 43–54, 59, 61, 65, 67–71, 118, 120, 125, 141–44, 157n18, 158nn45,48, 160n17. *See also* sedimentation, soil erosion

sedimentation: at Katse, 46–48, 51–52, 142, 158nn45,48; at 'Muela, 4–6, 27–29, 34, 43, 45–48, 51–53, 59, 67–73, 157n5, 158n48; at Matsoku, 5–6, 34, 48; of Lesotho's dams, 4–5, 10–12, 14–17, 23–24, 43–54, 59, 61, 65, 67–71, 118, 120, 125, 141–46, 157n18, 158nn45,48, 160n17. *See also* reservoirs, soil, soil erosion

sehala-hala. See *Chrysocoma ciliata*

selingoana. See *Pentzia cooperi*

Senqu/Orange River, 6, 12, 37, 48–50, 174n13

Sepedi, 14

settler colonialism, 5–6, 9–10, 26, 31–33, 48–50, 106, 125. *See also* Afrikaners, borders, colonialism

Shand, Ninham, 5–6, 9–10

shrubs: as index of land degradation, 11, 24, 45, 54–62, 81, 86, 120, 134, 144; burning of, 128, 134, 139; collecting for fuel, 27, 56, 60–61, 134; encroachment of, 25, 54–58, 120–22, 124, 127–28, 133–35, 137–39; in relation to grasses, 11, 54–55, 59, 81, 86, 128, 134, 139, 159nn52,58, 173n36; uprooting of, 59–61. *See also* grasses, plants, vegetation

silt: as soil particle type, 44, 52; silt traps, 24, 40, 59–66, 68–69, 76–79, 144. *See also* sedimentation, soil, soil erosion

siltation. *See* sedimentation

silt traps (stonelines), 24, 40, 59–66, 64*fig*, 68–69, 76, 77–79, 144. See also *fato-fato*, soil conservation, soil erosion

social engineering. *See* engineering

social theory. *See* theory

soil: parent materials, 31, 47, 50–51, 127; soil particle types, 44, 52; soil solution, 66; types and descriptions of soils in Lesotho, 12, 17, 50–52, 126–28 126*fig*, 136. *See also* basalt, sandstone, sedimentation, soil conservation, soil erosion

soil conservation: and US Dustbowl crisis, 48–49, 149n36, 157n18; history of soil conservation in Southern Africa, 17, 44, 48–50, 73–78; physical conservation works (gabions, silt traps, check dams, diversion furrows), 24, 39–40, 40*fig*, 59–66, 68–72, 71*fig*, 76–79, 144; social engineering for, 25, 41, 54–61, 66–67, 69–77, 80–92, 97–99, 104. *See also* sedimentation, soil, soil erosion

soil erosion: causes of, 5, 11–12, 16, 20, 23, 45, 47–50, 53–59, 61–62, 64, 69–70, 80, 85–86, 97, 107, 120–21, 125–26, 134–39, 145, 151nn68,71, ·158n45, 160n1; gully erosion, 4, 19, 40, 43, 48–54, 64, 68, 70–71, 122, 125–26, 126*fig*, 128, 133; measurement and monitoring of erosion, 17, 45, 47, 52–53, 67, 144; modelling erosion and sedimentation, 47, 51–53, 158n45; sheet erosion, 51, 53. *See also* sedimentation, soil, soil conservation

Smuts, Jan Christian, 49

Sole, Masupha, 52, 154n42

South Africa: apartheid, 1–3, 6–8, 7*map*, 10, 102, 108, 149n42; independence struggle of, 2, 6, 8–9, 30, 36, 73, 102, 114; in relation to the Lesotho Highlands Water Project, 1–7, 7*map*, 9–10, 28–29, 34–37, 44–46, 48–56, 152n2,

154n40, 155nn49,61, 174n13; relationship to Lesotho, 1–3, 5–10, 25, 30, 36, 64, 73, 102, 108, 114, 122, 145; settler colonialism in, 5–6, 9–10, 26, 31–33, 48–50, 106, 125; water demand in, 2–3, 34–35, 141, 173n1. *See also* apartheid, Bantustans

South African Development Community (SADC), 34

sovereignty, 3, 28–30, 147n8. *See also* Lesotho Peoples Charter Movement

space: niche space, 143, 174n17; rangeland spacetime, 11, 13, 25, 61, 81–85, 87–88, 92, 96–98, 118, 130, 132–34, 164n36, 171n13; spatiality of water in Lesotho, 37–38, 41–42, 44, 61, 144; spatial relations under apartheid, 4, 6–8, 8*map*, 10–11, 25, 64, 75–76, 125, 145, 171n2. *See also* core-periphery relations, degradation, rangeland ecology

species diversity, 81, 83, 124, 135, 137, 172n27, 173n34. *See also* degradation

sponge: as metaphor for wetlands, 18–19, 151n66; Khubelu Sponges Project, 11, 14, 17–19, 84–85, 87–92, 96–99, 113, 120–21. *See also* metaphor, theory

Sponges Project. *See* Khubelu Sponges Project

state, the, 58, 66–67, 73–74, 83, 88, 91–97, 95*table*, 160n9, 163n17, 165n44. *See also* chieftaincy, legal dualism

statutory government. *See* state, the

stonelines (silt traps), 24, 40, 59–66, 64*fig*, 68–69, 76–79, 144. See also *fato-fato*, soil conservation, soil erosion

storage: dead and live storage, 46, 50–51; engineering storage, 5, 10, 25, 66–67, 139, 144; Lesotho as storage reserve, 2, 26, 145; pump-storage scheme, 35; storage infrastructure, 3, 6, 10, 18, 24, 29, 35, 64, 66, 143–44. *See also* apartheid

summer: climate during, 17, 37, 41, 58, 63, 106, 133; grazing areas during, 12, 87–88, 137, 169n46; use of livestock medicines during, 133–34

suspended load, 14, 53. *See also* sediment

Swaziland (eSwatini), 49, 153n28

tariffs, 6–7, 32–33

taxes: as colonial tool, 6–7, 32–33, 93–94, 137–38, 153nn29,30; export tax for livestock, 170n74; non-tax revenue, 154n40. *See also* "hut taxes"

"temples of modernity," 3. *See also* dams

temporality. *See* time

terra nullius, 3

terrestrial demands (of water and livestock production), 4, 10, 14, 19, 80, 143

terrestrial politics, 1, 5, 78, 123

territory: establishment and loss of Lesotho's, 29–33, 49, 106, 125, 169n43; in relation to water production, 3, 5, 7–8, 8*map*, 24, 28–29, 35–38, 41–42, 44, 61; Lesotho's "conquered territories," 8*map*, 32, 148n26; of principal chiefs and grazing associations, 88–89, 97; reterritorializing ecological process, 88. *See also* borders

textiles: industry in Lesotho, 34; international industry, 103, 105, 110, 119, 135–36, 169n55

Thabane, Tom, 3, 35, 76

Thaba-Tseka District, x*map*, 31, 129–30

theft: of livestock, 115, 117, 130–31

Themeda triandra (*seboku*), 11, 55, 159n52, 173n29. *See also* forage, grass

theory: ecological, 11, 24, 80–81, 83, 87–88, 97, 99, 135, 163nn20,23; equilibrium theory of rangelands, 163nn20,23; fluvial, 1, 10, 16, 22, 48–50, 135, 143, 162n43; landscape theorizing, 10–12, 16–23, 45, 54–61, 71–73, 87–88, 124–25, 135–38, 143; social, 22, 80–81, 83, 96, 162. *See also* landscape, metaphor, rangeland ecology

thotho-li-roalana. See *Inulanthera thodei*

time: compensation timeframe, 78, 162n43; longevity of dams, 50–51, 78; seasonal change, 17, 37, 41, 58, 63, 106, 133, 169n46; seasonal grazing movements, 12, 87–88, 137; temporal arbitrage, 78. *See also* rotational grazing

topography: influence on erosion in Lesotho, 16, 51, 145; influence on rainfall in Lesotho, 31, 37

townships in South Africa, 146

trading posts: and livestock sales, 113; and the wool and mohair trade, 106, 168n39, 169n59, 173n34

Trans-Caledon Tunnel Authority (TCTA), 152n2, 155n49. *See also* Lesotho Highlands Water Project (LHWP)

transhumance, 87, 137. *See also* rotational grazing

Transkei, 8*map*, 33. *See also* Bantustans

translation: between an ecology and a sociology, 80–81, 83; of a fluvial imaginary, 62, 67; of "*fato-fato*," 65; of "*motebong ha ho lisoe*," 13, 84–85, 121 of Sesotho proverbs and phrases, 13, 59, 65, 74, 84, 113, 124, 134–35, 150n46, 156n75, 163n22, 171n11. *See also* metaphor, theory

Transvaal, 5, 8*map*, 9, 148n21, 153n28

trees: forests and deforestation, 66, 150n66,

173n30; Lesotho Woodlots Project, 161n36; tree-planting initiatives, 49, 53, 63, 73, 85, 161n36

Tsing, Anna, 16

tunnels, 1, 5–6, 7*map*, 28–29, 34, 45–46, 48, 51, 78, 120, 145–46, 152n2. *See also* Trans-Caledon Tunnel Authority

Turner, Stephen, 83, 97

United Nations: recognition of Bantustans, 33; United Nations Development Programme, 65, 97

United States: and global dam industry, 141–42; Dustbowl crisis, 48, 149n36

unpalatable forage, 11, 15, 25, 54, 60, 85–86, 121, 133–34, 139. *See also* forage

upstream: as site of water production and anxiety, 4–5, 11, 14–17, 20, 24, 40, 46–48, 50, 62, 66, 98, 118, 120, 144–45; upstream impacts of dam projects, 16, 34, 69–70, 72, 78, 142, 146, 162n43; upstream mechanisms for storage reserves, 10

USAID, 96–97. *See also* aid

user associations (*mekhatlo*), 82, 97. *See also* grazing associations

use: of water, 3, 36, 41–42; underutilization as settler colonial rationale, 3, 36, 42

vegetation: patterns of, 12, 14, 17–18, 20, 24, 58, 61, 120–28, 138–39. *See also* plants, shrubs, grasses

Venda, 8*map*, 33. *See also* Bantustans

Verwoerd, Hendrik, 6, 73

veterinary care, 15, 25, 106–7, 111, 117, 133. *See also* livestock, medicines, *nyopo-nyopo*, salt

village development committees, 95

volumes: of water in dam reservoirs, 4, 34–35, 47, 53, 142; volumetric water, 3–4, 6, 15, 34–36, 43–44, 67, 144. *See also* fluvial, hypervolume

war. *See* Gun War

ward chiefs, 93. *See also* chieftaincy, principal chiefs

water: abundance of, 3–4, 24, 27–30, 36–42, 44, 46, 144, 155n61; commodification of, 1, 5, 10–11, 15–16, 23–24, 29–30, 36–37, 41–44, 67, 77, 100, 102, 121–22, 145; export of, 1, 3–5, 9–16, 22–23, 29–31, 34–38, 41–45, 61–62, 66–67, 73, 77, 80–81, 90–93, 97, 100, 102–3, 109, 118–21, 124–25, 139, 143, 161n39; national water, 15, 29–30, 38, 41–44, 53, 61, 67, 131, 143–44; production of, 1, 5, 10–11, 15–16, 23–24, 29–30, 36–37, 41–44, 67, 77, 100, 102,

121–22, 145; scarcity of, 3–4, 37–38, 41, 156n64; water meters, 53–54, 146; water royalties, 34, 38–39, 75, 77, 154n40, 161n39. *See also* fluvial, hydrology, volumes

water abundance: as contradicting local realities, 24, 29–30, 36–38, 41–42, 144; as political artifact, 4, 27–30, 36–38, 41–42, 44, 46, 144, 156n64; as feature of "national water," 29–30, 36–38, 41–42, 44; as justification for Lesotho Highlands Water Project, 3–4, 24, 36–38, 41–42, 144, 155n61; as property of Lesotho's territory, 24, 27–30, 36–38, 41–42, 44, 46, 144, 155nn61,67; as rationale for Lesotho's sovereignty, 4, 29–30, 36–38, 41–42, 144; as tool for economic development, 3, 28, 36–38, 42, 161n39, as rationale for water commodification, 3–4, 24, 27–30, 36–38, 41–42, 44, 144, 155n61; in relation to colonization, 3–4; in relation to floods, 38–39; in relation to scarcity and drought, 3–4, 37–38, 41, 156n64; in relation to tourism industry, 27–28; of rain through orographic precipitation, 31, 37; overflowing Katse Dam as icon of, 27–28, 37, 46, 47*fig*; patchiness of, 30, 37–39, 41–42, 144. *See also* drought, floods, national water, water

"water-exporting country," 1, 15, 30

water royalties, 34, 38–39, 75, 77, 154n40, 161n39

Weberian state bureaucracy, 66

Westcliff, South Africa, 122

wetlands: conservation of, 11–14, 17–19, 37, 57, 59, 84–85, 120; degradation of, 17–19, 46–48, 57, 84–85, 122, 125–26, 126*fig*, 133, 139, 150n66; descriptions of, 12, 17–19 18*fig*, 47, 50–51, 59, 125–128, 133, 150n64, 151n69, 159n61; herder use of, 17–18, 23, 48, 121, 128, 136; importance to Lesotho Highlands Water Project, 13, 15, 17–19, 46–48, 54, 81, 120–21, 145, 151n68; Khubelu Sponges Project, 11, 14, 17–19, 84–85, 87–92, 96–99, 113, 120–21; metaphors about, 18–19, 39–40, 59, 150n66. *See also* Khubelu Sponges Project, sponges

Williams, Raymond, 15–16, 139

winter: climate during, 17, 41, 63, 133; grazing areas during, 12, 87–88, 169n46; use of livestock medicines during, 133–34

Witwatersrand, 1, 6, 32, 141

Wolpe, Harold, 33

women: collection of shrubs for fuel, 27, 134–35; participation in livestock production and sale, 90, 101, 103–4, 112, 117; participation in soil conservation projects,

69, 75, 88; perceptions of landscape change, 134–35

wool, 4, 23, 25–26, 47–48, 98, 100, 103, 105–110, 115–18, 121, 124, 126, 130–33, 136–39, 157n15, 164n39, 168n39, 169n59, 170nn66,76. *See also* Lesotho National Wool and Mohair Growers Association (LNWMGA), meat, mohair, woolsheds

woolsheds, 110, 116, 118, 169n59. *See also* Lesotho National Wool and Mohair Growers Association (LNWMGA), mohair, wool

work parties: difference between *matsema* and *fato-fato*, 166n57; *fato-fato*, 24–25, 63–67, 70, 72, 75–78; history of, 24–25, 73–75, 77–78, 93–94, 165n48, 166n57; *matsema*, 93–94, 165n48,

166n57; relationship to political authority, 24–25, 67, 72–78, 165n48, 166n57

work permits, 8, 33, 114. *See also* apartheid, passbooks

"world city": Johannesburg's aspiration as, 2–3. *See also* leaky water infrastructure, water scarcity

World Bank: development and conservation initiatives by, 75, 113, 161n39, 166n60; financing for Lesotho Highlands Water Project, 4, 6, 34, 36, 38; report on sedimentation, 4, 65, 68

workshops, 14–15, 39–40, 59, 85, 96. *See also* bureaucracy, conservation, meetings

Zimbabwe, 84, 86

Zuma, Jacob, 3, 78

Founded in 1893,
UNIVERSITY OF CALIFORNIA PRESS
publishes bold, progressive books and journals
on topics in the arts, humanities, social sciences,
and natural sciences—with a focus on social
justice issues—that inspire thought and action
among readers worldwide.

The UC PRESS FOUNDATION
raises funds to uphold the press's vital role
as an independent, nonprofit publisher, and
receives philanthropic support from a wide
range of individuals and institutions—and from
committed readers like you. To learn more, visit
ucpress.edu/supportus.